RISK, RESILIENCE, AND POSITIVE YOUTH DEVELOPMENT

Developing Effective Community Programs for At-Risk Youth

LESSONS FROM THE DENVER BRIDGE PROJECT

Jeffrey M. Jenson

Catherine F. Alter

Nicole Nicotera

Elizabeth K. Anthony

Shandra S. Forrest-Bank

OXFORD
UNIVERSITY PRESS

OXFORD
UNIVERSITY PRESS

Oxford University Press is a department of the University of Oxford. It furthers the
University's objective of excellence in research, scholarship, and education by publishing
worldwide.

Oxford   New York
Auckland   Cape Town   Dar es Salaam   Hong Kong   Karachi
Kuala Lumpur   Madrid   Melbourne   Mexico City   Nairobi
New Delhi   Shanghai   Taipei   Toronto

With offices in
Argentina   Austria   Brazil   Chile   Czech Republic   France   Greece
Guatemala   Hungary   Italy   Japan   Poland   Portugal   Singapore
South Korea   Switzerland   Thailand   Turkey   Ukraine   Vietnam

Oxford is a registered trade mark of Oxford University Press in the UK and certain other
countries.

Published in the United States of America by
Oxford University Press
198 Madison Avenue, New York, NY 10016

© Oxford University Press 2013

Library of Congress Cataloging-in-Publication Data

Risk, resilience, and positive youth development: developing effective community programs for
at-risk youth: lessons from the Denver Bridge Project/Jeffrey M. Jenson ... [et al.].
   p. cm.
Includes bibliographical references and index.
ISBN 978-0-19-975588-2 (alk. paper)
1. Youth—Services for—United States.   2. Problem youth—United States.
I. Jenson, Jeffrey M.
HV1431.R58 2013
362.7'5250973—dc23
2012015123

9 8 7 6 5 4 3 2 1
Printed in the United States of America
on acid-free paper

Risk, Resilience, and Positive Youth Development

For Mary Krane,
champion of children, youth, and families

CONTENTS

FOREWORD

We live in a current state of economic uncertainty and great fiscal challenge. One upside to a down economy is that when businesses, communities, and governments must tighten their belts, the result can often be new solutions and ideas. Like many states, Colorado faces difficult challenges in funding for education, social services, transportation, health care, prisons, the environment, and many other programs. To meet these challenges, the state relies on innovative ideas and bold collaboration between the public and private sectors to provide services traditionally funded by government. Social programs are an excellent example of how, in the face of limited economic resources coupled with increasing demands, a little innovation between government and private entities can reshape services and improve their outcomes.

In this book, a team of authors from the Graduate School of Social Work at the University of Denver describes how a university–community partnership is an effective approach to promoting the success of at-risk children and youth. The authors describe the Denver Bridge Project, a community afterschool program that serves more than 500 young people residing in public housing communities. The Denver Bridge Project is an innovative, cost-effective, public and private collaboration that is effectively helping young people solve their individual and social problems. The program has endured as an important resource in four of the city's most disadvantaged neighborhoods because of its ability to efficiently and effectively bring positive changes to hundreds of children and families.

The Bridge Project is a partnership between the University of Denver's Graduate School of Social Work and the Denver Housing Authority. As described by Dr. Jenson and colleagues, children and youth attending the Bridge Project benefit from education and social work services provided by trained staff and from weekly tutoring and mentoring sessions offered by university students and community volunteers. This book provides both the theoretical knowledge and the practical tools necessary to involve young people in positive activities and promote healthy child and adolescent development.

Thanks to everyone involved in the important work being carried out at the Bridge Project. Special thanks to the children and youth whose efforts have brought change and hope for better lives through education and mentoring. This book brings the Denver Bridge Project to life. May it inspire other towns and cities to bring opportunity and hope to the lives of children in Colorado and across the country.

John Hickenlooper
Governor of Colorado

ACKNOWLEDGMENTS

This book is the product of many remarkable people. We would like to thank the staff of the Bridge Project for their countless hours of service and hard work on behalf of children and youth. It is impossible to name every one of the committed staff members who have worked at the Bridge Project since its inception in 1991. All of them have had a great impact on the lives of young people. We also acknowledge the many children, adolescents, young adults, and parents who have participated in Bridge Project activities and programs. Without them, there would be no Bridge Project. Students, faculty members, and administrators of the Graduate School of Social Work at the University of Denver have played an important role in supporting program activities, managing financial resources, and procuring grants at the Bridge Project. The unwavering commitment of the Denver Housing Authority to provide program space and key infrastructure support has been a major source of support over the years.

We owe special thanks to several people who encouraged us to write this book. Mary Krane, former Executive Director of the Bridge Project, sparked the idea of documenting events and writing individual case stories at the Bridge Project. Mary gave her heart and soul to the Bridge Project for 13 years and for that we are ever grateful. Jeanne Orrben, a former site and program director, worked with countless students from the Graduate School of Social Work at the University of Denver during her tenure at the Bridge Project. Jeanne's passion and commitment to community practice with children and youth inspired all of us to write this book. Molly Calhoun, the present Executive Director of the Bridge Project, is laying the groundwork for new program innovations and directions. Our team was privileged to work with Molly during the course of writing this book. Current Dean of the Graduate School of Social Work, James Herbert Williams, has been instrumental in supporting our writing and scholarly activities at the Bridge Project. A number of Bridge Project Board members have made significant contributions to the program over the years. Philip D. Winn was instrumental in starting and sustaining the Bridge Project. In 2007, Philip and his wife Eleanor established the Philip D. & Eleanor G. Winn Professorship in the Graduate School of Social Work at the

University of Denver. The professorship has supported many of the resources that were necessary to write this book. Gary Yourtz, Charles Biederman, Jerry Gray, Kathy French, Robert August, Neil Oberfeld, and all former and current Bridge Project board members—many who are profiled in Chapter 4—have also been a source of inspiration to all of us. Finally, special thanks to Kevin Von Qualen for the photographs of Bridge Project participants that appear on the cover of this book. Thanks, everyone.

INTRODUCTION

Children and youth face unprecedented social, psychological, economic, and educational challenges in today's world. Most young people navigate these challenges successfully and become healthy young adults. Unfortunately, some youth find it difficult to avoid involvement in problem behaviors like delinquency or substance abuse and fail to thrive at school or in the workplace.

What makes it so difficult for some children to find a positive developmental path while others seemingly navigate a path to success with relative ease? The answers to this question are complex. On a positive note, we have learned a great deal about the developmental processes of young people in the past few decades. For example, risk factors for child and adolescent problem behaviors have been consistently identified and addressed by many of the nation's school-based prevention programs (Jenson & Fraser, 2011). Interventions that aim to reduce risk and increase protection among young people have been effective in preventing and reducing problems such as substance abuse, aggression, and crime (Catalano, 2007; Woolf, 2008). Programs that seek to reduce risk and increase protection have also helped at-risk children and youth become more successful in school (Anthony, Alter, & Jenson, 2009).

Recent advances in preventing childhood and adolescent problems, while promising, represent only a beginning point for efforts aimed at helping young people become successful adults. Theories of positive youth development (PYD), discussed in Chapter 2 of this book, reveal that a young person's path is influenced by a number of complex individual traits and family conditions (Lerner, Dowling, & Anderson, 2003). Yet we know relatively little about the specific interactive processes that influence risk, protection, and healthy development over time.

Deeply rooted social and economic inequities in the United States further exacerbate the road to success during childhood and adolescence. In practical terms, these inequities mean that many young people grow up in neighborhoods and communities that lack the supports necessary to avoid trouble and find success at school. These inequities are perhaps most obvious in public education.

Education practice and policy, particularly as they affect at-risk children and youth, are at a turning point in the United States. The past decade has witnessed an intense focus on academic achievement, an outcome that is evaluated generally by school grade point average and standardized test scores. Unfortunately, despite more than a decade of reform, the emphasis on achievement has led to mixed outcomes. It is true that children and youth in some towns and cities have demonstrated significant improvements in reading, math, and other cognitive skills in the past 10 years. However, young people living in conditions of poverty and children and youth who lack the opportunity to attend high-quality schools have not experienced similar gains in achievement (Tough, 2009).

In this book, we argue that poor academic outcomes among at-risk children and youth are a product of marginal schools and inadequate extended education opportunities in disadvantaged neighborhoods and communities. Others have noted the importance of high-quality schools in the context of educational outcomes (e.g., Buckley Barry, Schoales, Levy, & Montague, 2008). We focus our discussion on the importance and promise of implementing community-based education support programs to children and youth in disadvantaged neighborhoods.

STRUCTURE OF THE BOOK

The book is divided into two parts. In the first section, we describe three common theoretical approaches to providing community-based programs to children and youth. Established theories of risk and resilience (Jenson & Fraser, 2011) and PYD (Lerner et al., 2003) are described in Chapters 1 and 2. The basic assumptions and relative strengths and weaknesses of each theoretical framework are delineated. In Chapter 3 we stress the importance of interorganizational collaboration in developing and sustaining programs in community settings.

Part II presents a new intervention model that integrates elements of risk and resilience, PYD, and interorganizational collaboration into a single framework called the integrated prevention and early intervention model (IPEI). The IPEI synthesizes elements of risk, protection, PYD, and collaboration in a way that is intended to help policymakers, program planners, practitioners, and researchers design, implement, and test community-based programs for children and youth. We believe that the integration of risk, protection, and PYD principles produces a single model that, when followed, is most likely to yield positive outcomes in the lives of at-risk youth. The IPEI extends earlier work aimed at examining commonalities and differences between risk-based frameworks and PYD (Catalano,

Hawkins, Berglund, Pollard, & Arthur, 2002) as well as methods shown to be successful in generating the commitment and resources necessary to implement these models (Alter, 2009; Alter & Hage, 1993).

In Chapters 4, 5, and 6, we apply the IPEI to a case study of the Bridge Project, an extended education support program serving children and families in four Denver, Colorado, public housing communities. The Bridge Project is a unique collaboration between the Graduate School of Social Work at the University of Denver and the Denver Housing Authority. The history and current status of this partnership is described in Chapter 4. Bridge Project interventions include structured education curricula and social and emotional learning activities during the afterschool hours. The program emphasizes literacy, math, and technology skill training and relies on a trained corps of qualified tutors and mentors. We present findings from an organizational analysis of the Bridge Project and results from a mixed-method investigation of participant outcomes in Chapter 6.

In the final chapter, we argue that community programs like the Bridge Project are an essential part of a comprehensive plan to improve academic achievement among the nation's youth. Recommendations for advancing extended education support programs for at-risk children and youth are delineated.

SUMMARY

The history and outcomes associated with community programs like the Bridge Project demonstrate the promise of implementing theoretically based, extended education interventions in high-risk communities. We hope the IPEI framework presented in this book will be used by policymakers and practitioners to increase community-based educational supports for at-risk children and youth. We encourage readers to apply lessons learned from our work at the Bridge Project to children and families in their own neighborhoods and communities. Together, practitioners, educators, administrators, and researchers are in a unique position to affect the lives children and youth. We hope this book provides the necessary path and the requisite tools to make a positive difference in the lives of young people.

PART ONE

Theoretical Models and Community-Based Programs for Children and Youth

CHAPTER 1

A Risk and Resilience Framework for Child and Youth Programs

Effective community-based programs for children and youth use theory to inform the nature and direction of interventions and services. Knowledge gained from a well-tested theory provides important insights about why some young people develop problems at school or participate in problem behaviors like delinquency or drug use. Theories also help us think about the timing of intervention in relation to normal developmental phases experienced by children and adolescents. In this chapter, we review briefly the evolution of theories and program strategies that seek to explain, prevent, and treat child and adolescent problems. We then turn to a detailed description of the risk and resilience framework as a relatively new approach to addressing problems experienced by young people. Finally, we apply principles of risk, protection, and resilience to program design and interventions used commonly with at-risk children and youth.

BACKGROUND

Preventing and Treating Child and Adolescent Problems: A Brief History

Theoretical ideas and strategies aimed at preventing and treating problem behavior among young people have a long history in the United States. The earliest efforts to help troubled youth date to the 1800s and were largely institutional in nature. Houses of refuge were created in 1825 to hold runaway, neglected, and deviant youth. These large and often unsavory facilities emphasized principles of education and hard work. By all accounts, very little rehabilitation occurred in houses of refuge (Empey, Stafford, & Hay, 1999). By 1870, Massachusetts and New York developed juvenile reformatories that aimed to provide a less punitive environment for troubled youth. However, reformatories became quickly overcrowded and soon resembled the adverse conditions found in houses of refuge.

Significant changes in the public's attitude toward the rehabilitation of troubled children and youth occurred in the latter decades of the 1880s. Charles Loring Brace created a program in which at-risk and troubled youth from large cities were relocated to rural farm families in the Midwest (Pecora & Harrison-Jackson, 2011). While met with mixed reactions from policy reformers, Brace's program was among the first to formally acknowledge the importance of environmental characteristics such as poverty and industrialization as a determinant of child and adolescent problems. This initiative soon gave way to systemic efforts to save children from adverse conditions that became a critical part of early social work practice and policy.

The origins of what became known as the *child saving movement* are found in Chicago in the late-1800s (Platt, 1969). Concerned about high rates of school dropout and crime, community volunteers and early social work reformers such as Jane Addams and Mary Richmond advocated for the rights of at-risk and wayward children. Addams was instrumental in opening Hull House, the first community settlement house in Chicago. The program offered children and parents a respite from the adverse conditions of poverty, unemployment, and crime (Addams, 1912). In an influential book, Richmond (1917) stressed the importance of identifying and addressing the individual, family, and community problems that were so apparent in the lives of poor children and adults living in American cities in the early 1990s. She called for the expansion of family- and community-based resources to assess and treat troubled children.

A formal recognition of the rights of children and the separation of juveniles from adults in the nation's legal system coincided with early social work interventions. Mandatory education laws enacted in the late 1800s required children to be in school and reduced youth involvement in the labor market (Empey et al., 1999). The nation's first juvenile court in 1899 created a separate legal system for handling at-risk children and adolescent offenders. The court was intended to act as a wise and benevolent parent and to place the best interests of children above all other considerations (Krisberg & Austin, 1993). It was also responsible for relegating legal dispositions and for rendering placement decisions for children and youth who had no option of remaining at home. This dual function created a conflict between the principles of punishment and rehabilitation and made difficult the court's effort to strike an appropriate balance between the two. This conflict persists to this day (Barton, 2011).

Early sociological and social work efforts to prevent and treat child and adolescent problems highlighted the importance of understanding the broader social conditions that led to antisocial behaviors. The Chicago Area studies of the 1930s conducted by Shaw and McKay (1931) highlighted the relationships among poverty, social disorganization, immigration, and crime. The Mobilization for Youth projects in the 1950s concentrated on improving opportunities for youth in New York City (Weissman, 1969). Evaluations of these early projects yielded mixed results in preventing or reducing behaviors such as juvenile delinquency and drug use (Berleman, 1980). However, the emphasis placed on understanding the conditions that led to child and adolescent problem behavior paved the way for significant theoretical, program, and policy changes that occurred in the 1960s and 1970s. Below we describe important developments in prevention and treatment efforts targeting children and youth since 1960.

Prevention. Modern prevention programs are generally traced to the 1960s, when intervention approaches based on principles of information dissemination and fear arousal were implemented in many of the nation's schools and communities. These strategies stressed and dramatized the dangers and adverse consequences of drug use and delinquent conduct in an attempt to discourage young people from participating in these problem behaviors. Public policy advocates and practitioners agreed that conveying information about the consequences and risks associated with problem behaviors such as delinquency and drug use is an important component of prevention programs. However, the effects of knowledge-based or fear arousal techniques were largely unsuccessful in changing attitudes, intentions, or individual behaviors in children and youth (Bangert-Drowns, 1988; Tobler, 1986).

A typical student experience from public education illustrates the theoretical orientation and nature of prevention programs commonly found in the 1960s. At the time, most middle school students in the United States were exposed to educational films and messages about the serious consequences of drinking and driving while intoxicated. Predictably, these films were often followed by movies that discussed human sexuality and described the dangers of smoking marijuana. Little or no classroom discussion ensued after the films. Rather, students often left class that day with a general curiosity about what had been so graphically depicted—in many cases exaggerated—on the screen. Teachers tried their best to convey messages about the dangers of risky behavior to their students, but they simply were not equipped with the proper prevention or intervention tools. Clearly, just illustrating the risks associated with problem behaviors was not enough to effect change in young people. In fact, several studies showed that exposure to information-only programs actually led to increases in drinking and drug use (Hawkins, 2006).

Affective education strategies and alternative programs for children and youth were a focus of prevention activities in the 1970s. Affective education was designed to increase responsible decision-making skills and enhance self-esteem. In this model, students were exposed to problem-solving and experiential activities based on the assumption that effective decision-making skills would deter involvement in antisocial behavior. Unfortunately, early affective education programs were only loosely tied to theory and did not prevent or reduce antisocial behavior itself (Botvin & Griffin, 2003).

Another strategy of the 1970s, alternative programming, was based on a belief that extracurricular or positive community activities could serve as a deterrent to antisocial behavior. This assumption implied that students who participated in after-school programs such as sports, arts, academic tutoring, or community activities would avoid involvement in problems like delinquency and drug use. Programs were intended to improve participants' relationships with positive peers and adults through experiential learning and cooperation. Studies, however, revealed that this approach also had only a limited effect on preventing problem behaviors (e.g., Schaps, Bartolo, Moskowitz, Palley, & Churgin, 1981).

In sum, early prevention approaches in schools and communities suffered from a very weak theoretical foundation. Programs were based on the "best thinking" of the time, and interventions were seldom linked to theoretical explanations about why children and youth did or did not experience problems. It is not surprising, therefore, that early efforts produced little in the way of positive outcomes among the children and youth who were exposed to school- and community-based programs.

Treatment. Theories and treatment approaches for child and adolescent problems are often categorized by their relative attention to individual, social, neighborhood, and community levels of influence or change. For example, the earliest theories of antisocial behavior in young people relied on individual and biological markers such as gender or race and were quickly dismissed for lack of credible evidence (Gould, 1996). These very early accounts were subsequently replaced by a host of sociological and psychological theories.

Sociological accounts of child and adolescent problem behavior recognize the importance of behavior in the context of the larger social environment. Theories such as differential opportunity (Cloward & Ohlin, 1960), anomie (Merton, 1957), and strain (Agnew, 2001) emphasize the availability of positive opportunities for children and youth as a key ingredient in helping young people succeed in school and avoid problems like school failure, crime, and drug use. Social disorganization (Bursik, 1984; Shaw & McKay, 1942) and differential association (Sutherland, 1939) theories suggest that quality schools, access to health care, and the availability of positive community supports are critical factors in helping young people become successful.

A particularly influential framework for practice with children and youth has been social control theory. Developed by Hirschi (1969) in the late 1960s, control theory emphasizes the importance of strong social bonds in the context of a young person's family, school, peer group, and community. Hirschi argues that effective social bonds are characterized by strong attachments to positive adults and peers, commitment to education, involvement in prosocial activities, and belief in the moral order. Strategies that promoted the creation of strong social bonds in children and youth became an integral part of community and school interventions following the 1960s (Empey et al., 1999).

Psychological explanations of child and adolescent problem behavior were developed simultaneously with the sociological theories described above. Social learning theory reinforced earlier work in criminology that viewed antisocial conduct as a learned behavior (Akers, 1977). That is, children and youth participate in behaviors such as delinquency and drug use because of what they see and experience in their family and social environments on a daily basis. Using this key proposition as a starting point, social learning theorists suggest that children and adolescents can learn new and positive social, behavioral, and cognitive skills that lead to positive decision making and less negative behavior (Bandura, 1989).

In recent years, theories purporting to explain child and adolescent problem behavior have integrated sociological and psychological traditions. For example, Patterson (1982) notes the influence of early dysfunctional parenting practices on young children's behavior. Further, he asserts that social disadvantage exacerbates inadequate parenting, leading to a pattern of coercive demands and responses between children and parents that increases the risk for serious antisocial behavior over time.

Catalano and Hawkins (1996) created the social development model, a theory that integrates perspectives from social control theory (Hirschi, 1969), social learning theory (Bandura, 1989), and differential association theory (Sutherland, 1973; Matsueda, 1982). The theory proposes that four factors inhibit the development of antisocial behaviors in children: (1) *bonding*, defined as attachment and commitment to family, school, and positive peers (Garmezy, 1985); (2) *belief in the shared values or norms* of these social units; (3) *external constraints* such as clear, consistent standards against antisocial behavior (Hansen, Malotte, & Fieding, 1988; Scheier & Botvin, 1998); and (4) *social, cognitive, and emotional skills* that provide protective tools for children to solve problems in social situations (Anthony, 1987; Rutter, 1987). Other integrated theories developed in the past two decades by Loeber (Loeber & Farrington, 1998), Elliott (Elliott, Huizinga, & Menard, 1989), Moffitt (1997), and Thornberry (Thornberry & Krohn, 2003) have also contributed greatly to theoretically based approaches to helping young people.

In sum, sociological, psychological, and integrated theories have played an important role in improving the design and effectiveness of treatment programs for at-risk youth. Many commonly used interventions and therapeutic models for young people are based on specific theoretical suppositions about child and adolescent problems. These interventions play a critical role in helping troubled youth in the nation's juvenile justice, mental health, substance abuse, and child welfare systems change existing patterns of antisocial and risk behavior.

Despite these theoretical and applied advances in understanding, preventing, and treating antisocial behavior, many practitioners still find it difficult to apply complex theoretical models about child and adolescent development to actual intervention strategies. Thus, the challenge inherent in applying theoretical ideas to prevention and treatment modalities remains a significant barrier to improving programs for at-risk youth (Jenson, 2006). Youth service workers and program administrators frequently ask for practical guides for building effective interventions and services for children and youth. The risk and resilience framework is one response to the request from practitioners for a more applied theoretical approach to explaining, preventing, and treating childhood and adolescent problem behaviors.

The late 1980s marked a significant shift in thinking about prevention and treatment programs for children and youth. In contrast to earlier methods, many prevention and treatment strategies began to systematically incorporate tenets of social learning theory to teach social, behavioral, and cognitive skills to children and youth. Manualized prevention and treatment curricula using structured skill-training techniques and lesson plans were essential components of the new strategy. Also important, practitioners and researchers began to recognize the value of developing community and school programs that targeted known risk and protective factors for child and adolescent problem behaviors (Hawkins, Jenson, Catalano, & Lishner, 1988). Principles of resilience—the capacity to be successful in the presence of risk and adversity—also gained credibility and popularity in the 1980s and 1990s (Luthar, 2003; Werner & Smith, 1982, 1992).

The use of risk, protection, and resilience as guiding program principles is compatible with a public health approach to addressing child and youth behavior. Shown in Figure 1.1, a public health strategy to ameliorating youth problems is one that considers the presence or absence of risk and protective factors for antisocial conduct when designing or selecting interventions (Centers for Disease Control & Prevention, 2011). Importantly, steps in this model incorporate empirical evidence about the characteristics and conditions that are most likely to elevate, or reduce, the likelihood of child or adolescent problem behavior. We describe the key concepts of risk, protection, and resilience below.

Risk Factors

In the context of childhood and adolescence, risk factors are individual, school, peer, family, and community-level influences that increase the chance of problem behaviors like drug use or juvenile delinquency. Intervention models based

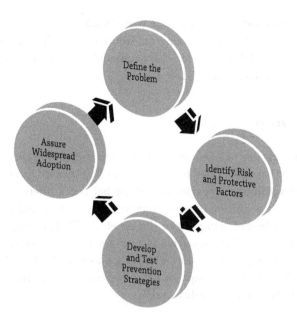

Figure 1.1
A Public Health Model of Preventing Child and Youth Problems

on principles of risk have gained widespread acceptance in the prevention field in the past decade (Biglan, Brennan, Foster, & Holden, 2004; Gottfredson & Wilson, 2003). The origin of risk-based prevention, however, dates to the 1980s when researchers and policymakers began placing greater importance on understanding the individual characteristics and environmental conditions present in the lives of troubled children and youth (Rutter, 1979, 1987). In turn, there emerged an increased emphasis on assessing the underlying causes of problem behavior, which led to the identification of specific individual traits, social influences, and environmental conditions that were significantly related to the onset or persistence of behaviors such as delinquency, drug use, and school dropout (Hawkins, Catalano, & Miller, 1992).

The earliest risk factor models were primarily lists of the known correlates of adolescent problems (e.g., Hawkins et al., 1988). Such lists often failed to consider the temporal relationship of risk factors to the occurrence of specific behaviors or to examine the additive and interactive effects of risk factors. Recent reviews of risk factors for adolescent problem behaviors (e.g., Fraser, Kirby, & Smokowski, 2004; Hawkins et al., 1998; Jenson & Howard, 1999, 2001; Jenson, Powell, & Forrest-Bank, 2011; Thornberry, 1998; Williams, Ayers, Van Dorn, & Arthur, 2004) have improved on earlier efforts by limiting their selection of studies to those in which the risk factor clearly preceded a problem behavior. Longitudinal studies have also been conducted to better understand the processes by which risk factors influence behavior over the course of childhood and adolescence (e.g., Hawkins, Catalano, Kosterman, Abbott, & Hill, 1999; Loeber, Farrington, Stouthamer-Loeber, & Van Kammen, 1998). Common risk factors for child and adolescent problems by level of influence are shown in Table 1.1.

Protective Factors

Experts favoring less of a deficit-based model to understand child and adolescent problems have advocated for a framework that is based on characteristics that protect youth from engaging in problem behaviors. There is some debate about the exact definition of what constitutes protection and about how to put protective factors into practice (Fraser et al., 2004; Rossa, 2002). Most investigators agree that protective factors are attributes or characteristics that lower the probability of an undesirable outcome (Rutter, 2001; Werner & Smith, 1992). There is disagreement, however, about the independence of protective factors in relationship to risk.

Table 1.1 RISK AND PROTECTIVE FACTORS FOR CHILD
AND ADOLESCENT PROBLEMS

Risk Factors	Protective Factors
Individual	Individual
Sensation-seeking orientation	Social and problem-solving skills
Poor impulse control	Positive attitude
Attention deficits	Temperament
Hyperactivity	High intelligence
	Low childhood stress
Interpersonal	Interpersonal
Family communication and conflict	Attachment to parents
Poor parent–child bonding	Caring relationships with siblings
Poor family management practices	Low parental conflict
Family alcohol and drug use	High levels of commitment to school
School failure	Involvement in conventional activities
Low commitment to school	Belief in prosocial norms and values
Rejection by conforming peer groups	
Association with antisocial peers	
Environmental	Environmental
Laws and norms favorable to antisocial behavior	Opportunities for education, employment,
Poverty	and other prosocial activities
Limited economic opportunity	Caring relationships with adults or extended
Neighborhood disorganization	family members
Low neighborhood attachment	Social support from nonfamily members

Note. Adapted from Jenson & Fraser (2011).

The knowledge base associated with the concept of protection emerged in the early 1980s when investigators such as Rutter (1979) and Werner and Smith (1982) expressed the idea that certain positive attributes or characteristics appeared to operate in the presence of risk or adversity. The exact definition of a protective factor, however, quickly became a topic of debate. Most of this debate centers on the confusion created when both risk and protective factors are conceptualized as representing the opposite ends of a single continuum (Pollard, Hawkins, & Arthur, 1999). For example, consistent family management practices are often identified as an important factor in producing positive outcomes in children. Inconsistent family management is construed as a factor leading to poor outcomes. In simple terms, consistent family management is identified as a protective factor while inconsistent family management is seen as a risk factor. Using risk and protection in this manner establishes the two concepts as polar opposites, with one pole representing positive outcomes and the other pole representing negative outcomes. We view protective traits as individual characteristics or environmental conditions that interact with specific risk factors present in a child or in her or his environment. We believe that protective factors serve to: (1) reduce or buffer the impact of risk in a child's life, (2) interrupt a chain of risk factors that may be present in a young person's life (e.g., disrupt a chain of risk that begins with peer rejection and leads to involvement with antisocial peers and then to delinquency), and (3) prevent or block the onset of a risk (Jenson & Fraser, 2011). Common protective factors are shown in Table 1.1.

Resilience

Resilience generally refers to successful adaptation in the presence of risk or adversity (Luthar, 2003; Olsson, Bond, Burns, Vella-Brodrick, & Sawyer, 2003). Numerous examples of young people and adults who have "overcome the odds" associated with the negative effects of risk come from child welfare (Festinger, 1984), juvenile justice (Vigil, 1990), substance abuse (Werner & Smith, 1992), and other service delivery settings. We conceptualize resilience as the outcome of a process that takes into account level of risk exposure and the presence of protective factors (Jenson & Fraser, 2011). When exposure to risk is high, evidence suggests that most children and adolescents experience some type of problem or developmental difficulty (Cicchetti, Rappaport, Sandler, & Weissberg, 2000). Protective factors exert influences on developmental outcomes where risk is high, but they may be relatively benign in circumstances where risk is low (Fraser, Richman, & Galinsky, 1999).

Sameroff and colleagues (Sameroff, 1999; Sameroff & Fiese, 2000; Sameroff & Gutman, 2004) have used the phrase *promotive factor* to refer to attributes or characteristics that have positive effects on people's lives, irrespective of the level of risk exposure. They argue that promotive factors (e.g., high intelligence) have direct effects on child and adolescent outcomes. Tests of the direct impact of promotive effects have been relatively limited to date (Sameroff, Bartko, Baldwin, Baldwin, & Siefer, 1999).

Increasingly, experts are viewing resilience as the outcome of an interactive process involving risk, protection, and promotion. Thus, adaptation—expressed through individual behavior—is interpreted as a product of an interactive process involving the presence or absence, level of exposure, and the strength of specific risk, protective, and promotive factors present in a child's life.

APPLYING RISK AND RESILIENCE TO PRACTICE

Principles of risk, protection, and resilience provide useful tools for practitioners and administrators because they help identify and specify interventions that are aligned with broader program goals aimed at preventing or treating a specific problem behavior. Figure 1.2 illustrates how risk and protective mechanisms are related to program goals, interventions, and outcomes in a typical community-based youth program.

The model begins with an understanding of the risk and protective mechanisms that are commonly associated with problems such as school dropout, delinquency, and drug use. As we noted earlier, risk and protective factors for youth problems vary widely among individuals. Risk and protective traits and conditions also vary by social context and environmental setting. Thus, a first step in applying principles of risk and protection to a youth program often requires an assessment of the most prevalent risk and protective traits among potential youth participants. Such an assessment should also include an evaluation of family, school, and community-level conditions that may increase risk and protect children and youth from involvement in problem behavior.

As shown in Figure 1.2, a program's goals, interventions, and anticipated outcomes should be directly linked to risk and protective factors. In our example, we show how knowledge of risk and protective factors can be used to articulate program goals, develop interventions, and identify outcomes for children and youth who participate in a community-based program aimed at promoting school success. Note that selected risk and protective traits are based on characteristics related to a specific child or adolescent problem. In our example, we are highlighting risk and protective factors most commonly associated with school dropout and academic failure. These factors, in turn, help establish program goals and lead to specific interventions that are effective in achieving such goals.

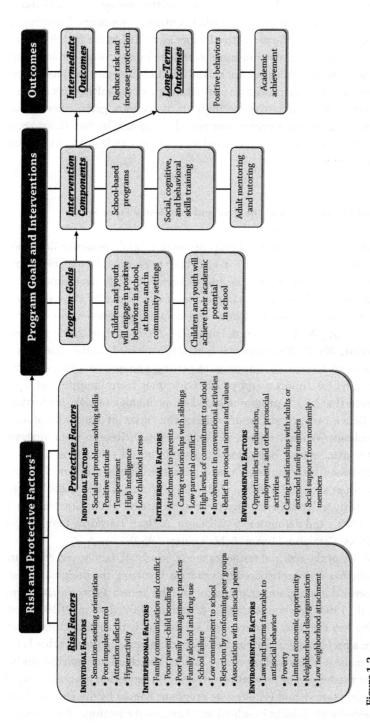

Figure 1.2
A Risk and Resilience Approach to Preventing and Treating Youth Problems
1. Adapted from Jenson & Fraser (2011).

Youth outcomes complete the final piece of the conceptual model shown in Figure 1.2. In our example, intermediate outcomes are defined as reducing the risk and increasing the protective factors identified in the far left column of the figure. Long-term outcomes are intended to measure academic success and involvement in positive behaviors. The selected outcomes complete a path of intervention that begins with an understanding of underlying risk and protective traits and leads to the specification of program goals, intervention approaches, and the measurement of stated outcomes. In Part II, we apply principles of the risk and resilience model to our case study of an after-school program in Denver.

Utility and Effectiveness of the Risk and Resilience Framework

The fundamental principles of risk, protection, and resilience described above have become a key feature in efforts to prevent and treat child problem behaviors. For example, risk and resilience models have contributed greatly to the development and implementation of specific clinical or programmatic interventions in school and community prevention settings (Cicchetti et al., 2000; Jenson & Dieterich, 2007; Luthar, 2003; Masten, 2001; Woolf, 2008). Also important, strategies based on the model have contributed to a renewed emphasis in testing prevention and treatment interventions for children and youth. Outcomes from longitudinal studies indicate that youth programs based on principles of risk, protection, and resilience can prevent and/or delay the onset of child and adolescent problems (Wilson, Lipsey, & Derzon, 2003). Recent meta-analyses and systematic reviews have identified a number of efficacious risk- and resilience-based interventions aimed at preventing aggression and violence (Hahn et al., 2007; Limbos et al., 2007; Wilson & Lipsey, 2007), drug use (Foxcroft, Ireland, Lister-Sharp, Lowe, & Breen, 2003; Gottfredson & Wilson, 2003), and delinquency (Catalano, Arthur, Hawkins, Berglund, & Olson, 1998; Catalano, Loeber, & McKinney, 1999).

The utility of the risk and resilience model in school, family, and community settings has also contributed to a process involving the design and testing of prevention programs that has come to be known as *prevention science* (Coie et al., 1993; Hawkins, Catalano, & Arthur, 2002; Jenson, 2010; Woolf, 2008). The key elements of prevention science imply that: (1) factors associated with a problem behavior must be changed in order to prevent that behavior, (2) malleable risk and protective factors identified in empirical studies should be the targets of prevention efforts, (3) prevention programs should be rigorously tested, and (4) effective programs should be disseminated and implemented with fidelity in school and community settings. The elements of prevention science, compatible with public health and risk and resilience models of intervention, have now become commonplace aspects of program design, evaluation, and funding in many youth service agencies.

Risk and resilience models have most commonly been applied to prevention programming. This is logical since the premise behind such models lies in reducing risks that lead to the onset of child and adolescent problems, and increasing protection. However, treatment approaches using principles of risk and protection have also been effective in predicting and reducing juvenile recidivism (Grunwald, Lockwood, Harris, & Mennis, 2010) and drug abuse relapse (Marlatt & Gordon, 1985). In these cases, knowledge of the risk and protective factors associated with reoffending or returning to drug use have been used to inform interventions that seek to interrupt the damaging cycles of repeated crime or drug abuse.

Translating Theoretical Principles to Programs and Services

Theoretical explanations that aim to specify the reasons why some children and youth have trouble at school or engage in behaviors like delinquency or drug use are measured ultimately by their translation to real-world settings. Most experts would agree that the risk and resilience model has been widely adopted by schools and communities because practitioners and policymakers have found the framework relatively easy to understand and put into action (Catalano, 2007; Hawkins, 2006; Jenson, 2010; Woolf, 2008).

The premise of the risk and resilience framework lies in using knowledge of risk and protective factors as specific targets of interventions and services. For example, studies suggest that attachment to teachers and other positive adults is an important protective trait in reducing risk for academic failure or school dropout (Hallinan, 2008). Thus, it follows that a school-based intervention that is consistent with the model uses strategies to increase school bonding and attachment. Similarly, a community-based youth service program might add a mentoring component such as those described in Box 1.1 in an attempt to increase positive attachments between at-risk youth and positive adults in the neighborhood.

Ideally, a continuum of interventions and services for children and youth will include program elements that address multiple risk and protective traits at all levels of influence. Clearly, no single intervention can effectively address all individual, social, and community risk and protective traits. Importantly, the risk and resilience model does allow practitioners and policymakers to identify and prioritize prevalent risk and protective traits in a targeted area and to then develop and select interventions that aim to reduce risk and increase protection. In Table 1.2., we show how knowledge of risk and protection has been used to inform the design of effective school, family, and community-based interventions for children and youth.

Yes, mentoring programs such as Big Brothers Big Sisters have reported positive outcomes for children and youth in several published studies (Herrera et al., 2007). Indeed, mentoring interventions have been associated with increased levels of positive social and emotional bonds that, in turn, serve as important protective factors for children and youth (Rhodes, 2002). Mentoring programs have also been shown to decrease important risk factors for school dropout, academic failure, delinquency, and drug use (Dubois, Holloway, Valentine, & Cooper, 2002).

What specific risk and protective factors are addressed by mentoring programs?

RISK FACTORS

- Norms favorable to antisocial behavior
- School failure
- Low commitment to school
- Association with antisocial peers
- Poor impulse control

PROTECTIVE FACTORS

- Opportunities for education, employment, and other prosocial activities
- Caring relationships with adults or extended family members
- Social support from nonfamily members
- High levels of commitment to school
- Involvement in conventional activities
- Belief in prosocial norms and values
- Social and problem-solving skills

An important aspect of mentoring programs is preparedness and training. Evidence indicates that consistent and sustained mentor training is related to increased participation rates and positive outcomes among youth who receive mentoring interventions (Herrera et al., 2007). Like all community and school programs, effective interventions require careful planning and consistent implementation!

Table 1.2 A TYPOLOGY OF EFFECTIVE SCHOOL, FAMILY, AND COMMUNITY YOUTH PROGRAMS

Effective Program Strategies	Targeted Risk and Protective Factors
Universal (General Populations)	
Early childhood education	Early onset of aggression, drug use, and
Antibullying programs in schools	delinquency; commitment to school; social
Classroom management and school organization	and cognitive skills; community norms about
Social, behavioral, and cognitive skills training	antisocial behavior
Changing community norms about antisocial conduct	
Selected (High-Risk Populations)	
Prenatal and infancy home visitation	Parental discipline and monitoring, attach-
Family support	ment to parents, school failure, family
Social, behavioral, and cognitive skills training	conflict, caring relationships with siblings,
Parent training	prenatal health
Increasing parent–child bonding	
Reducing family conflict	
Mentoring	
Indicated (Youth Populations with Identified Problems)	
Social, behavioral, and cognitive skills training	Social and cognitive skill, poverty, involve-
Wraparound services	ment in conventional activities, prosocial
Youth employment	beliefs

Note. Adapted from Biglan et al., 2004; Jenson et al., 2011; Limbos et al., 2007; Wilson & Lipsey, 2007.

INTEGRATION AND COMPARISON OF RISK AND RESILIENCE TO OTHER THEORETICAL MODELS

We earlier described the evolution of theory as it relates to the prevention and treatment of child and adolescent problem behavior. Risk and resilience models add several important components to other theories of child and adolescent behavior. First, unlike many theories, knowledge of risk and protective traits leads directly to the identification of specific intervention strategies. Pragmatically, knowing which risk and protective traits are most prevalent in a particular neighborhood or school allows practitioners and policymakers to more efficiently target services to local needs. These two related advantages run contrary to many theories in which constructs are stated in abstract terms or in ways that offer little direct application to intervention.

A second important contribution of risk and resilience to theories of child and adolescent development lies in recognizing that behavior is influenced by multiple levels and domains. This idea is not new. Ecological theory, a long-revered model in the social sciences, posits that child development is affected by interactions between the biological and psychological characteristics of an individual and conditions present in her or his environment. The ecological perspective is well known and widely applied in education, practice, and research across many disciplines and professions (Bronfenbrenner, 1979, 1986; Germain, 1991). However, the organization of risk and protective factors in a theoretical framework that is consistent with ecological theory marks a significant contribution to theory, practice, and policy with at-risk youth.

In earlier work (Jenson & Fraser, 2011), we noted that risk and resilience models afford policymakers a five-step design and implementation process for developing and implementing policies for children and youth. These steps include evaluating the prevalence of risk and protective traits in a given geographic area, assigning policy and practice needs to responsive care systems, using evidence to create policy responses, determining the course of specific individual and social interventions, and implementing and monitoring risk- and protective-based policies (Jenson & Fraser, 2011). While intended for policy-level discussions, these steps are easily converted to practice and intervention frameworks. The essential steps of assessing risk and protection, matching levels of risk and protection to appropriate interventions, and testing the effects of selected interventions on client outcomes are integral aspects of a risk and resilience framework. To that end, the model can be easily adapted for policy or practice applications.

No theory is immune from criticism or shortcomings. The risk and resilience model has been denounced for paying inadequate attention to differences in risk and protective traits by class, gender, race, ethnicity, and sexual orientation (Belknap & Holsinger, 2006). According to some practitioners and investigators, the model also falls short of recognizing the importance of understanding the nature of interactions between individual traits and the broader community conditions that lead to youth problems (Masten & Powell, 2003). Clearly, much needs to be done to increase the utility of the model across these and other potentially distinguishing characteristics or conditions. A final criticism of the risk and resilience model comes from practitioners who believe that the framework places too much emphasis on deficits. Proponents of the framework known as positive youth development have been the strongest voice addressing this concern. This model is the topic of the next chapter.

SUMMARY

Significant advances have been made in understanding the reasons why some young people develop problems at school or choose to participate in antisocial behavior. Isolating the individual, social, and community characteristics that elevate, or reduce, the likelihood of problem behavior among children and youth is the hallmark of the risk and resilience model. The model has been applied widely in community and school settings and used across a number of diverse prevention and intervention strategies. Among the strengths of the model is its ability to link etiological factors about child and adolescent problem behaviors to specific intervention strategies. In this regard, the model has had considerable influence on youth service workers and administrators. We discuss an alternative, yet complementary, model of understanding child and adolescent problems known as positive youth development in the following chapter.

CHAPTER 2

A Positive Youth Development Model for Child and Youth Programs

The application of risk and resilience frameworks to the developmental phases of childhood and adolescence has led to significant advances in preventing and treating social and behavioral problems experienced by young people. Yet many practitioners note that the emphasis on individual deficits associated with risk and resilience models limits their capacity to develop interventions and programs that acknowledge the many strengths and assets in a young person's life. Consequently, alternate models to risk and resilience that focus on aspects of positive youth development have been implemented by many community-based agencies. Interventions derived from these models promote the healthy development of children and youth by incorporating program elements aimed at maximizing positive social bonds and improving competencies in individual, social, and environmental contexts. In this chapter, we trace the origin and describe the evolution of the positive youth development framework. We also explore similarities and differences between positive youth development and the risk and resilience model presented in Chapter 1. We begin with a discussion of the fundamental principles undergirding the positive youth development model.

BACKGROUND

Healthy Child and Adolescent Development

Youth advocates, practitioners, and scholars have become increasingly aware of the relationship between young people's strengths, assets, and resources and their capacity to live healthy and productive lives (Catalano, Hawkins, Berglund, Pollard, & Arthur, 2002; Lerner, Dowling, & Anderson, 2003).

Indeed, studies indicate that children and youth who possess individual strengths and social and community resources are less likely than other youth to participate in problem behaviors like delinquency and substance use (Lerner et al., 2003; Phelps et al., 2007). Strengths and resources held by young people have also been identified as important change agents in interventions targeting children and youth (Catalano et al., 2002; Roth, Brooks-Gunn, Murray, & Foster, 1998). The increased orientation toward child and adolescent strengths has led to a relatively new framework known as positive youth development (PYD).

At its most basic level, PYD reframes existing risk-based explanations of child and adolescent behavior by focusing on the positive traits and resources in a young person's life. PYD underscores the healthy and adaptive development of children and adolescents. Advocates of the model advance the notion that all young people not only *have* resources but also *are* resources—to themselves, their families, and to others in society. They further suggest that healthy development is characterized by a sense of responsibility, connectedness, and positive values. The perspective stands in stark contrast to the early storm and stress viewpoints of adolescence (Freud, 1969) in which young people were thought to be in need of psychological intervention because of developmental conflicts that are now seen as quite normal during adolescence (Lerner, Almerigi, Theokas, & Lerner, 2005). In sum, from a PYD perspective, all youth possess, and indeed are, *resources* that should be developed rather than liabilities or problems to be handled (Roth et al., 1998).

THE POSITIVE YOUTH DEVELOPMENT MODEL

Origins and Influences of PYD

PYD has roots in several philosophical and theoretical traditions. The model emerged from interdisciplinary collaboration among practitioners and scholars who were interested in improving interventions for children and youth. Equally important, PYD also grew out of the grassroots efforts of youth workers who were interested in promoting programs and policies to support healthy child development (Lerner et al., 2005). Today, the on-the-ground proponents of PYD are social workers and other individuals who advocate for policy change and funding for interventions and community-based services aimed at promoting healthy youth development. The grassroots efforts of advocates and scholars have contributed greatly to the proliferation of PYD. Child advocates such as Geoffrey Canada in Harlem and representatives from groups like the Annie E. Casey Foundation are but a few of the national champions of PYD (Annie E. Casey Foundation, 2011c; Tough, 2009). The voices of these advocates alongside the diverse group of constituents interested in PYD have strengthened the connection between theoretical perspectives, policy, practice, and research in support of the model.

The PYD model is an extension of applied developmental science, an approach that builds on decades of research while extending easily from the ivory tower to communities and neighborhoods. Lerner, Fisher, & Weinberg (2000) explain that applied developmental science has roots in several traditions that include: (1) philosophy of science (Pepper, 1942), (2) developmental psychology (Cairns, 1998; Sears, 1975), (3) developmental theory (Lerner, 1998), (4) life span models of human development (Baltes, 1987; Baltes, Lindenberger, & Staudinger, 1998; Baltes, Staudinger, & Lindenberger, 1999), and (5) bioecological approaches (Bronfenbrenner, 1979; Bronfenbrenner & Morris, 1998). Borrowing from these influences, PYD suggests that human behavior changes during the course of development and that such change occurs in a bidirectional context involving interactions between individuals and their environments. Further, the model stipulates that developing strengths and competencies as opposed to treating deficits is the most effective way to prevent and treat problems among youth (Lerner et al., 2005).

Plasticity, or the idea that human behavior can and does change during the course of development, is central to PYD (Lerner et al., 2005). The concept of plasticity implies that there is always a possibility for change in human behavior and that supportive contexts can be mobilized to encourage and support such change (Benson, 2003). This hopeful perspective, which has not always characterized the study of child and youth development, is—perhaps not surprisingly—well received by supporters of youth development programs. A social work supervisor at the Bridge Project, the community-based program described in Chapters 4–7, supports the perception of PYD held by many members of the practice community:

> PYD has given my staff the ability to see and value the positive attributes of the kids we serve in our afterschool program. We know that children come to our program with significant risks in their daily lives. But seeing young people in the context of strengths and positive characteristics has really helped us redefine our interventions and practice approaches.

APPLYING POSITIVE YOUTH DEVELOPMENT TO PRACTICE

The key principles guiding PYD include respecting and identifying youth strengths, engaging and motivating youth to support change through these strengths, working with youth as collaborators, avoiding victim mind-sets, and harnessing resources that exist in the environment (Damon, 2004; Lerner et al., 2005; Pittman, 1992). The practice of PYD suggests that youth, families, communities, and systems can take proactive roles in the positive

Table 2.1 INTERNAL AND EXTERNAL ASSETS FOR MIDDLE
CHILDHOOD (AGES 8–12)

Internal Assets	External Assets
Commitment to Learning	*Support*
Achievement motivation	Family support
Learning engagement	Positive family communication
Homework	Other adult relationships
Bonding to school	Caring neighborhood
Reading for pleasure	Caring school climate
Positive Values	Parent involvement in schooling
Caring	*Empowerment*
Equality and social justice	Community values youth
Integrity	Children as resources
Honesty	Service to others
Responsibility	Safety
Healthy lifestyle	*Boundaries and Expectations*
Social Competencies	Family boundaries
Planning and decision making	School boundaries
Interpersonal competence	Neighborhood boundaries
Cultural competence	Adult role models
Resistance skills	Positive peer influence
Peaceful conflict resolution	High expectations
Positive Identity	*Constructive Use of Time*
Personal power	Creative activities
Self-esteem	Child programs
Sense of purpose	Religious community
Positive view of personal future	Time at home

Source: Search Institute (2006).

development of future generations (Benson, 1997; Edwards, Mumford, &
Serra-Roldan, 2007). Ultimately, PYD suggests that young people who have
mutually beneficial relationships with other people and institutions will enter
adulthood as positive and successful contributors.

PYD advocates also assert that risk-oriented frameworks fail to consider
the idea that preventing a problem from occurring does not guarantee that
youth are developing and growing in a healthy manner (Damon, 2004). That
is, healthy development (well-being, thriving, etc.) is not simply the absence
of problematic behaviors; it also includes the cultivation of multiple resources
and strengths within a child and her or his particular context (Anthony &
Stone, 2010). From the PYD perspective, children are seen as naturally competent and prosocial. Across cultures children universally show very early
signs of empathy, moral awareness, and prosocial behavior (Damon, 2004).

Therefore, rather than target pathology in an individual child, interventions based on PYD aim to promote positive behaviors by ensuring that there are positive influences in the individual, social, and environmental milieu of the child's life. These conditions and relationships provide the resources leading to the healthy development of young people (Lerner, Lerner, & Phelps, 2009). Understanding the importance of context creates the necessary foundation for interventions in school, home, and community settings.

Two additional related concepts have been linked to the promotion and evaluation of positive youth development. Below we describe developmental assets (Benson, 1997; Benson, Leffert, Scales, & Blyth, 1998) and the 5 C's of PYD—*competence, connection, character, confidence,* and *caring* (Lerner et al., 2000; Roth et al., 1998). We then extend the discussion of how these and other PYD concepts may be used in youth service agencies.

Developmental Assets

The developmental assets approach was conceived by Peter Benson in the 1990s at the Search Institute of Minnesota as a way to identify the variables that contribute to healthy child development (Benson, 1997; Benson et al., 1998; Scales & Leffert, 1999). The assets are grouped into external and internal assets for different age ranges (early childhood, ages 3–5; Grades K-3, ages 5–9; middle childhood, ages 8–12; adolescents, ages 12–18). Table 2.1 lists the assets for middle childhood. The first twenty external assets refer to people and institutions in children's lives and are categorized as *support, empowerment, boundaries and expectations,* and *constructive use of time.* In the developmental assets perspective, youth are equal and full partners in personal and social relationships and in community settings. Thus, they are expected to provide important and positive contributions to self and others (Damon, 2004). The model suggests that youth should be given roles with a purpose and the responsibility to provide service as members of their communities. Young people are expected to do well and are encouraged by parents and teachers to do so. Positive adult role models provide a context in which expectations for a sense of morality and spirituality are made (Damon, 2004).

Internal assets are defined by categories labeled *commitment to learning, positive values, social competencies,* and *positive identity.* These constructs pertain to internal qualities that promote positive development (Edwards et al., 2007). Caring, equality, social justice, integrity, honesty, and responsibility are among the personal qualities that instill a moral basis for identity. Promotion of positive moral development through engagement in civic society instills a set of aspirations toward socially and personally productive futures (Damon, 2004).

Research findings indicate that developmental assets are associated with positive educational and other life outcomes (Lerner et al., 2009). Roth et al. (1998) suggest the more assets youth exhibit, the less likely they are to participate in high-risk behaviors. Some studies report that developmental assets may be protective against risk behaviors such as adolescent tobacco use (Atkins, Oman, & Vesely, 2002) and violence (Aspy et al., 2004). Youth exhibiting more assets tend to participate in extracurricular activities and sports, display leadership, maintain good relationships with peers and parents, demonstrate academic competence, and become engaged in school at higher rates than other youth (Edwards et al., 2007). It remains unclear which particular assets are most influential since they are typically assessed together. We view the developmental assets approach as one way to describe and identify strengths in young people. Applying knowledge of assets to intervention and program design, however, has been limited to date.

The 5 C's of PYD

Lerner created the 5 C's acronym to describe the psychological, behavioral, and social attributes that are believed to be characteristic of a thriving and well-adapted young person (Lerner, 2005). Thriving represents a positive state, one desired outcome of PYD, and is described by Vazsonyi (2005) as "the process of developing functionally valued assets and behaviors" (p. 6). Thriving is a process rather than a trait or a state and is often viewed as the active reflection (rather than a passive outcome) of a range of adaptive behaviors in response to opportunities and challenges (Theokas et al., 2005). Table 2.2 summarizes the 5 C's, which include *competence, connection, character, confidence,* and *caring* (or *compassion*) (Lerner et al., 2000; Roth et al., 1998). A sixth C, *contribution,* was added more recently to reflect actions and behaviors resulting from the 5 C's (Lerner et al., 2005).

Competence refers to having a positive view of one's actions in domain-specific areas including social, academic, cognitive, and vocational settings. A young person with cognitive abilities and social and behavioral skills exhibits competence. Programs might support competence through various learning experiences in which a young person tries out new skills, with support and guidance.

Connection, on the other hand, refers to positive bonds with people and institutions that are reflected in bidirectional exchanges between the individual and peers, family, school, and community in which both parties contribute to the relationship. Positive bonds with adults and others involved in the young person's life, as well as connections to institutions, represent an experience of connection. Presumably, when a young person is connected, s/he is able to take full advantage of positive resources and support. Mentoring initiatives and other programs that support positive adult role models (including family members and extrafamilial adults) and relationships can contribute to building connection.

Table 2.2 THE "5 C'S" OF POSITIVE YOUTH DEVELOPMENT

"C"	Definition
Competence	Positive view of one's actions in specific areas, including social, academic, cognitive, and vocational. Social competence refers to interpersonal skills (e.g., conflict resolution). Cognitive competence refers to cognitive abilities (e.g., decision making). Academic competence refers to school performance as shown, in part, by school grades, attendance, and test scores. Health competence involves using nutrition, exercise, and rest to keep oneself fit. Vocational competence involves work habits and explorations of career choices. Effective entrepreneurial skills may be one instance of vocational competence.
Confidence	An internal sense of overall positive self-worth and self-efficacy
Connection	Positive bonds with people and institutions that are reflected in exchanges between the individual and his or her peers, family, school, and community in which both parties contribute to the relationship
Character	Respect for societal and cultural norms, possession of standards for correct behaviors, a sense of right and wrong, and integrity
Caring and compassion	A sense of sympathy and empathy for others

Source: Lerner, Lerner, & Phelps (2009).

Character reflects respect for societal and cultural rules, possession of standards for correct behaviors, a sense of right and wrong, and integrity. A child with character knows how to assess the functioning of the social world and makes wise decisions about her/his own conduct in relationship to these rules and norms. Character does not reflect simple-minded following of rules but, rather, an ability to critically examine situations and respond with well-reasoned decisions. Leadership and civic engagement programs often focus on character development through active participation in decisions and social initiatives.

Confidence is an internal sense of overall positive self-worth and self-efficacy: one's global self-regard, as opposed to the domain-specific beliefs. When a young person is confident, s/he feels good about her/himself and the ability to accomplish tasks. A confident young person will acknowledge limitations, in addition to strengths, and can therefore assert her/himself with assurance. Confidence can be encouraged formally via mentoring and tutoring programs, and more informally through positive relationships. The opportunity to try something new and learn through trial and error with support and encouragement promotes confidence.

Caring and compassion connote a sense of sympathy and empathy for others, the ability to see outside one's self. A caring and compassionate child can share the experience of suffering with others and relate to the basic human experience. Social justice, the notion of human rights and equity for all individuals, is also a part of caring and compassion. Caring and compassion can be reflected by positive adult role models and encouraged through stories and other ways of sharing the experience of others.

Lerner added a new "C" to the model in recent years (Lerner et al., 2005). Labeled *contributions*, it suggests that all healthy children and adolescents have a responsibility to give back to others in their individual, social, and environment settings. Contributions to self, family, and to the institutions of a civil society are ultimately what young adults who have developed adaptively will exhibit (Lerner, 2005). Giving something back is a natural and active extension of the original 5 C's. Lerner and colleagues (2005) suggest that contributions are made up of an ideological component (belief that something should be contributed to self and context) and an action or behavioral component that is responsive to the belief. Young people can make big and small contributions on an everyday basis as an outgrowth of the strengths they have developed within themselves. For example, programs like the Bridge Project—described in Part II of this book—encourage formal contributions by participants and alumni by creating opportunities to link young participants with older, more experienced participants (Anthony, Alter, & Jenson, 2009; Bender et al., 2011).

Recent studies have examined the conceptual framework of PYD, including the 5 C's, and the relationship between the key tenets of the PYD model and healthy development. Through the implementation and testing of the model in practice, largely via the national 4-H programs, the framework and associated outcomes have been identified. As depicted in Figure 2.1, the goal of PYD programs is to promote positive and healthy physical, intellectual/academic, emotional, psychological, and spiritual development. In other words, PYD programs promote thriving among young people in the various contexts (such as school, family, and community) of life. PYD programs accomplish this goal by assessing the needs of the child and delivering a structured curriculum and activities designed to promote academic and interpersonal skills, competencies, and positive personal attributes. The outcomes of the PYD model are the 6 C's—*competence, connection, character, confidence, caring* and *compassion*, and *contributions*.

In the next section, we discuss the empirical support for PYD and its utility as a program model for promoting healthy development among young people.

Utility and Effectiveness of the PYD Model

The U.S. Department of Health and Human Services commissioned a study in the late 1990s to examine the state of PYD programming and research

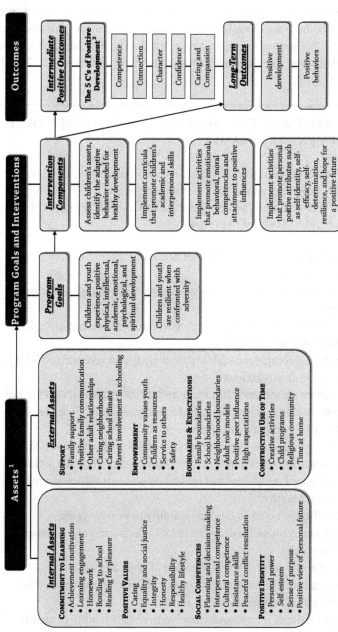

Figure 2.1
A Positive Youth Development Framework
1. Adapted from the Search Institute (2010)
2. Adapted from Lerner, Lerner, & Phelps (2009)

(Catalano, Berglund, Ryan, Lonczak, & Hawkins, 2004). Among the challenges facing the evaluation team was the considerable variability in definitions, mechanisms of intervention delivery, and intensity and dosage of PYD programs and practices. The project attempted to contend with some of these thorny issues by first clarifying what was meant by the term "positive youth development." The evaluation team also worked diligently to reach consensus on the objectives shared by PYD programs. Shown below in Box 2.1, the

---

Box 2.1 WHAT ARE THE OBJECTIVES OF POSITIVE YOUTH DEVELOPMENT PROGRAMS?

A team of researchers examined the objectives of positive youth development (PYD) programs across the country and found that PYD interventions shared 15 common themes (Catalano et al., 2004). Programs based on principles of PYD aimed to promote:

1. Bonding (emotional attachment and commitment to social relationships)
2. Resilience (capacity for healthy adaptation to change and stressful events)
3. Social competence (range of interpersonal skills integrating feelings, thinking, and action)
4. Emotional competence (ability to identify and respond to feelings and emotional reactions)
5. Cognitive competence (academic and intellectual achievement and cognitive skills such as reading and interpretation of social cues)
6. Behavioral competence (effective action)
7. Moral competence (respect for rules and a sense of social justice)
8. Self-determination (ability to think for oneself and take action)
9. Spirituality (components of religiosity or nontraditional applied spiritual practice)
10. Self-efficacy (belief in one's own ability to achieve goals)
11. Clear and positive identity (internal organization of a coherent sense of self)
12. Belief in the future (internalization of hope and optimism)
13. Recognition for positive behavior (positive response from others in the social environment)
14. Opportunities for prosocial involvement (availability of events and activities to encourage prosocial actions)
15. Prosocial norms (adoption of healthy beliefs and clear standards for behavior)

---

objectives reinforce the 5 C's described earlier in the chapter and emphasize the importance of healthy social bonds, competence, self-efficacy, positive opportunities, and prosocial beliefs in the lives of young people.

Catalano and associates (Catalano, Berglund, Ryan, Lonczak, & Hawkins, 1998; Catalano et al., 2004) conducted a systematic review of PYD programs that exhibit the 15 objectives shown above. Criteria such as clear use of PYD constructs, age of participants, and evaluation methodology were used in the review. Twenty-five programs that met the team's criteria for an adequate evaluation design and that had operational definitions of PYD components were identified. The 25 program evaluations ranged from single interventions such as the Big Brothers Big Sisters mentoring program (Tierney, Grossman, & Resch, 1995) to comprehensive programs such as the Adolescent Transitions Project (Andrews, Soberman, & Dishion, 1995) that uses youth and parent components as part of an overall strategy to promote healthy youth development. Positive outcomes pertaining to youth behavior such as increases in commitment to school and improvements in interpersonal skills were found in 19 programs. Twenty-four programs demonstrated significant reductions in negative behaviors such as substance use and high-risk sexual activity (Catalano et al., 2004).

Common PYD program components. Several common program elements or characteristics were found in the 25 effective PYD programs identified by Catalano et al. (2004). These components are discussed below and shown in Figure 2.2.

All 25 PYD programs reviewed by Catalano and colleagues (2004) *targeted at least five of the positive youth constructs* identified by the evaluation team. Competence, self-efficacy, and prosocial norms were the most common, appearing in all 25 programs. The ability to target multiple domains appeared

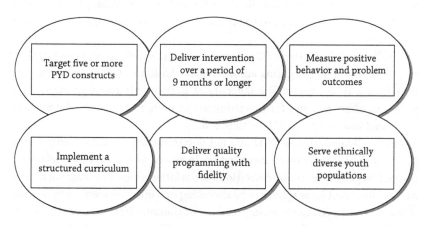

Figure 2.2
Characteristics of Effective PYD Programs

to strengthen the overall effect on PYD outcomes. This finding is consistent with prevention efforts that acknowledge common risk and protective factors for both problem and positive behavior among young people (Pollard, Hawkins, & Arthur, 1999).

Second, the effective PYD programs *measured positive behavior as well as problem outcomes*. While programs did not use the same measurement tools, the 25 effective programs used measures of problem behaviors such as substance use and positive outcomes such as self-efficacy in their evaluation protocols. Recognizing and measuring positive *and* problematic outcomes as distinct constructs and not simply opposite ends of a continuum (Anthony & Stone, 2010) are critical for evaluating PYD interventions.

Third, the 25 PYD programs implemented *a structured curriculum*, a function critical for replication of effective programs. In addition to providing a clear linkage between the theoretical framework and key tenets of PYD to the outcomes of interest, structured curricula allowed programs to specify intervention targets, goals, and evaluation measures.

Fourth, effective programs were *delivered over a period of 9 months or longer*. Longer periods allow young people the time to more fully accept and use content delivered in program components and to demonstrate some of the desired outcomes. It may also be that interventions taking place for longer periods of time are more likely to maintain effects in follow-up evaluations because of the young peoples' ability to try on skills in different settings and across different developmental stages.

Fifth, effective programs *delivered quality programming consistently (with fidelity)*. With the advantage of a structured curriculum, the effective programs were clear about the goals of the program and consistently and reliably implemented interventions as intended. In community-based programming in particular, fidelity can be a challenge when adaptations need to be made because of the diversity of the clients or the setting. Successful programs were able to stay true to the goals of the program and deliver high-quality programming consistently.

Finally, the 25 effective PYD programs *served ethnically diverse youth populations*. Effective PYD programs enrolled Black, Latina/o, Asian, and American Indian, and White youth. The diversity of participants found in many PYD programs offers promise for practitioners, administrators, and policymakers interested in advancing PYD for all youth.

The implementation of PYD as a guiding framework in community-based youth programs has grown significantly in recent years. Early models were plagued by poor operational definitions and relatively vague conceptual frameworks. These problems appear to be shrinking in scope as evidenced by studies that confirm the relatively widespread use of common PYD intervention components in a variety of youth service programs (Catalano et al., 2004). Results from recent studies also support the basic tenets of the PYD model, including the constructs associated with the 5 C's developed by Lerner and associates (King et al., 2005; Lerner et al., 2005, 2009).

Advances in the consistency and careful implementation of the PYD model are encouraging. Equally important, practitioners embrace the model as one that is compatible with individual, peer, and family interventions in community settings (National 4-H Youth Development Organization, 2010). While the acceptance of PYD among practitioners is a key marker in the evolution of the model, several limitations inherent in the framework still require attention. One concern is that most evaluative studies of interventions based on PYD have included only brief follow-up phases. In addition, a set of common outcomes to assess the impact of PYD on behavior has yet to be developed (Catalano et al., 2002). Questions, too, remain about the precise measurement of the indicators used to assess constructs imbedded in the developmental assets (Theokas et al., 2005) and the 5 C's of PYD (Lerner et al., 2005). Catalano, Gavin, & Markham (2010) recommend developing standardized PYD measures to aid in some of these challenges. Finally, few studies have examined the effects of PYD interventions for racially and ethnically diverse youth, and differential outcomes by factors such as gender and sexual orientation have also not been clearly delineated. Regardless, the model holds great promise as an effective organizing framework for community-based youth programs. In the next section, we offer ideas about how PYD can be integrated with the risk and resilience framework as a method of improving outcomes for children and adolescents.

INTEGRATION OF POSITIVE YOUTH DEVELOPMENT WITH RISK AND RESILIENCE MODELS

The risk and resilience framework and PYD models share the common goals of encouraging the development of individual and social competencies and promoting healthy youth development. Yet for much of the past decade, the two models have been presented as competing frameworks in the child and adolescent intervention and research literature (Catalano et al., 2004). We believe that the rather narrow discussion of the differences between risk-based and PYD models has been counterproductive to the larger goal of designing effective interventions for at-risk youth. Recently, other investigators have supported this assertion by noting the advantage of viewing risk-based and PYD models as complementary, rather than opposing, intervention frameworks. Evidence pertaining to the similarities between risk and resilience and PYD models is reviewed below.

The most direct comparison of similarities and differences in risk and resilience and PYD models has been conducted by Catalano and colleagues from the Social Development Research Group (Catalano et al., 2004). The authors' review highlights the striking parallels between the two models. First, both risk and resilience and PYD frameworks recognize the importance of protective factors and assets in young people's lives. To this end, constructs in each model extend beyond simple notions of risk and adversity by acknowledging the important role that individual, social, and community strengths and resources play in healthy child and adolescent development. Also important, both risk and resilience and PYD models reject the idea of targeting single child or adolescent behaviors. Rather, each framework recognizes the need to support the "whole person" by providing interventions and services that address a range of emotions, attitudes, and behaviors during childhood and adolescence. Catalano et al. (2002) note further that programs based on risk and resilience and PYD models are influenced heavily by ecological and systems theories. This is evident by the fact that both models acknowledge the influence of individual, peer, family, school, and community factors on child and adolescent behavior. Finally, both frameworks recognize the importance of environmental influences and contextual development in supporting young people, a major shift from earlier sociological and psychological theories that focused narrowly on individual pathology (Damon, 2004).

We believe that the similarities underlying risk and resilience and PYD models should lead to interventions and services that afford equal attention to the risks present in young people's lives *and* to the principles that comprise healthy development. In this context, the term *risk* should not be viewed as a negative individual trait that somehow inhibits intervention efforts aimed at promoting healthy development. All children and youth experience some level of risk in their lives. Recognizing and combating risk and adversity by promoting protective traits and resources are an essential key to promoting resilience and ensuring healthy development in young people.

The notion of risk is also fundamental to our understanding of the social injustices and inequities that many young people face. Unfortunately, many children and adolescents are raised in environments that offer few positive opportunities for a healthy life. Poverty, violence, addiction, abuse, unsafe neighborhoods, exploitation and child trafficking, and war are but a few of the problems confronting young people all over the world. Likewise, a child raised in a low-literacy home will face many challenges in school and in work. While all children have, and indeed *are*, resources, we cannot deny the reality of risk and separate young people from their contexts. Understanding the intersection of risk, protection, and promoting personal assets is at the heart of finding effective pathways to a positive and healthy childhood and adult life for all young people.

The intersection of risk and protection and the organizing principles of PYD also form the core of what is commonly known as resilience. Resilient adaptation describes a developmental process among young people who are exposed to risky environments in their everyday lives. In this context of significant adversity, Ungar (2011) offers an ecological definition resilience as:

> ...both the capacity of individuals to *navigate* their way to the psychological, social, cultural, and physical resources that sustain their well-being, and their capacity individually and collectively to *negotiate* for these resources to be provided and experienced in culturally meaningful ways. (p. 10)

SUMMARY

The PYD model has much to offer practitioners, community and program planners, and administrators seeking to develop or improve interventions and program services for children and youth. The positive focus on healthy child and adolescent development that embodies the model has stimulated a rapid increase in PYD programs in the past decade. More important, positive outcomes garnered from participants of PYD programs have now begun to support the utility of the model in real-world contexts.

PYD has been juxtaposed against risk and resilience models of understanding, preventing, and treating child and adolescent problem behaviors for too long. Empirical evidence and our own experience in youth service and community-based programs suggest that integrating principles of risk and resilience and PYD is a logical next step in improving the efficacy of interventions for children and youth. Principles embodied in risk and resilience acknowledge the significant influence that factors such as lack of opportunity, discrimination, and poverty have on healthy development. Clearly, not all children live in supportive homes, neighborhoods, and communities. It is crucial to acknowledge, and actively strive to ameliorate, the problems that exist in children's lives. Such problems include the frequent manifestations of social injustices associated with race, ethnicity, and social class that are prevalent in many American neighborhoods and communities. Disregarding or otherwise minimizing these risks could serve to perpetuate them.

Catalano and colleagues (2002) conclude their analysis of risk and resilience and PYD models by suggesting that "cooperation between the two frameworks would be the best strategy for progress in youth development" (p. 236). We agree heartily with this assertion. In the next chapter, we continue our discussion of integrating risk and resilience and PYD models by focusing on the tools needed to create effective youth service programs and interventions. Later, we describe how child and youth participants in a community program in Denver benefit from interventions that are based on an integrated risk and resilience and PYD model.

CHAPTER 3

Interorganizational Collaboration in Child and Youth Programs

Theories of risk and resilience and positive youth development provide a strong foundation for child and youth services. However, implementing and sustaining effective programs for at-risk youth also require strategic collaboration among community-based child and youth organizations. In this chapter, we describe key elements in relationships between organizations that affect community-based programs for children and youth. Discussed in the context of interorganizational relationship theory, these elements form the foundation of our proposed community collaborative model. Three themes are central to the discussion of interorganizational relationships and to this model. The first theme suggests that interorganizational network structures should be shaped to meet the needs of children and youth rather than vice versa. A second theme concerns the increasing number and specialization of nonprofit organizations found in community settings. Finally, a third theme informing our discussion of interorganizational relationships is the increased attention aimed at improving the quality and effectiveness of services for children and youth. Together, these trends provide the background necessary for understanding the importance of interorganizational relationships in community-based programs for children and youth.

NATURE OF HUMAN SERVICE ORGANIZATIONS

Over 50 years ago, American communities witnessed a phenomenal increase in the number and type of formal, human service organizations. As discussed below, this growth was the logical consequence of the 1960s freedom movements, the explosion of knowledge in the fields of psychology and sociology, and a deeper understanding of social problems by policymakers and community leaders. Over the last 30 years, the number of nonprofit human service organizations in the United States has grown by 115%, or about 23,000 organizations per year (Salamon, 1999, 2002), and their specialization and complexity have also increased. The enormous change in organizational landscapes has prompted considerable research on community organizations, and results from early studies produced a number of hypotheses that have stood the test of time.

Client Needs and Organization Resources

One important theoretical insight emerging from research on community organizations suggests that the form and work processes of nonprofit organizations are determined to a large extent by the nature and characteristics of their clients. In an influential article, Lefton and Rosengren (1968) set forth the premise that clients of organizations are integral factors that should influence an organization's shape and functioning. This assertion suggests that organizations should structure themselves to meet the needs of their clients rather than make clients fit into existing organizational frameworks (Klofas & Duffee, 1981; Potter & McKinley, 2005).

The first way that child and adolescent clients affect organizational form was originally labeled *longitudinal* and referred to the length of time that organizations must be prepared to offer services to a young person. As an example, children who have suffered injury due to accidents most often are treated in emergency rooms or inpatient trauma hospitals for relatively short periods of time, sometimes for only hours. At the other extreme, children with severe emotional disturbances are treated in child guidance clinics or community mental health centers, often for years. Thus, child and youth services range from extremely truncated to an almost indeterminate period of time.

The second way clients influence the form and operations of organizations is not length of service but, rather, by the breadth of service that is needed— a dimension termed *lateral* by Lefton and Rosengren (1968). For example, children who have witnessed or been involved in an incident of domestic violence usually are assessed by the community child abuse team for a single factor—safety of the child. Then, social workers will assess the child and family's problems and needs on a much broader scale—physical, emotional, social, financial—and create a comprehensive service plan. Thus, in this case the child's intervention is of narrow scope while the family's intervention is probably extremely broad in scope.

To complicate this picture, Lefton and Rosengren (1968) argued that short-term interventions can be broad in scope, as in educational assessment programs, while long-term interventions can be very narrow in scope, as in programs that provide a single service like school vouchers. Although the authors suggested four distinct categories of organizations—short-term/narrow scope, short-term/broad scope, long-term/narrow scope, long-term/broad scope—actually these dimensions form a continuum. This conceptualization of organizations underscores the following reality: not only has the number of human service organizations increased dramatically, but the range of organizations has also become highly complex. Today, people who start a service program for at-risk children and youth must understand the nature of their clients' needs as well as the organizational resources required to respond. In pulling together those resources, they will undoubtedly face a plethora of exceedingly diverse community-based organizations.

Children who are served in community-based programs have a wide range of needs. In some cases, young people receive services for many years. For example, ask anyone who has ever worked with children who live in public housing communities, and they will quickly identify resources needed to bring these children to the point where they can undertake school learning at the expected rate. These services would very likely include academic, medical, financial, enrichment, and family program components. To provide these resources, organizers face a number of challenges that arise when trying to bring together an array of services for a single child and her or his family. The problem is rooted in the fact that while the needed services may be available in a community, they are often not accessible because they are scattered among many different single purpose agencies.

The first challenge in building a community-based program for at-risk children and youth is to understand the field of organizations encompassed by the community. There may be hundreds or even thousands of organizations in a given urban area. On the surface they may appear to be autonomous and freestanding. However, beneath the surface one often finds that they are dependent on a complex web of interactions that is necessary to provide the many resources needed for their clients. Many are funded by federal or state categorical programs, each with different objectives and operating rules. Together, they comprise a many-layered, extremely complex organizational field that encompasses inconsistencies and contradictions in a barely discernible maze of embedded subsystems and subnetworks. Efforts to overcome the challenges of delivering effective youth services caused by this proliferation of nonprofit organizations have been many over the past half century.

Increasing Number and Complexity of Nonprofit Organizations

As noted above, the proliferation of community-level nonprofit organizations in the 1960s was driven to a large degree by an explosion of research and new knowledge in medicine and the social sciences, and financed to a large degree by a parallel expansion of federal welfare programs (Salamon, Musselwhite, & Abramson, 1987). As the federal government added departments in the fields of education, health, and human services, streams of funds that flowed from Washington to state capitals to local communities increased dramatically. Between 1970 and 2000, revenues to nonprofits increased by 144% after adjusting for inflation, nearly twice the growth in the nation's gross national product (Salamon, 2002). These streams created and supported categorical programs—programs that served young populations such as special needs children awaiting adoption, juvenile delinquents, and child victims of abuse and neglect. Community activists responded by creating nonprofit organizations that use these funds to improve the welfare of their citizens. However, this system of categorical funding created a crowded, complex, and fragmented organizational field in many communities.

The early 1970s witnessed an increase in the number of complaints about inaccessibility, gaps, and duplication in community service systems for young people. Concerned about overlapping and rule-driven bureaucratic processes, administrators in the Department of Health, Education, and Welfare (HEW) aimed to improve the quality of service delivery at the local level. To this end, they initiated reforms that would foster "service integration" across categorical program areas. HEW Secretary Elliot Richardson, an outspoken proponent of these service improvement efforts, is said to have once described the U.S. welfare system as "a hardening of the categories" (Kusserow, 1991, p. 3). Richardson led the effort to fund the Services Integration-Targets of Opportunity (SITO) program, which supported regional and local initiatives to overcome the problems of fragmentation and thus create well-coordinated services for children and with multiple needs (Agranoff & Pattakos, 1979).

However, in the late 1970s, services integration for children and youth lost its momentum, due partly to the disappointing results of the SITO projects and partly because HEW administrators shifted their attention to the integrative potential of state, regional, and local general-purpose governments. Thinking at the time was that service delivery would not improve until the capacity for human services planning and management was strengthened at the state and local levels. The proposed Allied Service Act, an attempt to overcome the federal structure of categorical funding by pooling funds in these umbrella state planning agencies, failed to pass Congress despite repeated attempts. By 1977, when Joseph Califano became HEW Secretary, service improvement efforts were losing ground fast, and throughout the 1980s, service integration efforts devolved to the states. Governors concerned about the rising costs of Medicaid and other social and educational programs moved toward greater centralization and measures of expenditure control rather than toward the decentralization required for service improvement.

In spite of the federal government's failure to reform its categorical funding structure, service integration efforts continued during the last two decades. Some of the more notable projects for at-risk children and youth have focused on targeted programs sponsored by private foundations and state agencies. For example, Massachusetts created an integrated HIV, hepatitis, and addiction treatment system (Hoffman, Castro-Dolan, Johnson, & Church, 2004); the Urban Institute sponsored the Serious and Violent Offender Reentry Initiative (Lattimore & Visher, 2009); and the Hogg Foundation for Mental Health funded programs for children with mental illnesses that integrated services from public schools, mental health centers, child protection agencies, and juvenile justice systems (Hogg Foundation, 2006). These are but a few of the many interorganizational collaborations that have been developed over the past several decades (Butler et al., 2008). History tells us that when a champion such as a government agency or a foundation takes the lead and the reform effort is focused on integrating services to a discrete target group, the quality of services can be improved (Gilbody, Fletcher, & Richards, 2006; Ouwens, Wollersheim, Hermens, Hulscher, & Grol, 2005; Swift et al., 2009; Zetlin, Ramos, & Valdex, 1996). Although comprehensive reform that collapses categorical boundaries in Washington may never be achievable, history suggests that the effects of federal fragmentation can sometimes be overcome at the community level (Alter & Hage, 1993).

Most recently, efforts to improve the quality of services have been fueled foremost by the continuous growth in knowledge and the resulting invention of new technologies. One example is youth homelessness (Greenberg & Rosenheck, 2010). Homelessness is not a new problem—runaways and young transients have always existed. What is new is the research that has yielded insights into the forces that drive youth into homelessness, as well as evaluation findings that show the effectiveness of a comprehensive community response. Large cities such as Denver, Colorado (Denver's Road Home, 2011; http://www.denversroadhome.org/) and middle-size cities like Madison, Wisconsin (Community Plan to Prevent and End Homelessness in Dane County 2011; http://www.cityofmadison.com/cdbg/docs/community_plan_to_end_homelessness_final.pdf) now have comprehensive and integrative plans and programs to serve homeless youth.

Another seemingly intractable problem being addressed by community collaboration is the achievement gap between African American and White students in elementary schools. A body of research begun in the 1990s shows a strong correlation between the amount and kind of language that children experience in early life and both their IQ and abilities in later life (e.g., Farah, Noble, & Hurt, 2006; Hart & Risley, 1995). This finding has the potential of changing how we think about poverty, how we reform the welfare system, and, especially, how we educate young children in poor urban neighborhoods and rural areas (Tough, 2009). Already, federal program announcements such as the 21st Century Community Learning Program (21st Century Community Learning Centers, 2011; http://www2.ed.gov/programs/21stcclc/guid-ance2003.pdf) and Promise Neighborhoods (The Bridgespan Group, 2011; http://www.bridgespan.org/promise-neighborhoods.aspx) are using this new knowledge to shape programs. Emphasized in both initiatives are afterschool and summer programs for extended learning as well as the need to integrate services and break down isolated agency silos.

Research findings concerning service improvement are unequivocal: categorical programs created to treat one childhood or adolescent problem with one intervention are less effective than those that take a comprehensive or lateral approach to human problems (Austin, 2004; Dryfoos, 1991; Jenson & Fraser, 2011). Thus, federal, state, and local communities should develop multidisciplinary and multisystemic approaches to a wide range of child and youth problems. Not surprisingly, professions, disciplines, and organizations are often discouraged from participating in interdisciplinary research and practice (Israel, Schulz, & Becker, 1998), but, ironically, they are also frequently mandated to form interorganizational relationships in order to provide more comprehensive and accessible services (Agranoff, 1991).

Summary

Postindustrial society in the United States is characterized by an exponential growth in knowledge and technology, made possible, in part, by our increasing willingness to be guided by research findings from the social sciences. As a result, a proliferation of community-level nonprofit organizations has developed, forming complex and overlapping service delivery subsystems and networks. Regardless of their intraorganizational administrative skills, policymakers and community leaders will likely not be successful in developing effective youth service community programs if they lack an appreciation of environmental complexity, the ability to think in multisystemic ways, and the capacity to create interorganizational relationships (Alter & Hage, 1993; Carlson & Donohoe, 2003).

INTERORGANIZATIONAL RELATIONSHIP THEORY

Academics are fond of saying that "the concept and outcomes of collaboration are not well understood" (Longoria, 2005, p. 123). Be this as it may, we contend that the models created when youth service organizations work together to deliver or improve services can be clearly described and that resultant outcomes can be specified, measured, and evaluated. The next section outlines such a theoretical approach to creating effective interorganizational programs.

Definitions

Interorganizational relationship theory emphasizes the importance of interorganizational partnerships and collaborations. In this context, interorganizational realationships refer to *the links between an autonomous organization and one or more other organizations that connect them in order to meet a mutual need, achieve an agreed-upon goal, or deliver a service.* In other words, interorganizational relationships are collaborations across boundaries of organizations that lead to specific and definable forms of collaboration (Alter, 2009; Hudson, 1987; Mathiessen, 1971). The frequently professed confusion about the nature of interorganizational relationships stems perhaps from this tautology—the term collaborations serves as both the means and the ends of an effort. Confusion also stems from the fact that many different terms have been used for the same phenomena. For example, many nouns are used to designate interorganizational relationships—*joint venture, partnership, collaboration, cooperation, cartel, network, alliance, consortia, collective, service system, system of care*—and many pages in the literature have been used to create a typology that is acceptable to everyone. Likewise, many verbs have been employed to describe the methods necessary to create and maintain interorganizational relationships—*boundary spanning, cooperating, collaborating, networking,* and *integrating.* For simplicity's sake, in the balance of this book we refer to an interorganizational relationship between two organizations as a *partnership,* and a relationship between three or more organizations as a *collaborative, network,* or *system,* depending on its purpose and structure.

Elements of Interorganizational Relationship Theory

The literature on interorganizational relationships lacks a grand encompassing theory; thus, several different concepts must be used to describe and predict best interorganization practices. One efficient way of providing this background knowledge is to organize these strands of theory under four topics: (1) determinants related to the formation of interorganizational relationships, (2) types of interorganizational relationships, (3) interorganizational work processes, and (4) outcomes of interorganizational relationships.

Determinants of interorganizational relationship formation. Our theory concerning the reason why interorganizational relationships are created includes five factors. First, before an interorganizational relationship can form, leaders must recognize that their organization cannot make it on its own and therefore must adopt collaboration as a survival strategy (Alter & Hage, 1993). Willingness to collaborate starts with the awareness and understanding of one's own needs as well as others' needs and the perception that they are in some way compatible. However, awareness of the need to reach out and willingness to do so are two different attributes. An attitude that is open to new ideas and new terrain and the ability to trust in others are the basic conditions needed for the formation of interorganizational relationships.

Second, the most frequently cited reason for interorganizational relationships in the literature is the need to acquire resources to accomplish organizational objectives (Beder, 1984; Benson, 1975; Contractor & Lorange, 2002). Partnerships and networks can be a successful way to gain resources, especially those that are specialized (such as grant-writing skill), tacit (such as in-depth knowledge of a target population), and require the experience that is gained from political and policy practice. Once embedded within an organization, these competences can be leveraged into expanded activities and programs. For example, the staff at a community public health clinic realized they were reaching only a small percentage of children eligible for the Child Insurance Health Program (CHIP). Although they tried public information media campaigns, the number of children served by their program remained relatively stable. As a last resort, staff members sponsored a half-day conference to which they invited all child- and youth-serving organizations in town. To their delight, attendance was greater than expected, and organizations they knew nothing about showed up. When they explained their problem and asked the assembled group to brainstorm solutions, many excellent ideas surfaced. As a result of subsequent planning sessions, the city now has a coordinated plan and program that brings CHIP information to all new mothers at the hospitals and does an annual door-to-door canvas to locate new resident families. In addition, through a collaborative with the elementary schools, information gets to all families in the community. Because of this action, the city now has one of the highest percentages of CHIP recipients in the state.

The third determinant associated with the formation of interorganizational relationships is the need to create a new product or service or to improve an existing one. The economy of the past decade has forced many child and family organizations to downsize, and simultaneously, to produce higher quality outputs or expand their market in order to survive (Vervest, 2005). In order to do more with less, they must obtain new human resources. By collaborating with one or more other organizations, separate skills and knowledge can be combined to produce new interventions that are better than the sum of the previous parts (Yuen & Owens, 1996). For example, the staff of a well-known social service organization serving children with special needs on the East Coast knew that a specialized program for children with head and spinal cord trauma was badly needed, but were reluctant to develop such a program because they did not have the required medical expertise. At the urging of the staff, members of the board of directors contacted a university teaching hospital that specialized in adult trauma and found it willing to explore the development of a specialized treatment facility for children and youth. Together, the available human and financial resources of the two organizations were sufficient to build the needed program. Later, the organization leveraged its newly gained knowledge to initiate an extensive national training program for caregivers of children with brain injuries.

The fourth motive for creating a partnership or network is to gain the ability to react quickly to potential opportunities at the moment they present themselves. Unfortunately, government agencies and managed care systems today often require organizations to respond to program announcements under unreasonable timelines. Fast response requires excess organizational capacity not available in many health and welfare organizations today. One means of meeting this challenge is to form interorganizational collaborations with an agreed-upon division of expertise and labor. For example, in a collaboration between three youth-serving organizations, each provided one specialist—a planner, a researcher, and a grant writer. Working as an interorganizational team, they developed grants and marketing programs that benefited each of the organizations equally and as a result were able to build a comprehensive program for at-risk teens.

The fifth and last determinant of interorganizational relationships is the need to compete (Stabell & Fjeldstad, 1998). In seeking grant and contract dollars, competition cannot be avoided. However, an approach that relies on interorganizational relationships can sometimes be successful in situations where competition will fail. An excellent example of using interorganizational relationships strategically in a competitive environment is described by Rodriguez and colleagues (Rodriquez, Pereira, & Brodnax, 2004). A small community-based mental health center needed to win a state-funded contract to support a program for emotionally disturbed children, but it knew it stood little chance in competition with a national for-profit behavioral managed care company that was seeking the same funds. The small community clinic, because it had the needed local contacts and political capital, knew it could probably develop a partnership with the national firm. However, it also knew this would be a marriage between David and Goliath. What to do? The winning strategy turned out to be a partnership with another organization, a local Latino/a service organization, bringing together the assets of diversity and community relationships, which outweighed the advantages offered by the national corporation. By choosing to compete by using the strength of community relationships, the small center not only won the contract but also was able to expand service to Latino/a children and youth. In an age of competition and managed care, strong interorganizational relationships can make the difference between an organization having to struggle for survival and one that realizes stability and growth.

Types of interorganizational relationships. As noted above, organizations are not such autonomous entities that they are completely free to shape their own future. Rather, they are anchored in networks of interactions with other organizations that provide intrinsic (information, sanction, technologies, political power) and extrinsic (raw material, parts, clients) resources. These networks of interactions take many forms depending on their function. In Figure 3.1 we apply a typology originally developed by Alter and Hage (1993) that uses a network's purpose as the organizing variable. The scheme describes obligational, promotional, and systemic interorganizational relationships.

Obligational partnerships and networks come together for the sole purpose of exchange. Loosely linked and informal, they may be grounded and sustained by personal and friendship relationships. For example, they can be a source for obtaining strategic information that is unobtainable through other channels (Das & Teng, 2002). Obligational partnerships and networks are built on the principle of reciprocity—you give me something I need and I will return the favor. In terms of duration, they can be formed to meet a time-limited need or may be maintained for many years. In terms of structure, they are flat with relatively little centralization of control because of their reciprocal and low-risk nature. A common example is a welfare council that is open to all community nonprofits and which meets once a month to share information and strategies.

Promotional partnerships and networks form to accomplish a goal or objective that no single organization can achieve on its own. Because they are action oriented, they tend to be more formal and tightly linked than are obligational relationships, and they are structured so that members may pool their resources through various means. Because they function to accomplish a joint action, they require a good measure of task coordination to insure that the left hand knows what the right hand is doing. A greater degree of centralization is also characteristic in order to provide coordination and control over member investments. Similar to obligational forms, promotional partnerships may

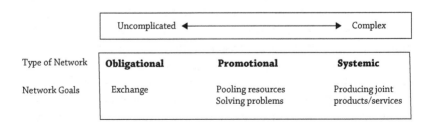

	Uncomplicated ◄──────────────────► Complex		
Type of Network	**Obligational**	**Promotional**	**Systemic**
Network Goals	Exchange	Pooling resources Solving problems	Producing joint products/services

Figure 3.1
A Model of Network Development

be ad hoc, formed to lobby for needed legislation, or they can be enduring, as with a trade association that represents the members' interests for many decades.

Systematic partnerships and networks enable organizations to jointly manufacture a product or provide a service. These are the most tightly linked and most formalized interpersonal relationships because members must integrate their resources and actions across organizational boundaries. Most important, systematic partnerships usually require a high degree of centralization in order to control the complexity of managing multiple work processes. In integrated service delivery systems, members work together to create and maintain common plans and protocols, and their staffs are often combined so they can work together face to face. When a service delivery system is functioning efficiently and effectively, children and their families may not be able to tell which organizations are serving them at any one time. In current parlance, this type of interorganizational relationship is said to be seamless.

Interorganizational relationships can also have a mix of forms when structural elements are mandated by funding agencies such as in state and county child abuse programs. Within these networks can be found subclusters with different forms. For example, a portion of the network may operate as an obligational interorganizational relationship, a different cluster of organizations may work as a promotional network, and a third cluster may function in a systematic manner. By definition, mixed forms are large networks that almost always contain a mix of public and private organizations.

In sum, interorganizational relationships can be differentiated by their unique organizational forms and work processes. Theory concerning forms of interorganizational relationships stipulates that as functions become more complex, viz., from linking to pooling to integrating, the degree of administrative control must become greater. In other words, interorganizational relationships will move in one direction or the other as the needs of their clients change. Theoretically, a network can originate as a production system, especially if mandated by law as in child welfare or juvenile justice systems. We turn next to a discussion of work processes associated with interorganizational relationships.

Work processes. As noted above, community-based partnerships serving multiple children and youth often must encompass multiple organizations if they are to meet the needs of at-risk children and youth. Thus, they must find ways of linking these organizations together in exchange or interactive relationships that solve problems or produce joint outcomes. The activities associated with joining together are called work processes.

The basic principle of the community approach is that the needs and preferences of clients and customers should determine organizational function and structure if programs are to be effective (Kirst-Ashman & Hull, 2009; Lefton & Rosengren, 1968). This theoretical statement applies to interorganizational relationships just as it does to single youth service organizations. If, for example, organization A must provide information and referral services to the parents of children with behavioral problems, then the relationship it has with organization B to which it must refer its children will differ in kind from other organizations, such as inpatient hospitals and schools, with which it must coordinate services on an ongoing basis. The recognition that *different types of interorganizational relationships and interactions demand different work processes* is a critical point.

In delivering services, work processes occur at two different levels: methods used by administrators and those by staff. In other words, managers use *administrative* methods to form working relationships with other administrators while staff members and volunteers use task methods when working with their counterparts at other organizations. At the conceptual level, these two sets of work processes are similar in many ways, but in practice they differ in a number of details.

All interorganizational work processes involve cooperation, but cooperation comes in numerous forms that are analytically distinct. In the context of the interorganizational principles presented here, *cooperation* is a broad term meaning to act in a helpful manner; *collaboration* is equally nonspecific and means to work together but with a mutually conceived and agreed-upon aim; *coordination* infers that both cooperation and collaboration are present but, further, that deliberate adjustment, modification, and regulation are taking place during the work process; and *integration* means that parts of the work process are being incorporated into an integral whole. In this framework, obligational partnerships are described as needing only cooperative and collaborative work processes, promotional interorganizational relationships must achieve coordinated activities to achieve their common goals, and systemic relationships require integration of work processes in order to produce a joint output. These distinctions are at the center of interorganizational relationship theory.

Interorganizational Coordination

Coordination is about control. Coordination is used to reduce the number of independent variables in the workplace that must be controlled (Turvey, 1990). Early in the study of organizations, sociologists identified two basic ways of controlling organizations as they work together: coordination by plan and coordination by feedback (March & Simon, 1958). Although these researchers concerned themselves almost exclusively with intraorganizational processes, their theory has enjoyed wide application (Hage, 2005). In brief, they hypothesized that the type of work process that should be used depends on the degree to which the work can be standardized.

As we know intuitively, standardization is achieved via plans, rules, protocols, timetables, guidelines, and agreements. The more work processes can be standardized by these means, the greater the degree of control over program elements. Visualize the assembly line, where the manufacturing process is broken down into minute steps that can be planned in complete detail. Each motion is specified and made concrete; each interval is timed. Little or no judgment is required to produce the output because all uncertainly has been removed from the process.

At the other end of this spectrum, information as feedback can achieve control but in a very different way. In work processes where tasks cannot be specified ahead of time, where many alternative methods exist and thus significant uncertainties are present regarding best practice, then simple rules and plans are not possible. When ambiguity and complexity dominate, the work process can only be shaped, improved, and adjusted by learning from the work experience. Information feedback is another powerful but a different form of coordination. Unlike rules and plans, however, feedback requires intelligence and judgment, and feedback processes are time consuming and expensive.

If interorganizational relationships are to be effective, then somehow they must monitor problems as they arise, monitoring made difficult because the work process resides in different organizations where staff have different perspectives about how children and youth should be treated. If the service is a child immunization program, for example, then a good deal of the work process can be standardized, and monitoring the frequency and timeliness of inoculations provided in clinics and schools is a fairly routine matter. However, what if the goal is to keep children with emotional and behavioral problems at home and in school and out of institutions? These work processes are far more complex, requiring much more judgment and decision making, and thus information sharing between organizations becomes absolutely critical. Without it, this goal simply cannot be met.

Administrative coordination. Thus, as a method of control, coordination can be thought of as varying with regard to the amount of information feedback required in order to produce quality (Argyris, 2002; Park, 1996; Solansky & Beck, 2009). This conceptualization concerning the amount of feedback produces three categories of administrative coordination: (1) *impersonal methods*, including the utilization of plans, rules, regulations, agreements, contracts, or any mechanism that removes discretion from member organizations and requires little feedback; (2) *personal methods*, meaning the use of person-to-person contact between administrators or the designation of an individual to act as coordinator so as to expedite decision making across organizational boundaries; and (3) *group methods*, including feedback obtained through face-to-face communication by two or more administrators who make decisions by consensus.

When little discretion in decision making is needed by organizations in the course of delivering services, then impersonal methods are preferable because they are the least costly. On the other hand, when decisions are complex and nonroutine, then administrators are better off using group methods and face-to-face interaction to solve problems and reach consensus about the best direction to take. Group methods are, of course, the most costly. Personal methods are the middle road because, although they require personal interaction, they do not have to be face to face.

Staff coordination. The second type of coordination used in community programs for young people has to do with workflows, the degree to which tasks performed by staff and volunteers are done separately or together: in other words, the degree to which tasks are integrated during the delivery of a service. As Thompson (1967) first proposed, time is a useful variable to use in understanding task coordination. If work tasks are accomplished separately, time intervenes between tasks. On the other hand, if staff members work face to face together and with a youth, such as in interagency treatment teams, then tasks are completely integrated and no time separates the decision making. This conceptualization concerning time applied to work systems produces three types of task coordination: (1) *sequential* client flows whereby the client is served by one organization, service is terminated, and the client is referred to the next organization for service; (2) *reciprocal* client flows whereby the client is served simultaneously by more than one organization but not in face-to-face interventions; and (3) *collective* client flows whereby the client is served simultaneously by staff from several organizations in face-to-face activity that develops plans and delivers the service (Alter & Hage, 1993).

Client flows. The reason for making these distinctions is that different client flows demand different types of staff coordination. Matching the way staff work together in interorganizational networks to the way clients flow between organizations is the key to good practice. A good way to understand this matching in child and youth client flows is to imagine you are a photographer in a helicopter hovering over the interchange of major highways in a large city. You have a time lapse camera, and you photograph this network of roads so that the headlights appear as luminescent corridors, forming circles that connect with each other and with the on- and off-ramps as depicted in Figure 3.2.

This image is a useful way of thinking about client flows in a crowded organizational field because it reduces confusion and illuminates the most frequent pathways that children and youth take as they go from organization to organization, distinguishing those with the heaviest traffic from those with the lightest traffic. As shown in Figure 3.2, when this approach is taken to understanding client flow, three basic patterns of client flows emerge (Alter & Hage, 1993), each demanding a different approach to managing child and youth interventions.

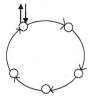

In sequential client flows, children and youth are served by one organization at a time; they then move on to the next organization. Tasks are primarily one-way information and referral.

In reciprocal client flows, children and youth are served by more than one organization at a time. Tasks are information and referral as well as case coordination from a central organization.

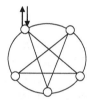

In collective client flows, children and youth are served by one interorganizational relationship intervention team using a single service plan and face-to-face interaction. Tasks are service integration.

Figure 3.2
Matching Client Flows to Interorganizational Relationship Work Processes

To describe these three basic patterns in practice, consider the following:

(1) Sequential client flows are illustrated by interorganizational relationships that serve seriously emotionally disturbed children who live at home and are treated at a community mental health center but who also must be treated periodically at an inpatient mental health facility. The work process priority in this interorganizational partnership must be the smooth, timely, and accurate transmittal of case and treatment information between the child's school, mental health center, and hospital. This type of network is relatively uncomplicated and best coordinated by plans and protocols that are established ahead of time between the cooperating organizations. These networks usually do not require expensive and time-consuming meetings between administrators or staff.

(2) Reciprocal client flows are illustrated by interorganizational relationships that aim to strengthen families and thus promote the academic success of their children. The primary need in this relationship is to assure that services are synchronized so that they work in harmony and do not conflict and undermine each other. This type of network is best coordinated by a case manager who knows what the "right hand" and the "left hand" are doing at all times and who guarantees accurate information flow between all organizations involved with the family. More expensive than one-way information

flow systems, the personal one-on-one nature of case coordination requires personnel trained in these work methods.

(3) Collective client flows are illustrated by interorganizational relationships that work to return child victims of abuse and neglect to their families through stabilization service and family therapy. Because of the complexity of child abuse and neglect services, all of the previous work methods are required in this type of partnership as well as face-to-face meetings where assessment, information sharing, and decision making can be integrated within the interagency team. With multiple agencies' involvement and periodic team meetings, this is the most expensive and labor intensive type of interorganizational relationship.

General Interorganizational Performance Objectives

As noted above, coordination is best thought of as a type of work method or as an intervention, not as an end itself (Alter & Hage, 1993). If an interorganizational partnership is using the appropriate work processes and they are the best fit for its type of interorganizational form, then there are general performance standards that can be expected. These standards include comprehensiveness, compatibility, and accessibility.

The first objective of coordination is to assure that interorganizational relationships are *comprehensive* and that all necessary resources and services are, in fact, available to those who need them. Comprehensiveness, while seemingly a basic concept, is often omitted from discussions of coordination, implying that focus is on the quality of the linkages between the organizations already in the network and not on the expected outcome of those linkages. The issue is not just whether organizations are working well together, but whether by working well together children's need are truly being met. Further, this objective applies to all levels of interorganizational relationships; to wit, all necessary expertise needs to be available among staff, all resources to support the continuum of care need to be available to the member organizations, and all children's needs must be met. If this is not the case, then the first task of coordination should be to focus on what can be done to generate the needed resources. Using comprehensiveness as outcome criteria, consider this scenario. An interorganizational network serving behaviorally disturbed children is running smoothly, but in-home assistance and respite for parents are missing from its service package. Therefore, rates of unnecessary institutionalization are unacceptably high. Is this network well coordinated? The answer is obviously "no."

Second, the component parts of interorganizational relationships must work together harmoniously. By this definition, compatibility is the effective linking and sequencing of the member organizations. Again, this objective is applied to all three levels of interorganizational relationships—the administrative, staff, and client levels. At the administrative level, *compatibility* between organizations means that goals and values are in agreement and correspond to those of clients. At the staff level, compatibility requires that expertise and technologies are congruent and that work processes complement rather than diverge from one another. Finally, compatibility means that children and youth are treated consistently by the different member organizations, and elements of a service or case plan mesh without contradiction. This definition is the meaning most often given to compatibility, and by implication it equates compatibility with the absence of conflict.

Compatibility is not enough, however. The availability of all necessary resources and their relative "seamlessness" does not of itself guarantee quality outcomes. In interorganizational relationship theory, a system is not sufficiently coordinated until services are *accessible* when and how children and youth need them. This objective is perhaps the most difficult to accomplish because of two problems. First, depending on funding, organizations most probably will have eligibility or access criteria that are incompatible or simply in conflict. For example, income eligibility standards of one organization may exclude an entire subset of the population being served, or intake requirements may be duplicative, requiring multiple and tedious intake sessions with a single youth. This is a problem decried by community planners for decades, and at this point no simple solutions have been found. Some communities have experimented with computer networks that permit intake through a single organization, which is then available to the others as needed. Many barriers to accessibility exist, but like comprehensiveness, it is a very worthy objective.

Summary

Our theoretical conceptualization hypothesizes that interorganizational networks fall into categories that lie on a continuum and are shaped and driven by the type of network needed to meet clients' needs. The type of network predicts what level of control and thus what work processes will be most effective. Figure 3.3 shows the three types of interorganizational relationships distinguished by increasing amounts of activity needed for goal accomplishment. This activity ranges from negligible in obligational relationships, to considerable in promotional relationships, to intense in systemic relationships. Work processes are categorized by two types—administrative and task—each having a type of work process effective for one of these three forms. Note the hierarchical nature of task processes. That is, as complexity of the administrative and staff work increases, the number of task types and breadth of tasks increases proportionately. This theory is descriptive as well as proscriptive

Embryonic ← → Mature		
Type of Network Obligational	Promotional	Systemic
Network Goals Exchange	Pooling resources Solving problems	Producing joint Products/services
Level of Control Negligible	Considerable	Intense
Work Processes:		
Administrative Informal	Formal	Group
Task Sequential	Sequential Reciprocal	Sequential Reciprocal Collective

Figure 3.3
Network Types Derived from Interorganizational Theory

and serves as a guide for choosing the best method of working together to achieve desired outcomes.

APPLICATION OF INTERORGANIZATIONAL RELATIONSHIP THEORY TO PRACTICE

The concepts of interorganizational relationship theory are useful tools for practitioners and administrators because they identify and specify network structures and work processes that fit well with the goals of the organization. These concepts represent important knowledge for those who are creating or maintaining programs for at-risk children and youth because they help organizations work cooperatively with other organizations in the community.

The Community Collaborative Model

The interorganizational concepts discussed above appear in Figure 3.4 as a logic model that we label the community collaborative model (CCM). This model links the overarching goal of children's well-being with the interorganizational methods needed to achieve intermediate results—service comprehensiveness, compatibility, and accessibility—and the long-term outcomes such as high school graduation. In other words, this hypothesis states that given the risks associated with childhood and adolescent antisocial behavior, youth service organizations must work with others in one of the three

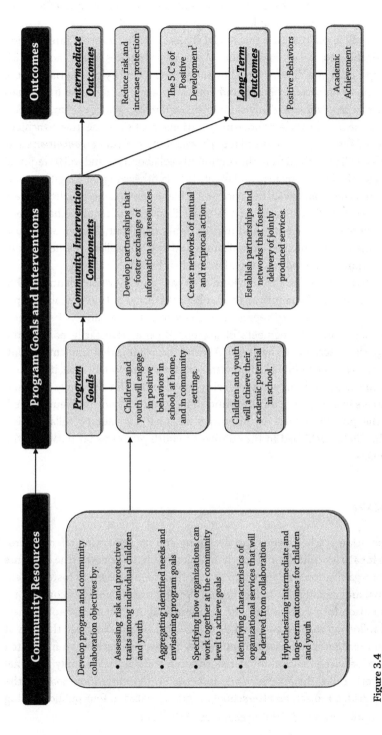

Figure 3.4
A Community Collaborative Model for Preventing and Treating Youth Problems
1. Adapted from Lerner, Lerner, & Phelps (2009)

suggested modes to design and implement quality services and efficacious interventions for young people.

Some will argue that that this model spans too many levels of intervention to be doable, much less measurable. After all, it requires one to accomplish five steps, each at a different level of analysis: (1) identifying the risks to the well-being of *individual* children and youth, (2) aggregating these individuals into at-risk *populations* and envisioning an overarching goal for them, (3) specifying at the *community* level how organizations must work together to achieve this goal, (4) stating the performance characteristics of your *organization*'s services that will be derived from the community collaboration and will be required to achieve the long term goal, and finally (5) hypothesizing the long-term outcomes in terms of *individual* behavior and achievements. Conceptualizing these five phases, each linked to the next by proscribed actions, requires that leaders think complexly, coherently, and multisystemically about children and youth within the context of their organization and staff as well as the network of organizations that is working together on their behalf.

Granted, dangers lurk in this kind of broad, multisystemic planning. One is the possibility of committing an ecological fallacy, of thinking about specific individuals as if they represented the group. It must always be remembered that individual members of a group do not necessarily possess the average characteristic of the group. Another problem is that implementation is extremely challenging. Nothing can counter the argument that it is much easier to design and carry out a service program that involves only staff and volunteers in a single organization and that targets only one problem or need. Still, the positive effects of interorganizational community collaboration and the quality achieved in the context of youth programs far outweigh the challenges.

SUMMARY

Collaboration is a key element in designing and implementing effective programs for at-risk children and youth. In this chapter, we reviewed the elements of interorganizational relationship theory that are necessary to foster organizational and community collaboration. We proposed a model of community collaboration for youth service organizations and its intermediate outcomes. In the following chapter, we use the CCM and previously described theories of risk and resilience and positive youth development to develop an integrated model of service provision for at-risk children and youth. We apply this final framework, called the *integrated prevention and early intervention model*, to the Denver Bridge Project, an afterschool program located in four public housing communities, in the remaining chapters of the book.

PART TWO

The Integrated Prevention and Early Intervention Model

Integrating Theory, Intervention, and

Evaluation at the Denver Bridge Project

CHAPTER 4

The Integrated Prevention and Early Intervention Model

Bridge Project Intervention Components

The principles of risk and resilience, positive youth development (PYD), and interorganizational collaboration described in the first three chapters are often used as separate entities in the design and implementation of youth service programs. Indeed, each model has had its advocates, and considerable energy has been spent detailing differences between the three approaches. In this chapter, we advocate for the creation of an integrated model that combines elements of risk and resilience, PYD, and interorganizational collaboration. We believe that together these three frameworks form an important summation of research and practice conducted in the past several decades aimed at preventing and treating child and adolescent problems. We describe how a perspective that combines elements of these three approaches, called the integrated prevention and early intervention model (IPEI), can guide the design and implementation of community-based programs for children and youth. A case study of the Bridge Project After-School Program in Denver, Colorado is used to illustrate the utility of the IPEI framework.

INTEGRATING THREE THEORETICAL PERSPECTIVES: THE INTEGRATED PREVENTION AND EARLY INTERVENTION MODEL

Integrating theories of risk and resilience, PYD, and interorganizational collaboration is not difficult; in fact, because their similarities outnumber their differences, the fit is logical and makes common sense (Catalano, Hawkins, Berglund, Pollard, & Arthur, 2002; Jenson & Fraser, 2011). The compatibility of the three models derives from the following characteristics.

First, all three frameworks bring a broad focus to the study and delivery of child and youth services. Rather than provide for one need, treating one problem or risk factor, or enhancing one protective factor, each approach argues for comprehensive assessments that consider children and youth in the context of their environment. As noted above, a narrow approach obviates the opportunity to see young people in holistic or ecological ways or as individuals who have unique strengths and weaknesses. Thus, through integration we minimize the use of one-dimensional labels and the adverse consequences of categorizing young people as dropouts, juvenile delinquents, drug abusers, or pregnant teens.

A logic model of the IPEI framework is shown in Figure 4.1. As shown in this figure, IPEI provides a multisystemic approach to designing, implementing, and evaluating interventions for children and youth. This integrated model, in turn, results in an ecological framework that is likely to be more effective than traditional, single-theory programs in preventing and treating child and adolescent problems. By addressing not only an individual child's characteristics, but also those of the family and community, we account for social and environmental influences on young people. Thus, the actions of practitioners and program administrators are more likely to target not only the child in context but also the broader environment itself.

Unfortunately, youth service practitioners and policymakers are not typically trained to think holistically; that is, when thinking about working with children and youth they seldom consider the influence of the broader context. A useful metaphor for overcoming this problem is a camera. If we zoom in on you working with a child, we see you and the child clearly, but the background is blurred. However, if our camera's depth of field is deep enough, we can focus on the background at a midpoint and again at a still farther distance, but then your and the child's image becomes fuzzy and finally loses its detail altogether. The camera's ability to take in the entire context of a reality and focus sequentially on different points in the entire depth of field is a good analogy for thinking holistically about preventing or treating child and adolescent problems.

Risk and resilience, PYD, and interorganizational collaboration models provide a strong basis for integration because each framework recognizes, accommodates, and incorporates similar program goals. The contribution of the risk and resilience framework lies in its emphasis on identifying the needs and strengths of children and youth in their particular contexts. An additional asset of the model is its ability to guide the design of program components to address the most significant of these needs and strengths. As noted in Chapter 1, the risk and resilience model has been used to identify a number of correlates of child and adolescent problem behavior; the identification of these correlates has, in turn, led to a continuum of interventions and services for young people. Indeed, the particular theoretical power of

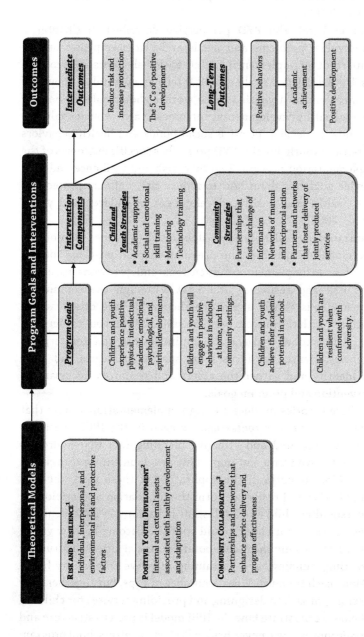

Figure 4.1
The Integrated Prevention and Early Intervention Model
1. Adapted from Jenson & Fraser (2011)
2. Adapted from Lerner, Lerner, & Phelps (2009)
3. Adapted from Alter & Hage (1993)

the risk and resilience model is its ability to forecast what elements of an overall program are likely to be the most effective in preventing or treating problems experienced by young people (Hawkins, 2006; Jenson, 2010; Jenson & Fraser, 2011).

On the other hand, the PYD perspective described in Chapter 2 minimizes individual problems and needs and places emphasis on the processes important for implementing intervention elements and program components. Unlike risk and resilience, PYD tells us a great deal about the actions and mechanisms a youth service worker should take in helping children achieve healthy developmental outcomes. It also provides valuable insights into how to develop positive social bonds and health behaviors among children and youth. Finally, PYD proscribes specific outcomes of the program implementation process. Together, risk and resilience and PYD theories provide guidance about how to reduce risk, enhance protection, *and* promote healthy and positive development in children and youth (Catalano et al., 2002).

Interorganizational collaboration, illustrated by the community collaborative model described in the previous chapter, provides specific advice about *how to* implement interventions and programs based on principles of risk and resilience and PYD. Although the community collaborative model is clearly a practice theory like the other two, it concerns itself not with the process between staff and child but rather with the specific activities conducted by staff, administrators, and counterparts in other agencies. Hence, the focus is on specific strategies and tools designed to identify and gather the assets and resources necessary to achieve intervention and program goals.

Together these theories produce a design implementation system that is *comprehensive, holistic, and contextual.* As seen in the IPEI, the three models offer an integrated and effective planning tool that addresses key risk and protective traits and important developmental processes in young people. More important, the application of these three theories is sequential: (1) risk and resilience form the foundation and etiological base for understanding child and adolescent behavior; (2) PYD identifies the processes necessary for children and youth to become healthy young people; and (3) the community collaboration model offers instructive steps for creating, building, and sustaining effective community-based programs. Alone each framework has a number of gaps, but together they produce a useful approach to designing and providing services for children and youth. Below we illustrate how the IPEI model is used to structure and deliver interventions in the Denver Bridge Project, an afterschool program located in four urban public housing communities.

Putting Theory to Work

The history of social intervention is littered with good intentions gone sour. If we make only one point in this book, it is that good theory is an essential aspect of developing successful programs for children and youth. Theory is required to develop social and educational programs in order to assure that the investment in effort and financial resources will lead to the desired outcomes (Polansky, 1986). In our case study of the Bridge Project, the desired outcomes are that children living in public housing neighborhoods develop and maintain academic skills, graduate from high school, and ultimately be accepted into local colleges and universities. To build a social or educational youth program without a practice theory is like starting across an ocean in a ship for a specific destination without a map. When the first storm breaks and pushes the ship off course, it has no means of finding its way back to the correct course. The early history of the Bridge Project, described in the accompanying pages (see Boxes 4.1 & 4.2), details the obstacles and progress experienced by the program since its inception in the early 1990s. Theoretical and program elements of the Bridge Project—and the relationship of these elements to the IPEI—are described next.

Box 4.1 THEORY AND PRACTICE IN ACTION: EARLY HISTORY OF THE DENVER BRIDGE PROJECT

The Bridge Project is a community outreach project of the University of Denver. The project was a fortunate confluence of forces that merged early in the 1990s. At that time, Chancellor Dan Ritchie was on a mission to transform the University of Denver's image to one of a top-level university that was integral to the economic and social fabric of the region. Ritchie believed that universities had an obligation to contribute to the welfare of their cities and/or regions and felt that valuable and largely untapped synergies were available through public–private partnerships. His success in developing initiatives between the university and the community is captured by the university's current desire to be *a great private university dedicated to the public good* (University of Denver, 2011; http://www.du.edu/ccesl/publicgood.html).

The story of the Bridge Project begins with a partnership between Chancellor Ritchie and Philip Winn, a former Secretary of the U.S. Department of Housing and Urban Development (HUD) and ambassador to Switzerland. Upon his return from Europe, Winn consulted

(continued)

---

with acquaintances such as Rabbi Stanley Wagner about the prospect of becoming involved in community service activities in Denver. Winn was seeking a change from the daily responsibilities associated with a long and distinguished career in the public sector. Rabbi Wagner, a personal friend of Chancellor Ritchie's, suggested that he and Winn meet with the chancellor to explore ideas about public service in Denver. Ritchie, excited about the potential of a community and university initiative, recommended that Winn and Rabbi Wagner explore possible program ideas with academic units on campus. Winn and Rabbi Wagner soon met Dean John F. Jones and Professor William Cloud of the Graduate School of Social Work. Jones and Cloud immediately recognized the value in partnering with Winn and a group of civic leaders in an effort to help young people living in poverty. The seeds of the Bridge Project were sown.

The Bridge Project, however, would not have come to life without the commitment and effort of a group of civic-minded individuals who were seriously concerned that the escalating negative conditions in the city's public housing developments were undoubtedly limiting the futures of children growing up in these neighborhoods. Winn, Jones, Cloud, and other supporters believed the odds were against young people in public housing because they had to contend with so many negative influences— gangs, violence, drugs, unstable families, adolescent pregnancy—and, that in many cases, children were prevented from concentrating on learning and school achievement as a viable pathway to a better future. Further, because the founders were business, industry, and service leaders, they realized fully the negative economic impact of perpetuating communities of poverty and violence.

Winn subsequently called on a group of citizens willing to invest in finding ways to intervene positively in the lives of children. From the beginning, the Bridge Project board established a culture that required members to give of their personal time, skills, and wealth in meaningful proportions. They were not just to sit in board meetings making decisions but were to involve themselves in the day-to-day struggle to help hard-to-reach kids, run a daily afterschool program, and help parents enable their children to learn.

In its infancy, this effort to help public housing kids had important assets that may provide lessons for others wishing to develop youth programs. First, a clear and imperative need was recognized and defined. Second, the initial impetus to act came from a respected institution, which provided sanction and prestige. Third, the effort drew on significant resources from board members who had knowledge of the community, political and financial connections, and personal commitment to both project development and children and families living in poverty. Perhaps most important, board members were motivated to act by personal

(continued)

altruism, believing that their investments could make a difference in the lives of poor, inner-city children.

Nonetheless, one crucial ingredient was missing. The Bridge Project founders agreed that they wanted to alleviate poverty, but they lacked a clear vision of how to achieve this end. While they thought a scholarship program for young adults was a good idea, they did not have a model that would be effective in encouraging children to stay in school so that they could attend college. Professor Cloud had served previously on the faculty at LeMoyne-Owen College in Memphis, where in the 1980s he adopted a public housing project across the street from the college. Cloud was involved in managing a number of program components, including a college scholarship initiative for at-risk youth. He was, thus, able to provide a program model that looked like it might be replicable in Denver.

The logical next move was to forge a partnership with the Denver Housing Authority. The director of the housing authority was willing to talk about a project and began meeting with the group. A citywide survey had just been completed, which found that the North Lincoln public housing neighborhood had an 89% dropout rate among its high school–age residents. The housing authority director initiated conversations with the chair of the North Lincoln Residents' Council, who, it turned out, was initially resistant to the idea of a program, saying, "we don't want to be studied...people have come here and studied us to death and we don't want to be guinea pigs anymore."

Overcoming the resistance of community leaders and neighbors was the first major barrier encountered by the Bridge Project. This resistance was subsequently overcome through the efforts of Denver City councilman Richard Castro and because of the founders' commitment to using community organizing as the means of starting a human service program. A planning group that included Philip Winn, University of Denver faculty members, Castro and his wife Virginia, and North Lincoln Resident Council chair Augie Martinez canvassed the neighborhood and talked extensively with residents to get their thoughts and suggestions about where help was needed. What emerged was a picture of great need—basic human services but also afterschool academic assistance for their children. Parents were clear that the help that was needed for their children during the afterschool hours had to be provided in a safe place. Thus, in attempting to build a bridge between the housing project and the university, the founders knew they needed an effective method of program development; in this case, the method was community organizing. This final asset—the understanding that program models must be rooted in the community—led to a vitally important conclusion. Based on parents' interest in locating the program within the community, the planning group requested physical space from Denver

(continued)

Housing Authority to develop an afterschool program. This was a logical decision—to place the Bridge Project next door to the children's homes—but at the time, the importance of this crucial choice may not have been fully understood. In retrospect, locating the program in the public housing complex was the most vital early decision.The early history of the Bridge Project reveals that the elements necessary to create an effective youth program in Denver's public housing complexes were in place and just waiting to be brought together. These elements included: (1) a clear and defined need that could be quantified; (2) political sanction derived from the University of Denver; (3) founders who were a well-connected, civic-minded group willing and able to invest personal assets in the long-term process of implementing the proposed project; (4) a sense of altruism that inspired the commitment and energy of volunteers; (5) a program model that would meet with approval of public housing parents; (6) political assets provided by neighborhood leadership; (7) a community organizing approach that put parents in control of the implementation process; and lastly, (8) institutional partners who, upon seeing that these resources were available, joined the effort and contributed the perfect location. These elements—*a clearly articulated need, political sanction and prestige, resources from committed volunteers, altruism, effective program models, neighborhood support, a method of organizing, and institutional partners*—are the primary essentials for program development.

Risk and Resilience: A Starting Point for Bridge Project Interventions

The Bridge Project adopted the risk and resilience framework in the late 1990s, and thereafter, this framework served to guide decisions large and small. With a risk and resilience theoretical model in place, staff and board members were able to think logically about the community problems they were attacking as well as the various ways and means of shielding children from the negative impacts of these problems. Given that the participants' social and educational problems were so multifaceted and complicated, staff at times had been overwhelmed with vast amounts of often chaotic and confusing information and observations. In order to bring order to program planning, they found that theoretical thinking about the factors contributing to child problems worked to reduce confusing information by identifying underlying regularities of cause and effect. The risk and resilience model thus acted as a filter to reduce the cacophony of white noise in public housing by highlighting the variables that would be useful for building a program model. The framework was also valuable in identifying factors related specifically to successful outcomes. In some instances, the risk and resilience model validated the activities that staff members were already doing. In other instances, the theory suggested new approaches and methods for reaching children and families. With a thorough grasp of the severity and scope of the problems, the Bridge Project staff designed interventions that logically linked together the elements of the causal sequence suggested by the risk and resilience model: risk and protection → goals → interventions → outcomes. Each of these elements is described below.

Identifying risk and protective factors. Bridge Project planners initially focused on the risks evident in public housing communities. Poverty was the first; program developers learned that by definition all public housing residents were poor and that 60% of parents received food stamps and participated in programs such as Aid to Families with Dependent Children and Medicaid. Public data also revealed that 90% of adult residents in Denver's North Lincoln community, the neighborhood targeted by planners as a first Bridge Project program location, did not have steady and adequate employment. Further, the North Lincoln community rated highest in the city for family violence, alcohol and drug abuse, and low parent commitment to education. Finally, crime statistics revealed that the neighborhood was unsafe and gang dominated, with few or no opportunities for safe afterschool activities. Perhaps most concerning, early analysis indicated that approximately 90% of neighborhood youth failed to graduate from high school (Denver Piton Foundation, 1991).

These findings pointed to poverty as the underlying cause of many of the problems experienced by children and youth. While optimistic about effecting positive change, the founders of the Bridge Project understood that a single university, together with a group of public-spirited individuals and a dedicated staff, could not lower the poverty rate among public housing residents. Nor could they create enough well-paying jobs to move a significant number of families into self-sufficiency or mount a successful effort for reducing crime and gang violence. However, inspired by the risk and resilience model, they could think about a set of interventions that would reduce risk and buffer children against the most negative neighborhood impacts. Further, new interventions could enable children and youth to identify their own interests and talents, which, over time, would help them persevere and prevail in the face of risk and adversity. This is a logical and seemingly simple set of theoretical concepts, but it encompasses complex assumptions and predictions that would not have become clear without the risk and resilience framework as a guide.

Differentiating goals. The Bridge Project, as first conceived by the founders in 1991, had a single long-range goal of ameliorating poverty. Initial program efforts focused on the idea of a scholarship program for high school students as a means to escape poverty. The assumption was that the promise of a college education would inspire adolescents to try hard in school, thereby making them college eligible. Thus, the Bridge Project had a single program goal

Box 4.2 REFLECTIONS ON THE POLITICS OF COMMUNITY ORGANIZATION IN THE BRIDGE PROJECT

John F. Jones, Ph.D. Dean Emeritus
Graduate School of Social Work
University of Denver

The Bridge Project started on a high note: Ambassador Philip Winn and Rabbi Stanley Wagner laid out a coherent socially responsible proposal to Chancellor Dan Ritchie, who wholeheartedly approved. But then came the difficult part, typical in a run-of-the-mill community organization. From experience, the community practitioner knows that the more complex the project, the more likely the possibility of conflict. Often the initial signs of controversy are rhetoric and moral posturing easily enough dismissed as insignificant, but underneath can lie a more serious clash of wills with far graver consequences. The clash of wills about the form that the Bridge Project should take, and indeed its very existence, was evident in the early days of the program.

Politics—the science and art of government—has a noble purpose, the common good, but self-interest is a factor that can run counter to the claims of others. That is quite normal; individual concerns and the right to promote them are taken for granted. But in community affairs, distinct institutional variables and patterns of behavior are more pronounced and troublesome. Policymakers, planners, and community organizers stand in need of a strategic approach to deal with competing demands. Two strategies are commonplace. The first seeks to accommodate the balance of power among stakeholders in a changing environment, where the environment is seen as the determining factor. The second strategy is more aggressive where a community activist, for instance, assumes that he or she is dealing with partisan political contests (Bryson, 1995). In the first year or two before the Bridge Project was firmly established and a routine administration put in place, a combination of these strategies was called for and used selectively.

A twofold set of circumstances was involved—the internal institutional environment and the external community environment. The internal environment, that of the University of Denver itself and its Graduate School of Social Work (GSSW), could not be easily altered in a short space of time. Like perhaps most universities, ultimate authority belonged to the University of Denver's Board of Trustees and the chancellor. Within that institutional framework, the university and GSSW each had its own fixed framework and customary way of doing things. Minor changes were possible, but the power structure and center of authority were apparent across campus. That, of course, did not prevent internal differences. Deans and department heads along with a number of faculty members were lukewarm, if not strongly opposed, to the radical changes implicit

(continued)

in a community project of the scale envisaged by Bridge advocates. This was most obvious in GSSW where faculty members were divided down the middle, one group in favor of the Bridge Project proposal, the other adamantly against the idea.

As the first political strategy mentioned above might have predicted, the outcome had less to do with ideology and rational discussion than the balance of power. Once it became clear that a decision had been made by the chancellor, department heads opposed to the Bridge Project either shrugged their shoulders and moved on, or experienced a change of heart and approved. There continued to be some dissent, but it was minimal, and as time went on it disappeared completely. Those favoring the Bridge Project had every reason to support a top-down policy on this occasion and did so. The end result over time was an embrace of the program by faculty and students to the benefit of the entire university. That, however, had little if any observable effect on the dynamics of faculty decision making.

The partisan political contest (strategy number two) held sway in the external community environment. Although the state and municipal structures have legislative standing, they are open to challenge in a way that an organization such as a university may not be. Local government is by its very nature an arena of partisan competition. The Denver Housing Authority was among the municipal agencies that Bridge Project advocates sought to influence and for the most part won over to their side. The North Lincoln Residents' Council initially resisted the threat of what might have seemed a public housing project coming under outside control. Persuasion and the prospect of educational, health, and other human service benefits carried the day, but the effort and commitment of community leaders like Denver Councilman Richard Castro were needed to bring the project to completion. Dedicated members of the Bridge Project Board used their status, political or otherwise, to gain support in the community for the North Lincoln program.At the risk of a generalization, one might suggest that the first political strategy paid off for the Bridge Project in the relatively tight-knit environment of the University of Denver, while a political partisan approach was required and proved successful in the larger community. Both strategies have a place in community organization, as its practitioners are well aware. Clearly, the Bridge Project has benefitted greatly from the operating principles and key tenets of community practice.

of providing college scholarships for all public housing high school graduates. This was an admirable goal, but within several years the founders came to the conclusion that their model was not working for the simplest of reasons— few college-ready high school graduates could be found in the neighborhood. Obviously, the goal had to be narrowed, the reach shortened, and by the mid-1990s a far more comprehensive approach to helping public housing children needed to be identified.

How the Bridge Project moved from one long-range goal using a one-dimensional program model (ameliorating poverty via college enrollment) to an intermediate goal using a comprehensive multifaceted program model is a case study of applying theory to practice. Today, the Bridge Project espouses one principle objective of *keeping children and youth in school*, with the intermediate goal of increasing the percentage of youth who graduate from high school. Although the college scholarship component is still one of the interventions and serves as a robust incentive, this component is no longer the major focus of the program. With the realization that meaningful change for a significant number of children would only come from targeting preschool and elementary school so they would have a chance at high school completion, the Bridge Project program model became increasingly more comprehensive and complex.

Linking interventions to goals. By the late 1990s, it became clear that in order to achieve the goal of high school graduation a much stronger emphasis had to be placed on improving younger children's reading, writing, and technology skills. Up until this time, supervised homework help in the hours following release from school was one of the primary interventions. However, by 1998 it became clear that academic instruction clearly had to be the first priority, and several other program components were created to support and enhance children's academic success. Thus, the Bridge Project went from offering one program component in the early 1990s to offering 12 components just 10 years later. These intervention elements were informed by principles of PYD and implemented by key components of community collaboration. In time, the Bridge Project model evolved to be an integrated approach to helping children and youth succeed in school. This integrated model became the IPEI. Additional reflections on the Bridge Project are found in Boxes 4.2 and 4.3.

BEYOND RISK, RESILIENCE, AND POSITIVE YOUTH DEVELOPMENT: THE INTEGRATED PREVENTION AND EARLY INTERVENTION MODEL

The risk and resilience framework provided the groundwork for initial program services at the Bridge Project. Focusing on improving academic outcomes, intervention components aimed to reduce risk factors for school failure such as low commitment to school, weak attachments to positive role models, school absenteeism, association with antisocial peers, and deficits in learning that hindered success. Interventions at the Bridge Project also aimed to enhance protective factors associated with preventing school failure such as involvement in school activities, social and problem-solving skills, positive

Box 4.3 A UNIQUE UNIVERSITY–COMMUNITY PARTNERSHIP

Today, the Denver Bridge Project is a unique partnership between the Graduate School of Social Work (GSSW) at the University of Denver and a community-based program that serves children, youth, and families in four public housing neighborhoods. The program is part of the organizational structure of the university and is under the fiduciary supervision of the Dean of the GSSW.

This collaboration offers several tangible benefits to the Bridge Project and to the university. First, the Bridge Project is supported by the general infrastructure of GSSW and the University of Denver. Thus, all four program sites receive assistance from the university's personnel, technology, and research divisions. In turn, GSSW and the University of Denver students have direct access to a host of applied learning experiences. GSSW alone sends approximately 10 graduate interns to the four Bridge Project locations each year. Students gain valuable experience in the tutoring, technology training, and social skills training intervention components at the Bridge Project. They learn first hand the many challenges of developing and sustaining a community-based program for children and families in four of Denver's poorest neighborhoods. On a broader level, the Bridge Project is closely connected to the University of Denver's mission to "be a great private university dedicated to the public good" (University of Denver, 2011; http://www.du.edu/explore/visionandvalues.html).

Faculty members in the position of dean at GSSW serve in a unique dual role. In addition to oversight of the education, research, and service missions of the school, GSSW deans also monitor program activities and financial status at the Bridge Project. This dual role poses challenges that are unique in the academic environment. Former Dean John Jones, the academic dean of GSSW at the time the Bridge Project was created, captures the original intent and challenge of placing the Bridge Project within the organizational structure of the University of Denver in Box 4.2. Jones was Dean of GSSW from 1987 to 1996. His term was characterized by the many challenges associated with starting and defining a community-based program. Jones and other program founders also established important and long-lasting ties with other community-based programs and with officials at the Denver Housing Authority. By the mid-1990s, the Bridge Project had begun to solidify its program and funding bases. Still, there was much to do before declaring the young program a success.

Catherine Alter assumed the deanship of GSSW in 1996. In a recent interview, she recalled one of her first interactions with Bridge Project board members:

(continued)

Several weeks after I became dean of GSSW I attended my first Bridge Board meeting. I arrived a few minutes early but members were already gathered, sitting around a table and chatting. As I waited for the meeting to begin, I realized they were talking about their children—their successes in school, problems with friends, activities and plans—normal concerns and anxieties of parents with young children. It wasn't until after the meeting, when I inquired about one of the children they had been discussing, that I realized these were not their own children, but Bridge Project children who they were mentoring. It was then that I realized this program was something extraordinary. The fact that busy, middle-class adults would invest of themselves so deeply that the boundaries between their own children and other children became blurred was truly amazing (C. Alter, personal communication, July 15, 2011).

Alter was Dean of GSSW from 1996 to 2006. During her tenure the Bridge Project grew from one program site near downtown Denver to three sites across the city. The school secured several large federal grants during this time, and the Bridge Project became widely represented as an important program for at-risk children, youth, and families in Denver's public housing neighborhoods (C. Molidor, personal communication, June 16, 2011).

The past several years witnessed the addition of a fourth Bridge Project site in northwest Denver. Interim Dean Christian Molidor oversaw the addition of this location. He reflected on his experience with the program in a recent conversation:

It is almost impossible for me to describe, in a few sentences, the impact that the Bridge Project has had in the lives of so many children and youth. This is a program that positively alters the cycle of poverty for kids living in Denver's poorest neighborhoods through mentoring and educational opportunities. I was hooked on the program after one visit. I think the integration of social work and education is what really makes it stand apart from other programs (C. Molidor, personal communication, June 16, 2011).

The University of Denver added additional faculty support to the Bridge Project in 2007 through establishment of the Philip D. and Eleanor G. Winn Professorship for Children and Youth at-Risk. This endowed professorship, currently held by Professor Jeff Jenson, allows a faculty member to concentrate on evaluation and research activities at the Bridge Project. When asked to consider the importance of the professorship, Jenson said:

Our research team has become increasingly active at the Bridge Project in recent years. We've created an effective longitudinal tracking system and have introduced systematic data collection at specific time points during

(continued)

the school year. Assessing the effects of community-based interventions like the Bridge Project is critical to advancing knowledge about effective strategies to help at-risk youth. Team members are now presenting papers at national conferences and publishing their work in professional conferences. I really think we are on the right track at the Bridge Project; we've learned a lot from some of our past mistakes and accomplishments (J. Jenson, personal communication, May 2, 2011).

Today's challenges at the Bridge Project include finding ways to sustain program efforts and financial budgets in the face of tight economic conditions. The program is also searching for ways to rigorously test and replicate the intervention in other localities. James Herbert Williams, the current dean of GSSW, recognizes the value of the Bridge Project and is striving to ensure its legacy as a University of Denver program. In a recent interview, Dean Williams noted:

> The Bridge Project is a perfect example of how a School of Social Work can partner with the community to deliver a community-based program that impacts the lives of youth and their families. The educational and prevention services provided by the Bridge Project support the mission and goals of both the University of Denver and the Graduate School of Social Work. We at the Graduate School of Social Work are very fortunate to have such unswerving community partners who see the value of this important community initiative (J. H. Williams, personal communication, May 10, 2011).

Ensuring the success of a community-based program for at-risk children and youth takes many hands and effective leadership. The students, faculty, and administrative staff at the Bridge Project and the University of Denver have formed a unique partnership to help at-risk children and youth in Denver's public housing communities.

attitudes about school, and caring relationships with teachers and other positive adults.

As noted above, Bridge Project staff members and members of the University of Denver research team began to see limitations of the risk and resilience model in the late 1990s. New applications and findings from the PYD field pointed to a need to incorporate additional aspects of strengths-focused approaches in the program's intervention strategies. To that end, tenets of PYD described in Chapter 2 were added to the Bridge Project's intervention model. This is best illustrated by the program's decision to intentionally link intervention strategies to the attributes identified by Lerner (2005) as key aspects of positive development: (1) competence, (2) connection, (3) character, (4) confidence, and (5) caring. Together with elements of risk and protection, these attributes form the basis of intervention elements at the Bridge Project. The Bridge Project currently provides interventions and operates year-round services through After-School, Summer, and Scholarship Programs.

The Bridge Project After-School Program: Child and Adolescent Interventions

Informed by principles of the IPEI, six core interventions are now provided in the context of afterschool programming at the Bridge Project. Shown in Figure 4.2, these program components are derived from the key theoretical constructs of risk and resilience and PYD that form the IPEI.

Program component #1: academic support. The heart of all Bridge Project interventions lies in promoting academic achievement. Academic interventions target underlying risk factors of school failure and low commitment to school and aim to enhance protective factors of involvement in school activities, having a positive attitude toward school, and social and problem-solving skills. Services aimed at improving school outcomes are also based on the PYD constructs of competence and confidence.

Structured tutoring to help children stay at grade level in reading, improve school grades and standardized test scores, and learn to read for pleasure is a key program activity in the afterschool hours. Academic achievement is also supported by: (1) daily homework help sessions, (2) reading readiness sessions for preschoolers, (3) specific reading instructional activities for children in Grades 1 through 5, (4) writing instruction, and (5) annual reading assessments in the fall and spring of each academic year. Educational assessments for all participants were added in the past 5 years as a means of identifying children who need extra help and instruction, as well as a means of evaluating the effectiveness of reading activities. These results are shown in Chapter 6.

The goal of academic improvement is one that cuts across all aspects of the curriculum. Opportunities for children and youth to practice their reading and writing are woven into many of the other intervention elements shown in Figure 4.2. For example, children who participate in mentoring, social and emotional learning, and leadership components are often asked to read books, write reports, and keep journals. Today, the expected result of the academic component is simply that *children learn to learn.*

Program component #2: technology training. In recent years, it became increasingly apparent that for children and youth to succeed in school the Bridge Project had to provide training in technology and access to computers and social network sites. Fewer than 25% of parents who live in Bridge Project neighborhoods own a computer, suggesting that most participants have very limited access to important types of technology (Jenson & Lopez, 2010). And although many public schools have computers, they often do not provide the daily access to technological resources that middle and upper class children

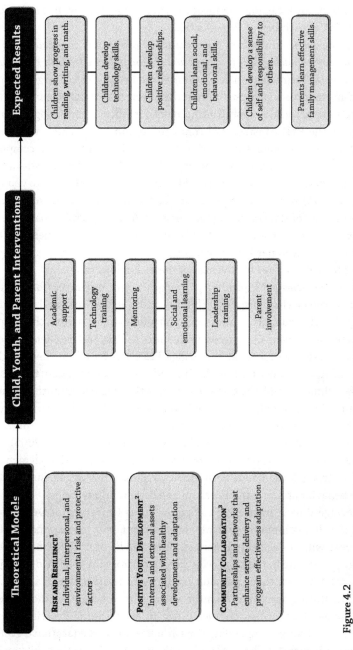

Figure 4.2
The Integrated Prevention and Early Intervention Model: Child, Youth, and Parent Interventions at the Bridge Project
1. Adapted from Jenson & Fraser (2011).
2. Adapted from Lerner, Lerner, & Phelps (2009).
3 Adapted from Alter & Hage (1993).

often take for granted. To counter this lack of resources, staff at the Bridge Project developed partnerships with technology experts from the University of Denver and with sources that provide hardware, software, and technology programming. The local housing authority cooperated by providing space for a computer lab at each Bridge Project site.

Today, the expected result of the technology program is that *Bridge Project children become technologically proficient and use computers effectively to complete their homework*. Technology interventions at the Bridge Project target the risk factor of limited prosocial opportunity and the protective traits of opportunities for education and social support from nonfamily members. Technology training also targets the PYD constructs of competence, connection, and confidence. The technology component includes: (1) daily assignments in the computer lab, (2) instruction in the use of standard software, (3) a technology team that trains youth between 14 and 18 years old to teach computer classes to younger children, and (4) part-time employment for technology team members who complete a series of structured training sessions. All Bridge Project participants are assessed each year for technological literacy as a means of helping staff identify children who need extra help and instruction. These assessments are also used to evaluate the effectiveness of the technology program.

Program component #3: mentoring. Bridge Project organizers had strong ideas about the merits of exposing children and youth to caring relationships with adults who support, encourage, and guide them across challenging developmental stages. Consistent with both a risk and resilience and a PYD framework, mentoring at the Bridge Project is based on the idea that having caring and consistent adults, in addition to one's parents, leads to secure attachments and positive social bonds that are useful in the broader community. Put in simple terms, children who are embraced by caring adults are more likely than other youth to see themselves as worthy of care and love (Herrera et al., 2007; Kuperminc et al., 2005; Spencer & Rhodes, 2005). The expected result of mentoring services at the Bridge Project is that all mentees will forge strong social bonds with prosocial adults that will in turn lead to positive behavior at home and in school and community settings.

The Bridge Project mentoring component uses University of Denver students and other community volunteers who commit to a relationship of at least 1 year with a designated mentee. Fifty middle and high school youth currently participate in the mentoring program across the four Bridge Project sites. A part-time mentor coordinator recruits volunteers and tracks and coordinates mentoring activities. Mentors spend 4 to 6 hours per month with their mentees. Mentoring activities range from attending sporting events and outdoor activities to spending time at museums and educational events. As shown in Figure 4.2, the expected result of mentoring is that *children will develop positive and supportive relationships with at least one caring adult beyond those already in their families*.

Program component #4: social and emotional learning. The social and emotional learning component at the Bridge Project exposes children to structured skills-training curricula and provides positive opportunities for social activities that enable participants to explore themselves and the outside world. The theoretical underpinning and rationale for this component evolved as the staff learned about PYD. One major tenet of PYD focuses on developing competencies in children and youth (Lerner, 2005). Children and youth at the Bridge Project participate in evidence-based prevention programs such as the Incredible Years (Webster-Stratton, Reid, & Hammond, 2004) and Youth Matters (Jenson & Dieterich, 2007) that aim to increase social, behavioral, and cognitive skills.

Bridge Project social and emotional learning activities also aim to make it possible for children with limited opportunities to develop new interests and competencies in things they like to do. This rather basic and intuitive idea is played out daily around the world in countless youth service organizations. In our program model, expanding children's horizons is a vital value-added component, not only because it builds competences, but because it is often the very thing that entices young people to come to the Bridge Project. Interventions include participation in: (1) afterschool groups focused on reading and literacy, (2) cultural activities, (3) life skills training, (4) sports, and (5) art activities. These activities are intended to help children develop social, cognitive, and behavioral skills that are beneficial in peer group situations and in school and community settings. The anticipated result of social and emotional learning activities at the Bridge Project is that *children and youth will develop social, cognitive, and behavioral skills, experience positive social development, and learn to self-identify their strengths, talents, skills and preferences.*

Program component #5: leadership training. In the early years of the Bridge Project, the staff recognized that developing social and academic skills was not sufficient to become successful in a complex world. To this end, middle and high school students at the Bridge Project now participate in intervention strategies that seek to develop personal responsibility and leadership skills. In this context, participants are encouraged to internalize the important values of inclusiveness, diversity, and respect for self, peers, and community in their daily lives. Today, leadership activities are used to instill these and other key values in the lives of older Bridge Project participants. Leadership interventions are most evident in the previously described technology training component and in the technology team intervention components. Adolescents are also exposed to structured leadership training by enrolling in an outdoor education program conducted in collaboration with a local family foundation.

Program component #6: parent involvement. The sixth program component shifts the spotlight from children to parents and aims to involve caregivers in the educational processes and careers of their children. Bridge Project staff have long recognized that many children in public housing neighborhoods face serious problems at home that make it difficult for them to learn at school. Children who are depressed, worried about problems at home, or who have unmet medical needs often find it hard to concentrate at school (Rounds, Huitron, & Ormsby, 2011). Staff members recognize the importance of providing social casework to some families. Today, parent interventions at the Bridge Project strive to help *parents and caregivers solve problems that act as barriers to their children's school performance and to support and take part in their children's academic career.* To implement this component, staff members seek to build positive relationships with parents and act as liaisons between parents and classroom teachers. Staff also attend parent–teacher conferences with parents, help parents find ways to remove barriers to their children's academic progress, assist families with concrete needs (e.g., food, furniture, home necessities), provide information and referral services, and offer adult language and computer classes.

Summary. The six program elements shown in Figure 4.2 illustrate the core interventions provided to Bridge Project participants through afterschool programming. Collectively, these strategies seek to increase academic and technology skills that will lead to success at school and in the community. Bridge Project interventions also aim to expose young people to positive adult role models; to enhance social, cognitive, and behavioral skills; and to develop leadership abilities. Finally, afterschool interventions strive to increase parents' involvement in their children's learning processes. The Bridge Project Summer and Scholarship Programs are described below.

The Bridge Project Summer Program

The Summer Program offers opportunities for children and youth to participate in daily literacy activities, attend outdoor education programs, and enroll in a technology program. The Summer Program was created in an attempt to maintain or continue improvements seen in the lives of children over the course of the academic year. Program components focus on academic and social skill development. The assumption behind offering summer activities is clear: children living in unorganized neighborhoods and dysfunctional situations need structure and continuity throughout the year in order to maintain newly acquired skills that are often at odds with their everyday lives (Anthony, Alter, & Jenson, 2009). By providing program continuity during the summer months, the Bridge Project makes clear to its participants that learning—especially reading and writing—is a continual and permanent part of life, not just something that is done at certain times and in certain places. The expected result of the summer component is that *children will continue to make academic progress during periods of time when school is not in session.* Available for 8 weeks, the Summer Program includes elements of the six afterschool program components shown in Figure 4.2 but focuses more intensely on academic strategies because daily exposure to school instruction is absent during the summer.

The Scholarship Program was the first component to be developed at the Bridge Project. As noted earlier, interventions at the Bridge Project evolved over the years to place greater emphasis on afterschool interventions for younger children. However, scholarship opportunities have remained a critical part of intervention services at the Bridge Project. Emphasis in the program is now placed on precollege preparation for those youth who qualify for scholarships. Follow-up support services are also available for currently enrolled college and university students. The stated goal of the Scholarship Program is that *youth will be accepted by local colleges and universities in increasing numbers and will have the personal strength and resources to earn a college degree.* Tuition grants provided by private and public donors are critical to meeting this objective. In addition to tuition grants, volunteers and private donors often provide the assistance necessary to build a bridge from public housing to higher education. Staff and board members also offer: (1) outreach to public housing parents with information about college accessibility and entrance requirements, (2) career and college counseling for high school students, (3) information sessions about college life (e.g., applying to a college or university, living in a dorm), and (4) support and assessment during the scholarship application process. The background and aspirations of a recent Bridge Project scholarship student is illustrated in Box 4.4.

Box 4.4 THE BRIDGE PROJECT SCHOLARSHIP PROGRAM: A YOUNG WOMAN'S QUEST FOR A COLLEGE EDUCATION

BACKGROUND

Husniyah's mother is from India. Her father "purchased" her mother when she was 14 and then immigrated to the United States. They had four children and were living in Denver's North Lincoln public housing community when the father abandoned the family and moved to Texas. When Husniyah was 11 years old, he returned to Denver and kidnapped all four children in the middle of the night while the mother was working and took them to Texas. Appealing to the Bridge Project for help, the mother sought to have her children returned to Denver. Eleanor, a Bridge Project staff member, an employee from a collateral agency, and a volunteer who had been working with the family located the father and asked Texas authorities to return the children to the mother. The state refused. However, after considerable detective work, Mary Krane and Jeanne Orrben of the Bridge Project learned that Husniyah's mother had never been divorced from the father and that no order of custody was ever issued. Subsequently, a Denver lawyer agreed to take the case pro bono;

(continued)

together this team of concerned persons took the issue to Judge Wiley Daniel, a Bridge Project board member. At about this time, Husniyah's father took the children to a swimming pool in Texas where, tragically, one of the children drowned. As a result of the father's incompetence, Judge Daniel was able to return custody to the mother, and Eleanor and a volunteer brought the children back to Denver. Husniyah and her two surviving brothers spent their teen years in the North Lincoln neighborhood and all of them participated in many Bridge Project activities. Through a partnership with a continuing education program, Husniyah's mother completed her GED and is now working full-time in a local nursery. Husniyah is now in college. Below, written in Husniyah's own words, is the admission letter to the Bridge Project Scholarship Program that got her there.

HUSNIYAH'S SCHOLARSHIP ESSAY

As a 17 year old girl I've had many chances to make the wrong decisions, but I learned once that your true character is who you are when no one else is looking. I grew up in the North Lincoln Projects with just my mom and siblings. Fortunately, there was a safe, caring, and peaceful place to go to after school, the Bridge Project. This wasn't like any other after-school program. There are staff we can go to when we need someone to talk to, or even just someone to guide us to the right path. Some of the people in my neighborhood were not exactly caring or even friendly. Someone you thought was your best friend today could be your worst enemy tomorrow. Kids would steal from everyone and everything, including their friends and family. In most ways my situation wasn't any different from the rest. My mom was always at work and we never really had money, but because of the values my mom instilled in me, and that Bridge helped reinforce, it never crossed my mind to fall into what everyone else was doing. I know right from wrong, and I know just because almost every single person in the neighborhood would do it every day, that doesn't make it right.

After growing up in that community I wanted to do what the adults did for me—help others stay out of trouble. I started volunteering at age 13. I moved up to be a Technology Team member at Bridge, and because of my leadership skills I moved up even higher to become a Computer Lab Manager. As a part-time employee at the Bridge Project I now see the same cycle of gangs, drugs, fights, stealing, and even murders. The worst part is the kids are all so young, some not even 10 yet, and they are experiencing all of this as just a natural part of life. Every day I do my best to show younger kids that there is another way, the honest way. The next step of my life is college. I am very excited about staying in Colorado, and getting a great internship at an honest business.

To this point in our narrative, we have discussed how the Bridge Project developed and maintains its interventions for children and youth. However, having a clearly articulated and theoretically based intervention model for children and youth is only half the challenge; the other half is managing such a model with intelligence and skill. The field of good intentions is littered with the corpses of good programs that failed to survive infancy. Several years into the development of the Bridge Project, when the program just started to expand, several organizational pitfalls emerged. Additional unknown hazards common to all social service and educational program development also lay ahead. Below we outline how the organizational and community capacity to deliver Bridge Project interventions was created and how such collaborative efforts evolved in a way that sustained and promoted the program.

Identifying organizational risk factors. The first risk to program integrity was a lack of organizational focus stemming from the fact that the Bridge Project board did not have a plan to guide the program's development. Because the program was initially a volunteer effort, everyone involved assumed that they held a common concept of what they were doing, why they were doing it, and what strategies and intervention methods were best. A theory-based organizational framework and a development plan were lacking to guide the young program. Subsequently, poor decisions were sometimes made regarding personnel choices, work processes, and fundraising.

Lack of focus can lead to another commonly encountered hazard known as *technological drift.* We use the term *technology* in a broad sense to refer to all of the methods used to accomplish the work of an organization. In our framework, *technological drift* refers to situations where a program changes, sometimes dramatically, after its initial implementation. The concept is similar to what other investigators have labeled *treatment or intervention drift* (Fraser, Richman, Galinsky, & Day, 2009). Drift occurs because a clear organizational model does not exist; or, drift occurs in a situation where a model exists but volunteers and staff members do not calibrate their work and actions to the model. In either case, programs drift because the organizational structure does not support, and sometimes actually undermines, intended program outcomes. In the early years, the Bridge Project coasted between being a scholarship program for older youth and a literacy program for younger children, and it accomplished neither particularly well. If the organizers of the Bridge Project had understood the difficulty of placing equal emphasis on two goals simultaneously, they would have prioritized their goals and perhaps been able to select strategies and protocols that would have avoided the drift and floundering of the early years. One caveat is important here: a failure to attain program outcomes can be due to technology drift, or conversely, it can be caused by failure to change.

A third hazard encountered by virtually every youth service program is the tension between resource dependency and regulation. As discussed in Chapter 3, community-based organizations are dependent on revenue from markets that generate fees and contracts; grants from government entities, corporations, and foundations; and gifts from individuals and corporate donors. In today's funding environment, agencies rely on all or a mix of these common sources. In the case of services intended to benefit low-income children and families, community-based programs are subject to both market forces and to the policies and intentions of those who control needed financial resources. The risk to fledgling programs of not finding a fit between what they planned to do and the preferences of their markets and funders is that their programs may be forced into making decisions that are incompatible with their values and goals. When community social service organizations accept funding from sources with goals and objectives that differ from their own, then their programs will not only drift but will be pushed, sometimes dramatically. How community-based programs approach the dilemma between the need to survive financially and the desire to maintain program integrity is a crucial issue. The strategy of the Bridge Project has been to avoid the worst effects of goal displacement by maintaining financial diversification via a balance between public and private support as well as by relying on a high level of in-kind support from volunteers and the community.

The way an organization develops its internal work processes and decision-making structures is another potential risk that can interfere with an agency's ability to realize its objectives. When an organization cannot accomplish what it promises despite sufficient resources, it is said to be a victim of intraorganizational dysfunction. Many community-based organizations experience varying degrees of dysfunction as did the Bridge Project in its early years. The behaviors that define dysfunction include: (1) staff that have difficulty completing a project, (2) leadership that is disingenuous in interactions and communication, (3) individuals or departments that constantly play one-upmanship, (4) organizational members who withhold information or create misinformation, (5) staff who do not question for fear of being humiliated and open to harsh criticism, (6) staff who are unhappy because of intense pressure from above, and (7) leadership that spends inordinate amounts of time on backtracking and damage control (Glisson, 2009). Internal work processes and communication systems that do not work, but that hinder progress, account for a high percentage of organizational failures (Packard, 2008).

The last serious risk to organizational success is the *silo syndrome*—a belief that one's organization is truly freestanding and autonomous, capable of pursuing its mission without having to work with or depend upon other organizations (Gulati, 2007). Organizational survival depends increasingly on the

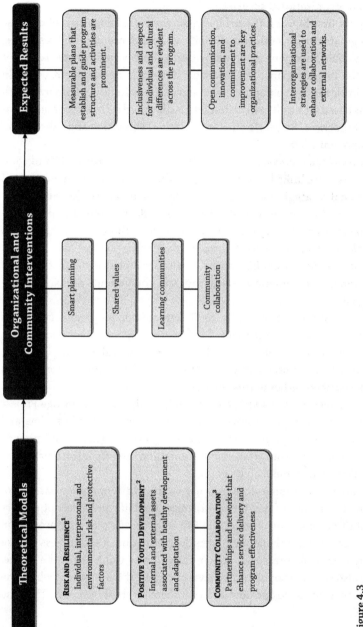

Figure 4.3
The Integrated Prevention and Early Intervention Model: Organizational and Community Interventions at the Bridge Project

1. Adapted from Jenson & Fraser (2011).
2. Adapted from Lerner, Lerner, & Phelps (2009).
3 Adapted from Alter & Hage (1993).

ability to network, cooperate, and coordinate with other organizations. The failure to scan the horizon, to see opportunities waiting in the distance that can be used for the benefit of clients and participants, is a threat to program success and organizational survival.

During its first 5 years, the Bridge Project was challenged by all of these risks to a greater or lesser degree. Despite an abundance of initial resources, the agency could have gone off course within a short period of time had it not been for the organizational skill available during its development years. In time, the Bridge Project became a community-based afterschool program with clear plans based on a well-articulated set of values and beliefs about organizational best practices. Below we offer an analysis of this vision and a discussion of its component parts.

Differentiating a common goal. In the IPEI model, both the child and community focuses are linked to the same goal; that is, intervention efforts and organizational strategies serve the same specific aims. By the late 1990s, the overall goal of the Bridge Project became clear. From this point forward, intervention and organizational capacity in the program have been *to help children and youth in public housing communities achieve their academic potential and graduate from high school.* The program has developed a set of organizational- and community-level program components aimed at meeting this goal.

Linking interventions to goals. By 2000, four specific program components were used by Bridge Project personnel and board members to enhance organizational capacity and collaboration. These components, shown in Figure 4.3, are intended to work seamlessly with the six child and youth intervention elements described earlier in this chapter.

Program component #7: smart planning. In its early days, the Bridge Project exhibited a lack of organizational focus and confusion about its aims and interventions. The program needed a planning process that would provide clear statements concerning the organizational and interorganizational methods it would use to accomplish its goals.

Unfortunately, planning does not just happen in community-based programs. The turbulence of day-to-day organizational life and a lack of managers and staff make it difficult to commit to a systematic planning process on the front end. Successful planning takes determination, a willingness to take time away from daily pressures, and an intention to think about the future. Planning also entails a sophisticated level of critical thinking about where the organization wants to go and how it can get there. In short, visionary thinking is required.

Planning is recognized widely as a critical step during the start-up phase of an organization (Austin & Solomon, 2008). However, smart planning should continue to be a central component of organizational life as an agency evolves and grows. Smart plans are conceptual structures that should be tested periodically to determine if they are still, in fact, describing what is actually happening in an organizational environment. Comparing actual practice with a plan also produces a helpful diagnosis about possible program and technological drift. Like an annual medical checkup, if vital signs have changed, then the problem should be investigated. Uncovering the underlying reason for drift and feeding this information back into a planning process comprise an important step in determining whether an organization's plan is working or should be adjusted.

Regardless of how carefully a plan is constructed and how often it is reviewed, if it was not created collaboratively, a total organization may not be covered. Further, if a plan is to serve as an action guide, then all people involved in the organization and in the interorganizational network should be included in creating and reviewing the plan. This inclusionary process of discussing means and goals often forces compromises and develops mutual agreements concerning the allocation of resources. In effect, the planning process produces a common cognitive structure that serves as a mutual agreement about technologies and strategies to be used in an organizational environment (Alter, 2008). If such a collective conceptualization is widely shared within and without the organization, a common ground is established based on mutual language, symbols, and beliefs about the efficacy of methods being implemented in a program.

As shown in Figure 4.3, planning efforts at the Bridge Project are intended to produce *clear, workable plans based on an agreed-upon set of values and beliefs about the best practices necessary to establish a common cognitive structure*. To implement this component, the entire Bridge Project community, led by staff, is actively involved in: (1) reviewing periodically the program's logic model, (2) adjusting the program components based on the results of the review, and (3) allocating time and resources necessary for determining if the results expected from all the components are being realized. Additional elements of shared value and leadership, expressed in the words of Bridge Project personnel and current and former board members, are described in Boxes 4.5 and 4.6.

Program component #8: shared values. Even though a clear plan has been mutually agreed upon and monitored by all involved, unless the program is grounded in an overall set of values, the delivery may still veer off course. What happens in the process of service delivery, in the thousands of interactions between staff, volunteers, and participants, cannot be fully legislated by a program plan. Further, everyday decisions made by staff and volunteers cannot be mandated by program protocols. A framework of values and practice principles, if clearly articulated within an organization, becomes the means by which staff and volunteers filter the myriad of options they face in the process of interacting and working with children and their parents. Often, when people speak about the culture of an organization, they are referring, in part,

Box 4.5 LEADERSHIP AT THE BRIDGE PROJECT: FOSTERING RELATIONSHIPS, COLLABORATION, AND RESPECT

Effective leadership is critical to the life of a community-based youth service agency. Fortunately, the Bridge Project has benefited from skilled and dedicated administrative and program directors since its inception in 1991. The program's board members have also played vital roles in creating and sustaining the agency.

What are the keys to effective leadership? Mary Krane, Executive Director of the Bridge Project from 1997 to 2010, attributes the sustainability and success of the Bridge Project to three essential elements. First, Krane emphasizes the importance of developing one-to-one relationships with children and parents who participate in the program. Reflecting on her years at the Bridge Project in a recent interview, Krane said,

> Personal relationships with neighbors—children, youth, and parents—have been one of the keys to our success. When we opened the doors at the Bridge Project I wanted it to be a place where children and parents felt safe. I also wanted them to interact with professionals who they trusted and valued. I think we have accomplished these things over the years. Today, children and parents come willingly to the program and feel very comfortable interacting with our staff (M. Krane, personal communication, December 15, 2010).

Krane identifies strong community collaborations and partnerships as a second essential element of leadership. In 1997, director Krane hired Jeanne Orrben to open a second Bridge Project program site. Orrben was a social worker with a deep community practice background that included extensive experience creating and working with community organizers and coalitions. In a recent interview, Orrben noted:

> Mary Krane wanted me to open the doors at Columbine, our second program site, the very same day I was hired! I had to work quickly to organize program activities and find other professionals in the community to help us become established. My experience in community organizing in Denver really paid off as I began to reach out to local schools and other youth service programs. They saw that we were intent on developing an effective program and we were in it for the long haul. Our credibility increased immediately among our fellow providers (J. Orrben, personal communication, January 6, 2011).

Krane and Orrben identify the importance of creating a culture defined by hope and respect as a third leadership component. Krane reflected on this point by noting the importance of modeling these values:

> I always believed that it was important for staff members to model and give respect to the children and parents who come to the Bridge Project. The families

(continued)

[86]   The Integrated Prevention and Early Intervention Model

we serve have typically experienced great risks and setbacks in their lives. I tried to make our program a place where all people's voices would be respected and valued. This was as important to me as the actual activities and services we provided (M. Krane, personal communication, December 15, 2010).

Orrben agreed, noting that,

When we were getting started, we wanted to make children and parents feel like the Bridge Project was their program, that they had ownership in everything that went on during the afterschool hours. I worked hard to begin a parent council and asked members for their input on all kinds of decisions. It was a busy and satisfying experience. Watching children and parents develop and grow along with the program was very rewarding (J. Orrben, personal communication, January 6, 2011).

Krane and Orrben look back fondly at the early days of the Bridge Project. There are twinkles in their eyes as they recount success stories of the many children and youth who they came to know over the years. Orrben points out that Phong Phan, current site director of the Westwood Bridge Project, was among the first youth to attend afterschool activities at the Columbine location she opened in early 1998. Krane points to the success of a former scholarship student, Kai Yeung, who now sits on the Bridge Project Board. There are countless stories, too many to convey in this book, that define the success of the program.

Molly Calhoun, current director of the Bridge Project, embraces the program philosophy and leadership elements articulated by Krane and Orrben. In a recent interview, Calhoun said:

For the children and families of the Bridge Project, we are a community safety net which gives them the foundation that they need to raise healthy, happy and successful young people. The Bridge Project lets our children and our families know that we believe in them. We believe in their potential to bring amazing gifts to our larger community. Families are not alone in raising their children through the sometimes difficult barriers that they face. The Bridge Project is a safe place—a place where all children and families can come for unconditional love, support, and opportunity. Many times, we are one of the only consistent supports in families' lives. We give our kids a chance to be human—to make mistakes and come back. We give them opportunities to go outside of themselves and outside of their community to reach their potential (M. Calhoun, personal communication, May 2, 2011).

Today, Calhoun works to stabilize Bridge Project interventions and bring a more evidence-based perspective to program choices and directions. Still, the importance of relationships, collaboration, and respect rise to the top of her priorities:

I think the Bridge Project is unique because our children can come to our programs from the time they are 3 years old through their college

(continued)

education. It is powerful for kids to know that they will never grow out of our programs. They are always welcome no matter what age or what type of support they need. We are in relationship with our communities. We have laughed and cried with the children and families of the Bridge Project. We have held parents' hands through difficult situations, and we have held the babies of a new generation. We have celebrated countless graduation ceremonies, and we have had heartbreak over the ones who took a different path. Our stories make us a strong organization which has been built on the success of individuals who just needed something to believe in (M. Calhoun, personal communication, May 2, 2011).

Additional key staff, such as current Director of Development Lynne Wilkey, and too many others to name, have contributed to the success of the Bridge Project over time. Krane, Orrben, and Calhoun would be the first to recognize and praise their dedication and many accomplishments.

to the system of beliefs and values that bind the organization's members to a common mission.

Beliefs and values differ, of course, by an organization's target population, mission, and goals. Given the diversity of children and youth who participate in Bridge Project interventions, values that recognize the importance of inclusiveness are paramount. Thus, as shown in Figure 4.3, the Bridge Project *encompasses the values of diversity and inclusiveness as well as the skills of cultural competency in all intra- and interorganizational interactions.* This commitment

---

Box 4.6 AN ACTIVE AND EFFECTIVE BOARD OF DIRECTORS

The Board of Directors has played an important role at the Bridge Project since the program's inception in 1991. Active, rather than token, participation in all aspects of the program has been a board trademark. Many board members have volunteered in annual agency events and fundraising activities. Some have served as weekly academic tutors or taught technology or business classes to participants. Other board members have even mentored youth over the course of many years.

Early members of the Bridge Project Board included civic and business leaders such as Philip Winn, Charles Biederman, Jerry Gray, Kathy French, Gary Yourtz, Robert August, and Neil Oberfeld. When asked about the origins of the Bridge Project in a recent interview, Winn noted:

The origin of the Bridge Project can be linked to a tremendous amount of hard work by many dedicated volunteers and community representatives.

(continued)

Dean John (Jack) Jones and Professor William Cloud of the Graduate School of Social Work at the University of Denver played a key early role by adopting and supporting the program. Original board members reached out to the community to gain support and build the program in ways that the university could not have done. It was clearly a team effort from the beginning; the board played an important role in establishing the program (P. Winn, personal communication, April 20, 2010).

Winn's enthusiasm and energy for the Bridge Project has been echoed by other members of the board of directors. Yourtz, a current member of the Bridge Project Emeritus Board, reflected in a recent interview on his involvement in the Bridge Project over the years:

> The Bridge Project has so much to offer young children and families. It has been rewarding to watch the organization grow over the years and to be part of something that is important to the community. The Bridge Project really reaches children living in difficult conditions and circumstances. I can't imagine what the neighborhoods would be like without the Bridge Project (G. Yourtz, personal communication, September 15, 2010).

In the past decade, chairpersons of the board such as Rhonda Kopp, Charles Jordy, and Alec Wynne made significant contributions to the growth and success of the program. Wynne, the current Bridge Project chairperson, noted the recent growth in Bridge Project activities:

> In 2010–2011, we served more children, youth, and families than at any point in our history. We had the largest number of students enrolled in higher education and the biggest college graduating class in the history of the organization. Participants at the Bridge Project revealed increases in reading scores, technology skills, and positive behaviors. We also added new community partners to enhance programming opportunities for our children (A. Wynne, personal communication, October 6, 2010).

An engaged and effective board of directors provides important community support and visibility to any community-based program for at-risk children and youth. The accomplishments of Bridge Project board members illustrate the impact that a committed board of directors can have on developing and sustaining community-based programs for at-risk children and youth.

is operationalized in a pledge to: (1) act with integrity, openness, and honesty in all relationships, dealings, and transactions; (2) keep faith with the public trust through efficient, cost-effective, and compassionate stewardship of resources; (3) ensure that policies and procedures of human relations are legally grounded, of high quality, and respectful of the dignity and rights of individuals; (4) respect all people's race, religion, ethnicity, gender, age, socioeconomic status, and sexual orientation; (5) reflect the diversity of the organization's constituencies and the broader community; (6) conduct programs in facilities that allow reasonable access to persons of all ability levels; and (7) manage resources in ways that promote a sustainable environment (Denver Bridge Project, 2011; http://www.du.edu/bridgeproject/).

Program component #9: learning communities. Plans and shared values are not helpful in the absence of organizational support. Organizational studies emphasize the importance of open and frequent communication between staff members, managers, and board members (Alter, 2008; Argyis and Schon, 1974). To become effective and sustainable, organizations have to become *learning communities.*

Learning communities are places where people continually expand their capacity to actively listen to and learn from each other and where there is time for reflection and feedback. Two realities of organizational life need to be understood before learning communities can develop. First, organizational work requires both explicit knowledge and tacit knowledge. Explicit knowledge consists of facts and their contexts, which are easily communicated through oral or written language. Tacit knowledge, however, refers to information that is often carried unconsciously. Individuals in organizations are often not aware of the extent to which they possess and rely on tacit knowledge, and they may be unaware that this knowledge might be valuable to others. Further, tacit knowledge tends to be embedded in organizational culture and thus is not readily accessible to those who are not part of that culture (Maierhofer, Kabanoff, & Griffen, 2002; Polanyi, 1983; Schein, 1992). Thus, the dissemination and infusion of tacit knowledge across an organization and among organizations are challenging, especially when those involved are from different educational and experiential backgrounds.

An understanding of tacit knowledge is important in youth service organizations because it is a vital element in innovative work processes (Alter, 2008). The difficult work of building an interorganizational plan and a common cognitive structure across organizational boundaries is rooted in the process of drawing out tacit knowledge from participants and transforming that knowledge into explicit knowledge (Terra & Angeloni, 2005). The Bridge Project's ability to modify its original ideas and invent a new and focused plan depended substantially on its ability to leverage its partners' tacit knowledge into effective communication, mutual understanding, and trust. By its very nature, innovation is a journey into the unknown and thus depends greatly on the shared tacit knowledge possessed by the innovators. Human service organizations, with their highly specialized intervention programs, need to continuously infuse tacit knowledge within and beyond their borders. This is a time-consuming but important process.

Uncovering tacit knowledge as well as practicing reflection and feedback are necessary if organizations are going to thrive in rapidly changing environments. Organizations that are flexible, adaptive, and productive are more likely to succeed because they are more capable of reacting to change. For organizations to develop self-correcting processes and create innovation, they need to become learning communities—places where learning is continual. Learning communities adapt and recreate themselves as their environments change. Members of learning communities see their work as a part of a whole system of youth services and know they have contributed not only to their part but also to the whole. This process assures that the continuous improvement of programs and services is at the very center of interorganizational life. Today, Bridge Project staff members define their *learning community as one in which open communication, innovation, and a commitment to continual improvement flourish*. The activities that achieve openness and innovation are similar, if not identical, to those of community collaboration and are listed below.

Program component #10: community collaboration. The discussion above concerning learning communities also applies to interorganizational relationships. Success in youth service organizations is determined to a large degree by whether agencies are open to and skilled at interorganizational collaboration (Schmid, 2008). As noted in Chapter 3, regardless of their size or number of intervention elements, programs must build collaborations and networks with other organizations in order to acquire the resources necessary to deliver effective interventions.

Community collaboration starts with a certain mind-set. If organizational members conceive of their jobs as residing within a space encapsulated by impermeable boundaries, then they may feel safe, but they certainly will not make full use of everything the community has to offer. On the other hand, those that view their organization as free of boundaries, or at least as having highly porous boundaries, will likely produce positive outcomes. Not only volunteers and staff, but also administrators and policymakers, need to be boundary spanners. Equate the common phrase *thinking outside the box* to *thinking outside the organization* and this point becomes clear. That is, the generation of new ideas, resources, and technologies often lies beyond old ways of individual and collective thinking. The Bridge Project captures the essence of this point by declaring that it is *outwardly focused, is enmeshed in a community of youth-serving organizations, and uses tested interorganizational strategies and tactics to the program's best advantage.*

The costs of collaboration are considerable. Thus, Bridge Project staff members have learned over the years to take a conservative approach to collaboration, viz., to use methods of collaboration that are no more intense and time consuming than is necessary. Today, the Bridge Project works from a matrix that views collaboration at the policy/administration, management/ supervision, and direct practice levels. Further, staff members understand that far less intensity of collaboration is needed in obligational networks than in systemic ones.

To make this insight concrete, we created the matrix shown in Table 4.1. To illustrate, if the collaboration is a referral system that involves only the exchange of information, then simple collaborative methods are sufficient. These methods might include referral agreements, written protocols, or joint training arrangements and seldom require extensive face-to-face staff time. However, if a joint effort requires the pooling of resources as in coordinated case management, then more intense methods such as interagency collaboration may be needed. Finally, if the aim is true integration, as might be represented by an ongoing interagency treatment team, then the most intense and expensive forms of collaboration are required.

It is also important to note that collaboration can sometimes be overrated or even viewed as a panacea for all organizational ills. Community collaboration in itself is not an answer for all problems faced by a given program. What it can do, under the right circumstances, is extend the organization's existing resources and competences to accomplish objectives that are beyond its current reach. Likewise, collaboration cannot compensate for mismanagement. In order to apply community concepts to programs, administrators must have more than a superficial understanding of strategic planning, and they must have the interpersonal skills to apply its principles to practice. Finally, all organizational members must be willing to spend significant time on external tasks without considering them to be extra work that lies outside of their daily responsibilities.

This last point raises a final caution. In the context of youth service programs, community collaboration requires considerable financial and time investments that must be balanced with the needs of at-risk child and youth participants and daily program activities. Collaboration is also increasingly mandated by a variety of funding sources. Although they are often unwilling to include the actual costs of collaboration in most contracts and grants, funders nevertheless frequently mandate that afterschool programs such as the Bridge Project coordinate closely with schools and health programs that serve the same participants. Such directives are intended to reduce service duplication, fill service gaps, and create more seamless intervention systems. However, in practice, they often ignore real costs inflicted on organizations. The Bridge Project, like other youth service organizations, has learned to think carefully and systematically about its collaboration efforts in the community.

Table 4.1 METHODS FOR INCREASING LEVELS OF COLLABORATION IN
INTERORGANIZATIONAL PARTNERSHIPS AND NETWORKS

Obligational Partnerships/ Networks Methods of Exchanging and Linking	Promotional Partnerships/ Networks Methods of Pooling and Meshing	Systemic Partnerships/ Networks Methods of Integrating
Policy-Making/Administrative Level		
Referral agreements concerning which agencies (units) will accept which children under what conditions	**Coalitions** that make and clarify policies, do collaborative needs assessment and planning, and solve systemic policy problems when they arise	**Interagency executive committees** that develop seamless services through the pooling of resources and co-location of staff
Program Management/Supervisory Level		
Protocols that operationalize the mechanics of a referral system such as information required by all participating agencies, forms to use, procedures to follow, timing, etc.	**Program plans** that implement coordinated service delivery; define the roles of participating agencies in terms of intake, assessment, and treatment services; and insure that all program components of the system operate smoothly	**Management tools** that support the collaborative operation of services: procedures for integrating the hiring, supervising, and evaluating of pooled staff; integrated budgets and operating plans; methods for integrated program evaluation
Direct Practice Level		
In-service training for staff of all participating agencies (units) that provide comprehensive information about services available to children in the system	**Case conferences/interagency staffings** that share information about child assessment, planning, and intervention, and offer mutual case adjustment/ planning opportunities	**Interagency teams** that jointly do client assessment, and develop and implement an integrated case plan
Social and professional functions that promote mutual awareness and understanding between staff who make and receive referrals in participating agencies (units)	**Case coordinators** who insure that all necessary child information is shared, detect intervention problems, and negotiate adjustments in participating agencies' case plans if necessary	**Case integrators** who insure that all necessary information is shared among participating team members, monitor team members' compliance with the case plan, and mediate changes in the case plan if necessary

Note. Adapted from Alter, C. (2008). Building community partnerships and networks. In R. J. Patti (Ed.), *The handbook of human services management* (pp. 411–434). Thousand Oaks, CA: Sage.

SUMMARY

A new approach to working with at-risk children and youth in community settings labeled the IPEI model was described in this chapter. The model is a synthesis and integration of commonly applied risk and resilience, PYD, and interorganizational collaboration frameworks. The IPEI recognizes that an effective community-based youth service organization must pay equal attention to the design and quality of child and youth intervention elements and to the elements of organizational and community collaboration that ensure its success over time.

The case study of the Denver Bridge Project presented in this chapter illustrates the utility and promise of the IPEI model. The origin and evolution of the Bridge Project captures what are very common challenges in designing and maintaining effective community-based agencies for at-risk children and youth. The program's six child and youth intervention components and four organizational and collaboration components represent the type of planned thinking that is necessary to implement and sustain community-based programs for at-risk children and youth. In the next two chapters, we describe efforts to assess the effects of Bridge Project interventions and present findings from recent evaluations with child, youth, and young adult participants.

CHAPTER 5

The Integrated Prevention and Early Intervention Model

A Guide to Evaluation at the Bridge Project

The integrated prevention and early intervention model (IPEI) described in the previous chapter provides a theoretical and programmatic framework for interventions delivered to children and youth at the Denver Bridge Project. In this chapter, we illustrate how the IPEI model is used to inform and guide the agency's evaluation plan. Specific evaluation strategies and measures used to assess child, youth, and program outcomes at the Bridge Project are described. To set a context for using the IPEI model as a guide to evaluation activities, we begin the chapter with a discussion of the importance of evaluation in community-based programs for children and youth. Evaluation strategies available to practitioners and program administrators in community settings are also briefly reviewed.

BACKGROUND

The Relevance of Program Evaluation

Evaluation efforts aimed at assessing the effectiveness of community-based programs for at-risk youth have gained new importance in recent years. One impetus for the renewed attention to program evaluation comes from a parallel decrease in public and private funding opportunities for youth programs. A decline in national and local funding options for community-based agencies has, in turn, led to intense competition for program dollars in many communities. To increase the likelihood of procuring financial support, programs must increasingly show evidence of effectiveness to potential funding sources.

Evaluation activities are conducted to assess the effects of a program's interventions and services on client outcomes. Outcomes in the context of youth service agencies often take the form of attitudinal and behavioral measures that are linked to a program's intervention model or theory of change. Thus, in their simplest form, evaluation activities seek to assess change in the goals specified in a program's logic model or intervention plan.

The importance of program evaluation, while obvious to researchers and evaluation experts, is not always readily apparent to practitioners and administrators in community-based agencies. Program personnel often lack the requisite training or the combination of skills that are necessary to envision or conduct a meaningful evaluation. In some cases, programs may simply lack the necessary funds to design and implement evaluation activities. Whatever the reason, evaluation tasks are often omitted or given diminished attention in a program's annual planning, budgeting, and implementation activities.

Evaluation studies serve several purposes in the life of an organization. Findings from evaluative studies inform the direction of a program's intervention elements and provide critical planning information related to an agency's long-term goals. Results from ongoing program evaluation studies can, and should, inform the type of services an agency chooses to develop and implement. More important, results from evaluative studies are necessary when submitting competitive grant proposals to public entities and private foundations. Funders now require potential grantees to include evidence of program effectiveness in nearly all competitive proposals. Community-based agencies that lack an evaluation plan or have no findings to describe the effects of their interventions on the lives of young people are at a distinct disadvantage in today's funding streams. This is particularly true given the rapid advance of evidence-based practice.

Evaluation in an Era of Evidence-Based Practice

The popularity and advance of evidence-based practice (EBP) in recent years has had significant implications for evaluating social interventions for children and youth.

Sackett and colleagues (Sackett, Straus, Richardson, Rosenberg, & Haynes, 2000) define EBP as "the integration of best research evidence with clinical expertise and client values" (p. 1). EBP, described elsewhere in detail (Gambrill, 2007; Sackett, Rosenberg, Gray, Haynes, & Richardson, 1996), encourages practitioners and agencies to select efficacious interventions for their clients. Adhering to EBP in practice requires an adequate knowledge base about the efficacy of interventions for children and youth. In addition, program administrators and practitioners must have the skills necessary to access dissemination sources that describe the results of efficacy trials or that synthesize findings from systematic treatment outcome reviews (Howard, Allen-Meares, & Ruffolo, 2007).

EBP has received considerable attention from local, state, and federal policymakers and funding sources in the past decade (Jenson, 2005; Jenson & Fraser, 2011). State and local systems of care, private foundations, and federal entities have entered the debate about the best ways to select and implement effective interventions for children and youth. Many community-based agency administrators and practitioners are working diligently to understand EBP in an effort to develop competitive research proposals and implement effective program components.

The flurry of activity associated with EBP is not confined to selecting and implementing well-tested programs. Developing new knowledge about the effects of interventions for children and youth requires continual attention to designing and testing new programs (Fraser, Richman, Galinsky, & Day, 2009). To this end, more evaluation research is needed to contribute to the knowledge base of efficacious community-based programs for children and youth (Jenson, 2010).

Community-based youth service programs, thus, have a two-pronged incentive for keeping abreast of developments in EBP. First, agencies are asked increasingly to select and implement tested program components and interventions when intervening with at-risk children and youth. Second, community-based programs should consider adding to the knowledge base of effective interventions for children, youth, and families by developing and testing their own interventions.

The evolution and widespread acceptance of EBP reinforces the need for ongoing attention to community-based evaluation and research. Below we describe briefly common quantitative and qualitative evaluation approaches and discuss mixed-methods approaches to evaluating community-based youth programs. Strategies from the Denver Bridge Project are used to illustrate these approaches.

EVALUATION APPROACHES IN COMMUNITY-BASED PROGRAMS

Quantitative Evaluation Methods

Quantitative methods are a traditional approach to assessing program impacts and outcomes for participants in community-based youth programs (Grinnell, Gabor, & Unrau, 2009; Royse, Thyer, & Padgett, 2009; Wholey, Hatry, & Newcomer, 2010). Quantitative program evaluation typically uses survey or official record data to evaluate child or parent outcomes. Indicators from quantitative data sources are important because they allow program and evaluation teams to link specific measures to a program's logic model and stated goals. For example, as shown previously in the IPEI model, a major goal of the Bridge Project is to increase academic performance among children and youth. To assess whether the program's interventions are achieving this goal, participants complete surveys in which they report their current level of involvement in school activities and describe their commitment to school. In this case, a series of quantitative indicators is helpful in determining whether children and youth are meeting stated program goals associated with academic performance.

Existing sources of information are also helpful in certain evaluation situations. To illustrate, the evaluation team at the Bridge Project has established an ongoing process with the Denver public school district that provides evaluators with standardized test scores, attendance, and disciplinary incident reports for all program participants. Schoolwide data such as average test scores or indicators reflecting the percentage of students receiving free and reduced lunches are also available to Bridge Project program administrators and evaluators. Such academic information provides important contextual and comparative information for a community-based youth service agency.

Programs can also benefit from data collected at a neighborhood or community level. For example, neighborhood-level census data allows an evaluation team to assess the prevalence of common risk and protective traits among children and youth who live close to a program site. In other cases, a larger census tract comparison may be useful. To illustrate, if a program objective is to increase the amount of time that parents spend helping their children with homework, it may be important for a community-based agency to obtain information about the percentage of single-parent families residing in the neighborhood. Finally, census-level data measuring delinquency, crime, or substance abuse rates in a neighborhood or city may be helpful in understanding the environmental context surrounding a community-based program. A detailed discussion of the strengths and challenges of different measures for neighborhood or community context is found in Nicotera (2007).

Evaluation designs. A variety of research designs are available to evaluate the effects of community-based youth programs (Grinnell et al., 2009; Royse et al., 2010). The most common design in community settings is a pretest–posttest design in which participants complete one or more surveys before they enroll in a program, followed by one or more posttests at predetermined time intervals. Many evaluation plans for programs serving children and youth administer pretests at the beginning of the school year and posttests at the end of the academic year.

One immediate limitation inherent in the evaluation of community-based programs involves the inability to create comparison groups or to randomly assign youth to receive or not receive programming. In many cases, ethical obligations to serve all at-risk children or logistical limitations including cost and difficulty involving nonparticipating children and families in an evaluation design prohibit the use of rigorous research designs that require comparison or control groups. Relying on youth to voluntarily enroll in programs such as the Bridge Project introduces an evaluation selection bias and may lead to questions about whether program effects are due to the interventions that are provided or to high levels of motivation among voluntary participants. Furthermore, variations in program approaches, structure, and exposure in many community-based programs create challenges in assessing program impact because it is difficult to determine fidelity of programming and mechanisms of change among multimodal programs (Anthony, Alter, & Jenson, 2009).

Comparison and control group designs in which participants in a community-based program are compared with similar youth who do not receive services are the best means to improve the rigor and quality of a basic evaluation design. When feasible, such designs improve a program's ability to assert that change observed among their participants is due to the services provided and not to some outside factors. Readers are referred to Grinnell et al. (2009) for a detailed discussion of research designs and methodological limitations of alternative evaluation strategies.

Qualitative Evaluation Methods

Quantitative forms of information and data provide *breadth* and an accurate numerical assessment of participation in community-based programs. Conversely, qualitative evaluation designs and qualitative data provide *depth*. A typical qualitative data collection method includes semistructured personal interviews with participants in one-to-one settings. Focus groups with 10 or fewer participants are also used frequently to evaluate the effects of interventions or services for children and youth. Other qualitative methods include client journals and observational strategies.

A variety of new and innovative qualitative evaluation strategies are also available to program administrators and evaluators. One such strategy involves the use of photo voice techniques (Wang, 2006; Wang, Morrel-Samuels, Hutchison, Bell & Pestronk, 2004). Photo voice strategies are used to ask participants to respond in writing or dictation to open-ended questions about photos they took themselves that are deemed to be pertinent to a selected intervention or program goal. Additionally, drawings and dictated stories are sometimes used to elicit children's perceptions or viewpoints about abstract or challenging questions. For example, in order to comprehend the neighborhood context in which the Bridge Project provides services, a sample of 45 participants engaged in discussions about the surrounding neighborhood and responded to queries to uncover assets and deficits within that context. Qualitative analysis revealed youth concerns related to risky people as well as to the presence of positive residents and neighbors. Additionally, neighborhood resources were defined along with concerns about the conditions of the built and natural environment (Nicotera, 2011). These findings have been used to improve volunteer training in the agency. They have also served to illuminate the context in which children live and play beyond the confines of the buildings where interventions are implemented.

Other evaluators have used qualitative accounts from participants in innovative ways. For example, Kibel (1999) describes a method for collecting client stories and systematically mapping them as part of an overall strategy to assess participants' outcomes. This systematic mapping, or what Kibel labels *results mapping*, allows evaluators to create a holistic view of program outcomes and impacts from the stories provided by participants. Such an approach is helpful because it moves beyond the use of anecdotal client stories that often amplify program outcomes or success in biased ways.

An example of a recent qualitative study at the Bridge Project illustrates the potential of using qualitative data collection in community-based programs. To assess barriers associated with their children's education, structured focus groups were conducted with parents whose children participated in the Bridge Project and attended public schools (Lopez & Yoder, 2011). Parents were recruited through referral from Bridge staff members and by using snowball sampling among parent networks. Interview topics prepared prior to the groups served as a semistructured guide and focused on how parents were currently involved in their children's academic experiences, barriers to involvement, and parents' service needs related to providing academic support to their children (see Box 5.1 for more details).

Box 5.1 PARENTAL VIEWS OF EDUCATION: A QUALITATIVE STUDY FROM THE BRIDGE PROJECT

Involving parents in their children's education is an important factor in improving young people's academic success. A qualitative study was conducted to better understand patterns of participation and to identify barriers to parent involvement among parents whose children attend the Denver Bridge Project.

METHOD

Two focus groups with 12 parents were conducted to examine topics associated with parental involvement in education. Interview topics prepared prior to the groups served as semistructured guides. Questions asked parents to reflect on their current involvement in their children's academic life, identify barriers to involvement, and speculate on services

(continued)

---

that might help them become more involved in their children's education. Focus groups lasted 90 minutes and were audio recorded and transcribed. Two cycles of coding included descriptive coding (Saldana, 2009) followed by theoretical coding (Saldana) to identify themes in qualitative data related to theory and existing literature.

FINDINGS

Parents identified specific barriers that limited their involvement in their children's education. Tangible barriers included difficulty participating in school-related activities due to time availability, lack of finances and transportation, cultural and language barriers, and limited access to technology used to communicate with teachers. Many parents indicated that they relied on family, neighbors, and staff from the Bridge Project to provide the support necessary to overcome these barriers. Parents also reported feeling marginalized in their interactions with school officials. For example, some parents felt frustrated and helpless when "dismissed" by teachers and administrators who, parents reported, discriminated against them due to their living in low-income communities. Other parents felt like their voices "did not count" and that attempts to "jump through hoops" or "work the system" were often unsuccessful, reinforcing the sense of powerlessness.

CONCLUSIONS

Prior studies reveal that parents who live in poor, urban communities often feel marginalized and stigmatized in the context of their children's academic experiences (e.g., Farber & Azar, 1999; Kelly, Raines, Stone, & Frey, 2010). Further, parents are sometimes "blamed" for being uninvolved or not invested in their children's life at school (Frey, Walker, & Perry, 2011). Contrary to these assertions, the parents interviewed in this study expressed a strong interest in supporting their children's academic performance. However, they face significant individual and social barriers that limit their desire to become more involved in their children's education.

The findings from this qualitative study led to several new initiatives at the Bridge Project. First, staff members increased efforts to advocate for parents in local schools by bridging communication between parents and school officials and by attending parent–teacher conferences. New training initiatives were also launched to teach parents the technology skills necessary to participate more fully in their children's education.

Many qualitative designs and evaluation strategies are available to program administrators and evaluators. Readers are referred to Padgett (2008) for an in-depth discussion of these designs.

Using Mixed-Methods Evaluation Approaches

In recent years, significant attention has been paid to implementing evaluation approaches that combine the best elements of quantitative and qualitative methodology. Termed *mixed-methodology* or *mixed-methods*, this approach aims to integrate conventional quantitative and qualitative strategies into a single evaluation plan that maximizes the precision of both strategies (Patton, 2002). Mixed-method approaches have now been implemented successfully in community-based youth programs (Bender, Brisson, Jenson, Forrest-Bank, Lopez, & Yoder, 2011; Nicotera, 2008; Nicotera & Matera, 2010).

Mixed-method evaluation designs use elements of quantitative and qualitative design to assess program and client outcomes (Creswell & Plano-Clark, 2011). Mixed-method studies take different forms but are characterized generally by identifiable quantitative and qualitative types of data collection and analysis. For example, a community-based day treatment program for troubled youth may collect quantitative data to assess changes in behavior or school performance before, during, and after intervention. Evaluators at the same program may also conduct focus groups with participants or collect qualitative data from the parents of youth who are enrolled in the program. Observational data may also be collected through systematic observation of young people's interactions in program, school, family, or neighborhood settings (see Box 5.2 for more details).

Box 5.2 WHY CHOOSE A MIXED-METHODS APPROACH TO EVALUATION?

Engaging in mixed-methods program evaluation is time-consuming and costly. Thus, it is important that researchers and practitioners have a clear rationale for extending the resources that are necessary to conduct mixed-methods studies. An ancillary Bridge Project program, called *neighborhood explorers* (Nicotera, 2008; Nicotera & Matera, 2010), was designed to teach participants skills for creating community change and to increase civic engagement among youth. A mixed methods approach using both qualitative and quantitative strategies was selected to evaluate the program. A convergent parallel mixed methods

(continued)

design was used to allow investigators to examine statistical change and to interpret the meaning of change among participants (Creswell & Plano-Clark, 2011).

WHAT DOES A MIXED-METHODS APPROACH TO EVALUATION ENTAIL?

All mixed-methods approaches require both qualitative and quantitative data collection and analysis; the type of design chosen determines the time points at which both types of data are collected and analyzed. The convergent parallel mixed methods design in our example required that the quantitative pretest surveys be administered simultaneous to collecting the qualitative data. Quantitative data collection involved administering a civic engagement-youth development instrument (Nicotera, Altschul, Munoz, & Webman, 2010) prior to and at the end of the program. Qualitative data were collected via focus groups with youth participants. The pretest focus group protocols were designed to encompass items drawn from the quantitative baseline survey; the posttest focus group protocols included additional queries that were not included in the pre-focus group.

Using simultaneous data collection procedures requires hiring research assistants with skills in both survey administration and focus group facilitation. Finding personnel with analysis skills pertinent to qualitative and quantitative data are also important considerations. In our case, the neighborhood explorers program and its evaluation plan was made possible by grant funding which made it feasible to conduct a more costly mixed-methods evaluation. Agencies interested in conducting a mixed-methods study should consider project costs prior to implementing an evaluation plan.

Issues of cost may be eased by the added benefits of mixed-methods approaches. In our study, important artifacts from the intervention itself played an important role in understanding program effects. The neighborhood explorers intervention included an empowerment practice for community change called Photo Voice (Wang et al., 2004; Wang, 2006). Participants took photographs as they assessed their neighborhoods, wrote explanations for each photo, and then used their pictures to express views about neighborhood conditions. The information derived from these interventions became important data sources when findings derived from the formal qualitative and quantitative data sets were analyzed and interpreted. Practitioners and evaluators who choose a mixed-methods evaluation approach should consider how artifacts from the intervention can bolster the evaluation process or even how data collection strategies can be embedded in the intervention itself as a cost and time saving device.

Summary

Numerous quantitative, qualitative, and mixed-method evaluation designs are available to help program administrators and evaluators assess the effectiveness of community-based youth programs. Selecting the best evaluation plan for a particular program requires linking a program's conceptual model to program objectives, goals, and desired outcomes. We believe that mixed-method approaches offer the most comprehensive approach to evaluating program effects and encourage their use in the field. Implementing a comprehensive evaluation plan requires the involvement of many stakeholders; engaging staff members in the evaluation process is critical to the success of a plan and anticipation of problems that will certainly arise. Challenges and strategies associated with implementing successful evaluation designs in community-based programs are discussed briefly next.

CHALLENGES IN COMMUNITY-BASED PROGRAM EVALUATION

Securing Parent Consent and Youth Assent

Program evaluation activities in youth service agencies should include parent consent and youth assent procedures. These processes can be time consuming and difficult to obtain in diverse community-based settings but are nonetheless essential. Parents must provide permission for their children to participate in survey or observational data collection. Parents should also be informed of an agency's intention to collect information about their children from schools or social service agencies. Following parent consent, all children and youth enrolled in a program's interventions should be approached and asked to give their assent to participation. These procedures help ensure that children and parents are aware of data collection activities that occur during a given period of time. Finally, parent consent and youth assent should be voluntary in nature to reduce any perceived or real forms of bias in the evaluation design.

Data Collection With Children and Youth

Unique concerns arise when approaching program evaluation research with children and youth (Hart, 2002; Hill, 2006). One issue involves the capacities of young people to represent themselves in the evaluation process. In addition, even though the problems of young people are often the subject of evaluation studies, children's voices are many times absent or viewed as unreliable unless they coincide with responses given by adults regarding the same topics

(Vandell & Posner, 1999). This viewpoint suggests that children may be unreliable accountants of their own lived experiences.

Other evaluators challenge this view. As Prout (2000) notes, "the idea that children are social actors, with a part to play in their own representation...is at last beginning to be absorbed into mainstream social science thinking..." (p. xi). The perspective that young people have the capacity for self-representation is also supported in a study by Borland and colleagues (Borland, Hill, Laybourn, & Stafford, 2001). In this investigation, the authors informed the Scottish Parliament about ways to improve the manner in which children and young people's voices can be considered in the design of policy and legislation in Scotland. Three approaches to gathering the views of young people included: (1) research *on* children in which adults set the agenda and projects are aligned with developmental stages, (2) research *with* children in which children are viewed as socially competent and as contributors, and (3) research as *empowering* for children in which their participation is central and viewed similar to adults. In our view, the last two approaches are most central to conducting evaluation studies with young people. We believe that it is the responsibility of programs serving young people to ensure that participants' voices are represented and valued in evaluation activities.

Handling Small Samples

Children and youth often participate in community-based programs on a voluntary basis. Therefore, they may have no direct incentive to complete evaluation and data collection tasks. In some cases, this leads to evaluation studies with very small sample sizes. This can be problematic because it reduces a program's ability to detect effects and limits the generalizability of results to similar programs.

Program personnel and evaluators must work together to offset the problems caused by small sample sizes. One effective strategy is to involve program staff members in all facets of an evaluation study (Royse et al., 2010). By participating in the development of initial research questions and in the design of the overall evaluation plan, program administrators and practitioners send an important message to children and youth about the importance of evaluation activities. Our experience at the Bridge Project suggests that when staff members feel they are valued in the development and design stages of the research process, they are more invested and better able to understand the importance of sampling and accurately tracking youth longitudinally. This involvement increases the likelihood that staff will be motivated to assist actively in data collection efforts. In addition, efforts to integrate data collection into the standard operating procedures of program staff are important and likely to increase efficiency and reduce staff fatigue.

Selecting evaluation measures that align closely to a program's interventions and goals is a critical step in the evaluation process. Measures should be linked theoretically and empirically to a program's conceptual and logic models. The IPEI framework we use at the Bridge Project allows us to carefully connect the program's intervention elements to goals and intermediate and long-term outcomes. To illustrate, the IPEI framework shows how self-report measures of a child's level of attachment to teachers and commitment to school are used as intermediate outcomes. We will return to the IPEI, and its application to the Bridge Project, at the end of this chapter.

Evaluators must also take considerable care in selecting data collection methods. Surveys and other instruments should be easy to administer and tailored to the developmental attributes of participants. At the Bridge Project, we have found that keeping participants' attention and engagement during data collection activities requires using incentives such as food, prizes, or books. Staff encouragement to participate in data collection is essential.

Differences in children's developmental stages and cognitive abilities may require the consideration of a variety of data collections methods. In our case, evaluation team members generally read survey items to younger children. For older youth, we've found utility in using online surveys administered in Bridge Project computer labs. Computer assessments also provide a level of privacy and confidentiality that we hope reduces social desirability bias.

Being Sensitive to Racial, Ethnic, Gender, and Sexual Orientation Differences

Program evaluation must attend to the racial, ethnic, gender, and sexual orientation differences that are present in the lives of children and families. Neighborhood and community factors related to such differences are also important in the context of evaluation. Evaluators should stop and consider individual and neighborhood differences among the people they serve when designing data collection processes, selecting measures, and analyzing information. Selecting culturally relevant measures when available, or considering adaptations when necessary, are critical issues in working with ethnically and culturally diverse populations.

The presence and complexity of language often comprise a critical issue in evaluation activities. Evaluators must be aware that simply translating survey questions from one language to another requires more than hiring someone who speaks and writes in the language of interest. Words and concepts can mean very different things in different cultures, and simple translation processes may be insufficient in conveying difficult or abstract concepts.

Conducting qualitative interviews, especially focus groups, is also challenging when there are multiple languages represented in the participant population.

Language differences among family participants can also be an obstacle in evaluation studies. At the Bridge Project, children and youth participants generally speak English while their parents often speak the language of their country of origin. This poses obvious communication and data collection challenges. An additional concern is that participants from different cultures often respond to evaluation activities in very different ways. Some participants may be comfortable sharing their views in a face-to-face setting with evaluators, while others may find such a process to be intrusive or even personally offensive. These language and cultural factors illustrate just a few of the many challenges confronting program evaluation teams in community-based settings. Additional concerns and strategies for addressing racial, ethnic, gender, and sexual orientation differences in program evaluation have been discussed by various scholars (Hood & Cassaro, 2002; Knight, Roosa, & Umana-Taylor, 2009).

Asserting Cause-and-Effect Relationships

Youth voluntarily choose to participate in many community-based programs. Thus, a major limitation in evaluation research pertains to the lack of comparison or control groups. Without adequate comparative groups, it is often unclear whether the youth most motivated to change were those included in the group being studied, and whether this motivation level was responsible for change rather than the program being evaluated (Bodilly & Beckett, 2005; Gottfredson, Gerstenblith, Soule, Womer, & Lu, 2004).

Threats to asserting causal relationships between program participation and outcomes can be addressed by creatively designing quasi-experimental and experimental studies. For example, community-based programs may consider comparing participant outcomes to outcomes of youth in other communities without available programs. In settings where the need for services is greater than available program slots, youth can be randomized to a waitlist control group where their outcomes are measured and compared with youth randomized to receive services. This option is challenging to community agencies that aim to serve as many youth as possible in the most equitable way and, as a result, often extend services to accommodate waitlists or serve youth on a first-come, first-serve basis.

Finally, evaluation designs can more rigorously test effects of additional intervention components by randomly assigning youth to interventions beyond services as usual. At the Bridge Project, for example, we plan to introduce new empirically supported skill-building groups to our programming. When we begin offering these services, we will randomly assign youth to receive services as usual or to receive services as usual with the addition of the new skills group. Once rigorously tested, new intervention components can then be offered on a broader scale to all youth participants.

Summary

Methodological concerns present in community-based programs require evaluation experts to play close attention to a host of interrelated issues. Evaluators should work closely with program staff to ensure that staff members are invested in the evaluation plan and to be certain that all evaluation activities are linked closely to a program's intervention components. Consent and assent procedures must be clearly articulated. Measures to assess change in young people should be connected directly to program goals and be sensitive to differences in race, ethnicity, gender, and sexual orientation. Finally, evaluation experts should consistently strike a balance between upholding traditional methodological concerns and ensuring that participants have an active voice in evaluation processes and activities. Below we outline the evaluation plan used to assess the effectiveness of the Denver Bridge Project.

THE IPEI MODEL AND THE BRIDGE PROJECT EVALUATION PLAN

Evaluation strategies at the Bridge Project focus on assessing changes in risk, protection, and PYD constructs identified in the IPEI framework described in the previous chapter. Critical elements of the program's evaluation plan are described below.

Agency–University Collaboration

Program evaluation at the Bridge Project is conducted with support from faculty members of the Graduate School of Social Work (GSSW) at the University of Denver. Since the late 1990s, a GSSW professor has designed and implemented evaluation activities at each of the program sites. Graduate students from GSSW work with the faculty member to collect, manage, and analyze data collected from children, youth, and parents. Bridge Project administrators and practitioners work collaboratively with the evaluation team to establish evaluation goals, select measures, plan data collection activities, and disseminate results. A research committee comprised of GSSW faculty, program site directors, educational specialists, and graduate student interns meets monthly to monitor evaluation activities at the Bridge Project (see Box 5.3 for more details).

Box 5.3 A TEAM APPROACH TO PROGRAM EVALUATION

The Bridge Project is part of a unique partnership with the Graduate School of Social Work (GSSW) at the University of Denver. Fifteen graduate student interns from GSSW work with children, youth, and parents at the four Bridge Project program sites each year. Graduate interns gain valuable clinical and administrative experience by interacting with individual clients, conducting groups on special topics, and learning supervision and leadership tasks. Undergraduate students from the University of Denver serve as academic tutors and participate in other volunteer activities at the Bridge Project during the academic year.

GSSW also provides critical evaluation support to the Bridge Project. A professorship endowed by two of the program's founders, Philip D. and Eleanor G. Winn, provides the support necessary for a GSSW faculty member to design and supervise the agency's data collection plan. This plan includes the involvement of one or two doctoral students who actively collect, manage, and analyze data at all four Bridge Project locations.

Evaluation activities encompass a great deal of complexity. In a recent interview, former Dean of GSSW, John Jones, noted the importance of objectivity in the political context inherent in program evaluation at the Bridge Project:

> The Bridge Project has significant political implications in regard to evaluation. Accountability in assessment is an important principle in case studies. Policymakers, practitioners, and the public, when reviewing social or economic intervention, want to know if they can trust the program evaluations that nonprofits, government bodies, and multilateral agencies conduct. After all, the question in many people's minds is: Does social or economic intervention work and how thoroughly is it measured? There has been criticism of planning bodies and the effectiveness of their outcome studies in local, national, and international projects... Too often program evaluation reports of community programs and projects are self-serving in the assessment of goal achievement.... Care must be taken, whether the evaluator comes from inside or outside the organization, that a high standard of research is demanded. The validity and reliability of a study benefits not only the organization and its clients but, equally important, the public that hopes for project assessments it can trust (J. Jones, personal communication, May 22, 2011).

Evaluation also involves technical, logistical, and methodological skills. Measures must be selected and reproduced in an easy-to-administer fashion for subjects. Interview schedules must be established and data collection resources located. Data must be managed appropriately and analyses must be conducted. Reports and articles must be written and disseminated. In short, it takes a team of people to design, implement, and maintain a strong program evaluation!

Evaluation activities at the Bridge Project represent an ongoing collaboration between the program's staff members and GSSW faculty and students. Evaluation elements have changed over the course of the program's existence, a common phenomenon among community-based programs for children and youth (Anthony et al., 2009). The adoption of the IPEI framework in the past several years, however, has helped stabilize evaluation activities at the Bridge Project. Today, evaluation efforts aim to assess the key elements of risk, protection, positive youth development (PYD), and collaboration that are specified in the IPEI model.

Evaluation Procedures

Children, youth, and parents are recruited to participate in Bridge Project activities at the beginning of every school year. Initial registration includes an explanation of all program components and related expectations and goals. Parents complete informed consent procedures, and youth sign assent forms at the time of registration. Evaluation team members are present during registration to explain consent and assent procedures and to outline the types of data collected during the school year.

All participants at the Bridge Project are assigned a unique identification number at the time of registration and subsequently tracked for participation and exposure (measured in standardized units) in each program component. Attendance at Bridge Project programs is recorded daily by program staff. These data are aggregated monthly and maintained in a longitudinal database managed by the University of Denver evaluation team. Program participation varies across intervention elements at the Bridge Project. Consequently, sizes pertaining to different research questions differ by purpose and activity. A pretest–posttest design based on the academic school calendar (August to May) is used to assess individual and educational outcomes and to evaluate levels of risk, protection, and traits associated with PYD.

Measures

Self-report and official record data are collected to assess participant outcomes at the Bridge Project. Measures used to assess risk and protective factors, the 5 C's of PYD, and academic performance are listed in Table 5.1 and described briefly below. Additional methodological details and information pertaining to the psychometric properties of measures are found in Appendices A and B.

Risk and protective factors. Risk and protective factors associated with academic achievement and other child and adolescent behaviors are assessed annually using the Risk, Protection, and Antisocial Conduct Inventory (RPACI)

Table 5.1 BRIDGE PROJECT EVALUATION MEASURES

Construct	Measures
Risk and Protection	Risk, Protection, and Antisocial Conduct Inventory[a]
The 5 C's of PYD	
Competence	The 5 C's of PYD-Bridge Project[b]
Character	The 5 C's of PYD-Bridge Project[b]
Connection	The 5 C's of PYD-Bridge Project[b]
Caring and Compassion	The 5 C's of PYD-Bridge Project[b]
Confidence	Piers-Harris Self-Concept Scale[c]
	Developmental Reading Assessment[d]
Academic outcomes	Morgan-Jinks Student Efficacy Scale[e]
	Colorado State Assessment Profile[f]

[a]Jenson & Anthony, 2003.
[b]Lopez & Jenson, 2011.
[c]Piers & Herzberg, 2002.
[d]Beaver, 2006.
[e]Jinks & Morgan, 1999.
[f]Colorado State Department of Education.

(Jenson & Anthony, 2003). The RPACI is a self-report survey constructed by the research team that evaluates risk and protective factors at individual, interpersonal, and environmental levels of influence.

The 5 C's of PYD. We found no single instrument in the published literature that comprehensively evaluates the 5 C's—competence, connection, character, confidence, and caring/compassion—of PYD (Lerner, 2005). Therefore, members of the Bridge Project team developed an instrument to measure each of the 5 C's specified in PYD framework (Lopez & Jenson, 2011). The instrument, 5 C's of Positive Youth Development-Bridge Project (PYD-Bridge), yields a total score that is obtained by summing scores from five individual PYD scales.

Items from several existing instruments were selected or adapted to develop individual PYD scales that measure each of the 5 C's. The PYD construct *competence* is a nine-item scale that asks participants to reflect on their ability to be successful in academic settings. *Connection* is measured using a nine-item scale that asks subjects to reflect on the quality of their relationships with adults. *Character* is a 10-item scale that examines how children and youth respond to antisocial influences and behavior. Several questions in this scale also assess participants' hope for the future. *Caring* and *compassion* are a seven-item scale that assesses subjects' ability to take the perspective of others and to feel empathy for peers. The Piers-Harris Self-Concept Scale (Piers & Herzberg, 2002), a 60-item survey used to assess young people's perceptions of self across domains of behavior, intellect, physical appearance, popularity, anxiety, and happiness/satisfaction, is used to measure the PYD construct of *confidence*.

Academic performance. The Developmental Reading Assessment (DRA) (Beaver, 2006; DRA, 2009), a standardized measure of reading abilities, is used to assess academic competence among Bridge Project participants at pre-test and posttest. The DRA evaluates accuracy, fluency, and comprehension through individual reading conferences in which students read selected texts with onsite educators. Colorado State Assessment Profile (CSAP) scores, from a statewide standardized achievement test, are obtained annually from Denver Public Schools. Official indicators reflecting academic grades and attendance are accessed through the school district database twice each academic year. Self-reported grades and measures of academic efficacy are also collected using the Morgan-Jinks Student Efficacy Scale (Jinks & Morgan, 1999).

Analysis

A pretest–posttest design based on the academic school calendar (August to May) is used to assess changes in risk, protection, the 5 C's, and academic performance over time. Paired comparisons (*t*-tests) assessing levels of change between fall and spring are used as a primary analytic approach. Ordinary least squares regression is used to assess the relationship between program participation and selected IPEI outcomes. Additional evaluation methods and tools are described in Chapter 6 and Appendices A and B.

SUMMARY

This chapter discussed the utility of the IPEI model for planning and guiding evaluation activities at the Denver Bridge Project. Common evaluation approaches and challenges in the context of community-based youth programming were also reviewed. We believe that the IPEI framework is helpful to Bridge Project personnel because it provides the basis for a comprehensive, agency-wide evaluation plan. Interventions and program activities specified in the IPEI model lead directly to preselected measures and data collection instruments. These measures, in turn, provide the basis for evaluating the key elements of risk and resilience, PYD, and collaboration found in the IPEI logic model. To this end, the model also helps minimize program uncertainty by articulating a set of consistent measures and outcomes over time. Finally, our experience at the Bridge Project suggests that practitioners, administrators, and researchers should work collaboratively to design and implement evaluation strategies to overcome the many challenges discussed in this chapter. In the following chapter, we present findings from the Bridge Project to illustrate how planning and implementation activities are related to child, youth, and parent outcomes.

CHAPTER 6

Community and Participant Outcomes from the Bridge Project

This chapter describes findings from mixed-methodology evaluations of the Bridge Project. The agency's evaluation plan, described in detail in Chapter 5, provides the foundation and operational blueprint for the evaluation activities described below. In addition, evaluation questions and study processes are guided by the program goals, interventions, and outcomes articulated in the integrated prevention and early intervention model (IPEI) in Chapter 4. Using the agency's evaluation plan and the IPEI, we present findings from assessments of community processes and participant outcomes from the past 2 academic years. Results from a community investigation of Bridge Project network members and staff are first described. Findings from a mixed-methods evaluation based on data from school records and from surveys, interviews, and focus groups with youth, parent, and former participants are then presented. Procedures, methodological details, and instruments relevant to each study are found in Appendices A and B.

THE COMMUNITY STUDY

A study of the Bridge Project and its niche in the Denver community was conducted to: (1) determine by empirical means the size and services offered by the network of organizations in which the Bridge Project is embedded, (2) identify and assess the types of mechanisms that the Bridge Project uses to coordinate and integrate its activities with the other organizations in its network, and (3) ascertain how staff members view the effectiveness of the network. Personal interviews and surveys were used to collect data from 16 staff members from the Bridge Project. See Appendices A and B for a detailed description of community study methods.

The Interorganizational Network at the Bridge Project

Children in the Bridge Project neighborhoods have multiple needs. To be effective, the program must be nested in a large network of organizations that provides the best opportunity to meet these needs. Our data confirm the assertion that such a network exists at the Bridge Project. Bridge Project staff members reported that they worked with 47 different organizations in the past year. The resources these organizations offer participants vary widely and include diverse activities such as computer training, hockey lessons, gardening, and social skills training. Because the array of enrichment opportunities is so broad, we have grouped the organizations into categories. As shown in Table 6.1, the largest category of network members provides (1) outdoor, recreational, and sports opportunities. This is followed by: (2) educational opportunities, (3) concrete resources, (4) physical and mental health care, (5) youth programs, (6) volunteers, and (7) jointly delivered social casework.

Two organizations in the interorganizational network defy classification because they provide less tangible but nonetheless varied resources and opportunities to Bridge Project participants. The first is Denver Public School (DPS), an organization that works with the Bridge Project on a daily basis.

Table 6.1 CHARACTERISTICS OF THE INTERORGANIZATIONAL NETWORK SERVING THE BRIDGE PROJECT

Type of Organization	Number in Network	Examples of Resources Provided to Participants
Outdoor, recreational and sports opportunities	11	Community gardening, outward bound, skiing and snowboarding, mountain climbing, yoga, hockey, sports camps
Educational and skill development opportunities	10	Art, music, and dance classes, computer program, animal humane program
Concrete resources	8	Food, clothing, rent assistance, books, Christmas toys, school supplies
Medical and mental health care	7	Dental and orthodontics, eye care, family public health and wellness services, school physicals, family planning
Sources for volunteers and tutors	5	Academic tutoring, teachers, guidance counselors
Youth programing	4	Social skills development (girls' group, college preparation), work internships, travel abroad
Social casework	2	Collaborative social casework
Total number of organizations in the Bridge Project network	47	

DPS supports the Bridge Project's evaluation process by providing academic grades, progress reports, and attendance data. DPS social workers are involved in joint casework and family support activities with Bridge Project staff. DPS classroom teachers and other school personnel, in addition to being important educational partners, work with Bridge Project staff to design afterschool learning goals for children and youth that go beyond what might be accomplished during the school day (see box 6.1 for an example).

Box 6.1 COLLABORATION BETWEEN SCHOOL PERSONNEL AND BRIDGE PROJECT STAFF MEMBERS

Bridge Project staff members frequently work with teachers to support academic success for individual children and youth. Interviews were conducted with Denver Public School (DPS) teachers and resource advocates to gain a better understanding of the collaborative elements that are necessary to improve academic performance for at-risk youth in community-based programs.

PERSPECTIVE FROM A DPS TEACHER

One DPS teacher states that his collaboration with the Bridge Project has persisted over 12 years and that it has transitioned smoothly from one site director to the current one. He noted that relationships between the teachers and the Bridge Project site director is characterized by mutual respect that revolves around commitment to promoting improved academic success for individual youth. Communication ensures both securing services and holding youth accountable, as illustrated in this quote:

> ...We have a great relationship where if she is noticing something about a student she will call me, we'll talk and usually we will find we are seeing the same positive or negative about that child and same with me if I am having trouble I will call her up and say hey so and so needs to be doing this for homework can you make sure he or she is doing that and it's taken care of, so yeah we have a great working relationship.

The teacher further expressed what he thinks would make the most difference in improving the lives of children at the Bridge Project:

> ...Find a way to get those parents so they feel comfortable with coming to Bridge and seeing what is going on, have an interpreter for every language, good luck but I could if I was King for a day this is what I would do, I would have every language covered I would have an interpreter for every language, show off the program for that day...show what the program does, show

(continued)

how it is connected directly to the school, bring some teachers over who say here is what I expect my students to do, here is how Bridge can help my student, show the correlation, you know show that connection....

Resource Advocates are hired to learn about programs in the community like the Bridge Project and to ensure that schools and parents are aware of local resources. One advocate explained that her relationship with the Bridge Project started when staff from the program showed up to help paint the school building when they were getting ready to open. The Resource Advocate explained that the relationship she had with the Bridge Project staff was practical and efficient and aimed at the mutual goal of improving academic performance. She noted that the tutoring services at the Bridge Project were "incredibly helpful in meeting the needs of the DPS school improvement plan and in raising our kids test scores."

The Resource Advocate also noted that what sets the Bridge Project apart from other available programs is that "there are a bunch of social workers working there, offering a scope and depth of skills and services that should be recognized and harnessed." Further illustrating this sentiment, she noted:

It's the social work component of it that's helpful, it's not just sitting a kid down to learn about reading and writing and math, its knowing that there's other services available, there's linkages in the community and there's people with really specified training available—it's to help kids.

The second hard-to-classify organization is the University of Denver, not only for its administrative role in the operation of the project but also for its ability to provide many program resources. For example, the university athletic department works with Bridge Project staff to develop summer programs including sports camps and skill development for hockey players. The university's international programs provide classes about study abroad options for high school students. In addition, the university's many academic units provide curriculum development consultation and academic tutors. Bridge Project staff members frequently noted that they relied extensively on network partners, noting that they "can't do it all" and that they "must rely on the community for meeting many of our kids' needs." In this case, the reference to community implies that 47 nonprofit, community-based organizations are willing and able to serve Bridge Project participants.

We mapped the intensity of interactions and resource flows between these 47 organizations and the Bridge Project and found an interorganizational network with multiple layers (see Appendix A for description of the mapping process). As shown in Table 6.2, a core of six network members characterized by intense interactions and resource flows surrounds the Bridge Project. The Bridge Project is situated in the middle of this network. Second, a group of 23 organizations with less intense communication patterns forms a middle ring. Finally, 18 organizations with weaker ties are on the periphery of network interactions with the Bridge Project. The pattern of interactions reported by staff members reveals that the six core organizations have more than 100 interactions with the Bridge Project per month. The 23 middle ring organizations have between 10 and 99 interactions, and the 18 outer ring organizations have 9 or fewer interactions per month. Table 6.2 categorizes the interorganizational network at the Bridge Project by intensity of interaction.

A number of interesting findings emerge from this interorganizational network. First, the intensity of interactions with organizations that provide educational opportunities and medical services varies from weak to very intense. Conversely, all of the organizations that provide concrete resources have very few interactions per month. This finding supports our earlier assertion about the connection between complexity of activity and intensity of interaction. Put in other terms, the more complex the activity, the greater the communication that is necessary to uncover tacit understandings of the situation. For

Table 6.2 INTENSITY OF INTERACTION WITHIN THE BRIDGE PROJECT
INTERORGANIZATIONAL NETWORK

	Number of Organizations	Number of Interactions per Month	Resources Provided
Core	6	100–400	Educational opportunities/skills (3)
			Other (joint casework) (2)
			Medical and mental health (1)
Middle Ring	23	10–99	Outdoor, recreation, and sports (8)
			Educational opportunities/skills (6)
			Medical and mental health care (3)
			Youth programming (3)
			Sources for volunteers and tutors (3)
Outer Ring	18	1–9	Concrete resources (8)
			Physical and mental health care (3)
			Outdoor, recreation, and sports (3)
			Sources for volunteers and tutors (2)
			Education opportunities/skills (1)
			Youth programming (1)

example, the two organizations within which staff members engage in joint casework are both in the core group because casework is complex and requires close working relationships, if not actual teamwork. By contrast, the eight organizations that provide concrete services are all in the outer ring because these flows can be standardized in a way that casework and medical services cannot. Thus, common sense dictates that the ongoing working relationships between the Bridge Project and the organizations with whom they do casework and those that provide concrete service should be quite different in nature. The differences in these linkages are the subject of the next section.

Types of Coordination and Integration

We next examined the types of coordination and integration mechanisms used by Bridge Project staff members to obtain resources. To assess these mechanisms, respondents were asked about "the *basis* on which they can make a request of another organization and have some assurance their request will be fulfilled" and then asked to report the percentage of time they rely on friendship, exchange, informal, and formal types of coordination to complete work tasks. Staff members were further asked to estimate the percentage of all their child-focused work with other organizations in which they used sequential, reciprocal, and collective mechanisms of integration.

As shown in Table 6.3, respondents rely more heavily on friendship connections to acquire resources than on any other coordinative mechanism. Clearly, the power of perceived friendships among colleagues in the human services is an important coordination mechanism at the Bridge Project. In regard to integration, our interviews with program staff members confirm our hypothesis that work patterns would be largely reciprocal or collective in nature. Because of budget and staff limitations associated with programs that serve public housing residents, we believed it would be highly unlikely that integration would be achieved by collective means (e.g., interagency teams using a single case plan), as this approach is time consuming and expensive. Therefore, reciprocal mechanisms were the expected choice. Not surprisingly, Bridge Project staff members report that approximately 62% of their interorganizational relationships are reciprocal.

As noted above, friendship relationships and reciprocal work flows are the most commonly reported collaborative mechanisms used by Bridge Project staff to meet work objectives. However, we wondered if differences in the use of types of coordination might be accounted for by differences in age of staff and position in the organization. To examine potential age differences, we categorized respondents as under or over 30 years of age. Using analysis of variance tests, we found a significant age difference in staff members' use of friendship coordination; staff members over 30 were significantly more likely than younger staff to rely on friendship as a form of coordination [F (1, 14) = 6.87, p = .02]. Effects were also found pertaining to job position and use of coordination. Relying on exchange mechanisms to obtain resources was significantly higher for supervisors when compared with other staff members [F (2, 13) = 4.48, p = .03]. Second, administrators were significantly more likely than supervisors and other staff to use formal agreements [F (2, 3) = 4.62, p = .03]. Finally, there were no significant differences in use of integration mechanisms by age. However, administrators used sequential mechanisms at significantly higher rates than other staff members [F (2, 12) = 5.13, p = .025]. Further, supervisors used reciprocal work efforts significantly more often than administrators [F (2, 12) = 4.28, p = .040].

Network Effectiveness

As noted earlier, respondents were asked to rate the actual performance of their service network and to assess its potential performance if all necessary practice resources were available. Table 6.4 shows differences between staff perceptions of the actual and potential performance of their organization. These "gap scores" are shown separately for administrators, supervisors, and other staff members. The average gap scores for administrators range from 1.3 to 2.0. The range for supervisors is .6 to 1.3, and for staff it is 1.2 to 2.0. There were no significant differences in gap scores by organizational position,

Table 6.3 PERCENT OF TIME SPENT ON COORDINATION AND INTEGRATION MECHANISMS BY BRIDGE PROJECT STAFF

	Administrators (N = 4)	Supervisors (N = 4)	Staff (N = 8)	Bridge Average
Coordination Mechanisms				
Friendship	40.0	33.8	40.6	38.1%
Exchange	2.5	27.5	5.6	11.8%
Informal	16.5	21.2	43.2	27.0%
Agreements	41.0	17.5	10.7	23.1%
Formal Agreements				
Totals	100%	100%	100%	100%
Integration Mechanisms				
Sequential	71.2	15.0	19.3	35.2%
Reciprocal	18.8	66.2	60.0	48.3%
Collective	10.0	18.8	20.7	16.5%
Totals	100%	100%	100%	100%

Table 6.4 STAFF PERCEPTIONS OF NETWORK EFFECTIVENESS

	Administrators	Supervisors	Staff	Overall Average
Goals of the Bridge Project are achieved.	1.25	1.0	1.2	1.14
Bridge, working with its network of organizations, can generate adequate resources.	2.0	1.33	1.7	1.66
The network works smoothly.	2.0	1.5	1.5	1.66
The network is productive.	1.0	1.3	1.3	1.22
The network is effective.	1.25	1.0	1.7	1.3
Overall, I am satisfied with the performance of our network.	1.5	.6	2.0	1.37
Overall average	1.5	1.1	1.7	

Note. Scores reflect differences in subjects' ideal versus actual ratings of network effectiveness. $N = 16$.

suggesting that staff members' perceptions of their performance and that of their network are largely in agreement.

In sum, the accounts of Bridge Project staff and board members highlight the importance of the community in sustaining program activities in public housing neighborhoods. Findings from the community study also confirm the importance of strong interorganizational networks at the Bridge Project. Clearly, it appears that the Bridge Project has succeeded in embedding itself in a large, lively, and dynamic network of organizations that works to provide children and youth in public housing the opportunities they need to succeed in school and later life. Implications of these findings are discussed further in the final section of the chapter. Results from a mixed-methods investigation of Bridge Project participants and intervention elements are described below.

MIXED-METHODS STUDY OF BRIDGE PROJECT PARTICIPANTS AND PROGRAMS

A mixed-methodology approach was used to identify patterns of participation and evaluate outcomes among Bridge Project participants. Qualitative interviews and focus groups with current and former child, youth, and parent participants were conducted to understand the experiences of people who attend the Bridge Project. Quantitative data were also collected to assess risk and protection, the 5 C's of competence, confidence, character, connection, and caring/compassion (Lerner, Lerner, & Phelps, 2009), and academic performance. Study approaches were based on the IPEI model described in Chapter 4. Methods and instruments used to generate findings from the mixed-methods study are described in detail in Appendices A and B. To provide a context for evaluation results, we begin this section with an overview of program participation at the Bridge Project.

Program Participation

Demographic and program participation data provide important information about patterns of involvement in any community-based program. Such data also allow an evaluation team to assess differential outcomes for children and youth by characteristics such as age, gender, and racial or ethnic background. Demographic and program exposure data are collected routinely at the Bridge Project.

Five-hundred and fifty-two children and youth participated in one or more Bridge Project programs across all four locations in 2009–2010. Child and youth participants averaged approximately 10 years of age. Fifty percent (N = 276) of participants were female and 50% (N = 276) were male. Forty-five percent (N = 248) of participants were Latino/a, 24% (N = 132) were African American, 9% (N = 50) were multiracial, American Indian, or White, and 9% (N = 50) were Asian American. Thirteen percent (N = 72) of subjects did not report their racial or ethnic membership. The Bridge Project served approximately 70 refugee children from Somalia, Liberia, and other African countries. Participation in Bridge Project program components is shown in Table 6.5. Homework help, tutoring, and technology training were among the most frequently attended intervention elements. More than 84% (N = 464) of children and youth received help with their homework during afterschool hours; 82% (N = 450) of youth at all four sites participated in technology training activities. Approximately 55% (N = 303) of participants participated in regular tutoring sessions. Eight percent (N = 46) of adolescents participated in one-on-one mentoring during the 2009–2010 calendar year.

Literacy programs included regularly scheduled reading classes and two special initiatives. First, 107 children participated in the Read, Imagine, Share, and Explore (RISE) Program. RISE aims to build and support community-wide literacy by equipping preschoolers and their families with fundamental reading and vocabulary skills. Preschool participants between 3 and 5 years old attend weekly classes that are facilitated by community volunteers and staff members. Students are engaged in fine and gross motor development, vocabulary and idea expansion, and problem-solving activities through books, music and movement, and artistic expression. Second, 142 fourth-grade students participated in a hands-on science program offered in collaboration with the National Renewable Energy

Table 6.5 PARTICIPATION IN BRIDGE PROJECT INTERVENTION COMPONENTS

Component	Participants	Average Hours	Total Hours
All Components	552	96.0 (*SD* = 98.7)	53,286
Academic Components			
Tutoring	303	13.9 (*SD* = 10.5)	4,218
Homework help	464	34.8 (*SD* = 33.0)	16,164
Mentoring	46	18.6 (*SD* = 24.2)	855
Literacy Components			
National Renewable Energy Laboratory	142	7.7 (*SD* = 6.8)	1,092
Read, Imagine, Share, and Explore	107	7.9 (*SD* = 7.1)	845
Reading classes	190	5.6 (*SD* = 6.6)	1,074
Technology Components			
Computer classes	450	20.2 (*SD* = 21.6)	9,103
Open computer lab	373	14.2 (*SD* = 16.4)	5,286
Technology team	33	50.8 (*SD* = 24.6)	1,669

Laboratory (NREL). NREL classes combined topical reading with related activities aimed at promoting renewable energy and energy efficiency skills designed to help students increase their reading comprehension and science skills. One-hundred and ninety participants accounted for approximately 1,000 hours of structured reading class attendance.

Participation in technology training is also shown in Table 6.5. Four hundred and fifty youth attended an average of 20 computer classes in the academic year under study. Technology team members (*n* = 33) logged more than 1,600 hours in technology-related programs and tasks. More than 370 youth attended open computer lab sessions. Two-hundred and forty-eight children and youth between 6 and 13 years old attended the Bridge Project Summer Program in 2009–2010. Finally, 45 young adults are currently enrolled in local colleges and universities through the Scholarship Program. We describe motivating factors for participating in Bridge Project activities and programs in Box 6.2.

Voices and Perspectives of Children, Youth, and Parents

Qualitative interviews and focus groups provide valuable insights into the perspectives of participants in community-based programs like the Bridge Project. Five themes emerged from our interviews and focus groups with

Box 6.2 WHY DO CHILDREN AND YOUTH ATTEND THE BRIDGE PROJECT?

One of the qualitative themes in our study concerned reasons why children, youth, and parents attended the Bridge Project. Here are some of the reasons participants learn about and choose to attend he program.

LEARNING THE BRIDGE PROJECT IS A NEIGHBORHOOD RESOURCE

Parents and youth learn about the Bridge Project through: (1) relatives and immediate family members, (2) parent–teacher conferences, (3) Bridge staff who actively recruit participants, and (4) flyers and the sign outside the buildings where each of the four sites is located, and (5) the physical location of the Bridge Project within participants' neighborhoods. One youth notes learning about the Bridge Project through word-of-mouth between family members and neighbors,

> My cousins in the other neighborhood they live close by another Bridge
> Project and I went there for a couple of weeks. Once my mom saw the same
> sign of the Bridge Project she asked if it was sort of the same thing as over
> there and they said yeah and my mom signed me up.

LENGTH OF PARTICIPATION

Youth's length of overall participation ranged from approximately 1 to 10 years. One youth noted a steady progression of involvement at the Bridge Project,

> Well, I've been a student with them at Columbine at first since I was in 4th
> grade and I grew up. Then I went to [name of one Bridge site] and worked
> [as tech team member] there for a year and then I worked at [name of
> Bridge site] for two years now. We've been going for like 8 years now.

Some youth noted disruptions in program participation due to a change in the location of where they or a sibling attended school. There are no policies at the Bridge Project restricting participation by where a youth resides or attends school. However, sometimes the distance between a youth's school and one of the program sites interferes with participation.

PARENT PARTICIPATION

Although primarily a program for youth, the Bridge Project periodically offers programming that targets parent needs as well. Most youth

(continued)

COMMUNITY AND PARTICIPANT OUTCOMES FROM THE BRIDGE PROJECT

participants indicated that their parents did not attend the Bridge Project on any type of regular basis. However, several participants noted that their parents were involved in periodic meetings and holiday parties. Others indicated that their parents attended English as a second language and computer classes; some parents noted that they go to the Bridge Project to ask about how their children are doing on school-related performance measures.

children, adolescents, young adults, and parents (see Appendix A for methods and procedures related to these results). Three common themes were identified across all respondents: (1) *assets of the Bridge Project*, (2) *Bridge Project challenges and problems*, and (3) *Bridge Project and school*. These themes reflect the quality of Bridge Project programs and transactions between participants, peers, staff, and volunteers. Analysis of the technology team focus groups and college scholarship participants revealed two themes that were unique to these samples of older youth. These themes reflect the underlying dimensions of positive youth development (PYD) and are identified as: (4) *what I bring to the kids*, and (5) *concern for others*. Table 6.6 provides additional definitions for the identified themes and shows the percentage of quotes related to each particular theme by age group.

In addition to the major themes present in the data, important contextual information emerged as subjects, particularly parents, responded to neighborhood- and community-level questions. We begin by noting the importance of context and follow with a review of the qualitative themes reported by child, youth, young adult, and parent respondents.

The Bridge Project in Context

Bridge Project interventions are embedded in a neighborhood and community context that poses significant challenges to children, youth, and parents. Statements from children, youth, and parents in the study samples illustrate clearly these many challenges. We found that elements of neighborhood *social cohesion, collective socialization, resources*, and *safety* were common concerns among children, youth, and parents.

Principles of social cohesion, the degree to which members of a neighborhood feel connected to one another (Sampson, Raudenbush, & Earls, 1997), are represented by parent's comments about how much or how little families

Table 6.6 THEME DEFINITIONS AND MAGNITUDE WITHIN AND ACROSS
THE PARTICIPANT GROUPS

Theme and Definition	Percentage of Quotes				
	Elementary	Middle	High School	College	Parents
Bridge assets: Positive factors participants noted about what they experience and get out of the Bridge Project. Includes the following areas: specific programs (mentoring), day-to-day activities, relationships with peers and staff, safety and respect.	72.6% (*n* = 48)	63.1% (*n* = 41)	50.0% (*n* = 30)	69.6% (*n* = 71)	58.6% (*n* = 41)
Bridge problems: Negative factors noted about experiences related to participating in the Bridge Project. Includes: actual experiences and recommendations youth made for changing or improving the program.	25.4% (*n* = 17)	21.5% (*n* = 14)	6.6% (*n* = 4)	11.8% (*n* = 12)	35.7% (*n* = 25)
Bridge and school: Participant references that made a direct comparison between school and the Bridge Project.	2.9% (*n* = 2)	15.4% (*n* = 10)	—	1.0% (*n* = 1)	5.7% (*n* = 4)
What I bring to the kids	—	—	23.3% (*n* = 14)	—	—
Concern for others	—	—	20.0% (*n* = 12)	17.6% (*n* = 18)	—
Total quotes by age	*N* = 67	*N* = 65	*N* = 60	*N* = 102	*N* = 70

interact with neighbors, how well they recognize people in the neighborhood who do not live there, and by how much or how little neighbors help one another. Statements from Bridge Project parents range from what one might perceive to be a total absence of neighborhood social cohesion to moderate levels of cohesion. For example, one parent notes that she does not really know her neighbors, but that she would recognize people in the neighborhood who do not live there. Another parent notes that she does not know a lot of the neighbors and that they don't all share the same values, but that she trusts neighbors ("I think people help us out when we need it . . . And uh, we help people out when they need it."). Parents' comments related to this theme suggest rather loose ties among adults residing in Bridge Project neighborhoods.

Parents in the study sample indicated that other adults in the neighborhood would be willing to discipline neighborhood youth if they were acting disrespectfully to adults or to report youth if they saw them skipping school or spray-painting graffiti. Comments of this type are illustrative of neighborhood collective socialization, a concept coined by Wilson (1987) to reflect a neighborhood's ability to provide appropriate social controls for children and youth. This sentiment, however, was not universal among respondents, as some parents noted that language barriers and lack of cultural familiarity might prevent them from intervening in child misbehavior in the neighborhood.

Access to neighborhood resources including grocery stores, public transportation, schools, employment opportunities, prosocial activities, and health care is an important aspect of any healthy community (Elliott et al., 1996). All parent participants noted that the Bridge Project provided an important neighborhood resource for their children's education; they also valued the program as a safe place for their children to spend time. A majority of parents believed that their local schools were inadequate. Comments pertaining to gaining access to health care, public transportation, employment, and groceries were mixed in nature, with some parents reporting relatively good access, and others finding it difficult to take advantage of services. To illustrate, one parent noted that she could access some groceries in her neighborhood, but that there was an absence of fresh vegetables and fruits. Another parent stated, "We usually get rides to um El Banza and um Save A Lot there's no place around here to shop." When the interviewer asked if it was easy to find rides to these stores, the parent replied by noting that she is only able to get to the grocery store about one time per month. This varation is likely due to the resources particular to the four different neighborhoods served by the Bridge Project.

Parents were also asked if they felt that their children could go to and from school safely. The safety concerns in the statements that follow are typical of concerns raised by parents. Parents felt that their neighborhoods were safe in a general sense, but many qualified their responses by noting they felt their children were only safe if they walked with them to school and back or if they took the bus. Other factors about neighborhood safety also surfaced in the interviews. For example, one parent noted the easy access that children and youth have to drugs in the public housing communities when she named the place in the neighborhood where people are actively using drugs and how this makes it difficult to protect her children, "there are drugs on the streets and it gets sometimes too easy to get marijuana...or any kind...it's difficult."

Elements associated with neighborhood and community context provide an important backdrop for the five themes discussed below. The importance of neighborhood context is illustrated by the case study described in Box 6.3.

Box 6.3 A DAY IN THE LIFE OF A BRIDGE PROJECT YOUTH

What is it like to live in a Bridge Project neighborhood? What is a typical day like in the Bridge Project After-School Program? The life of 10-year-old Jordan Walker offers some clues to the challenges of living in one of Denver's poorest neighborhoods.

Jordan gets out of bed at 5:00 a.m. to get ready for school. His mother starts work at 6 a.m., so she drives Jordan and two younger siblings to his grandmother's house before school starts. Jordan falls to sleep on his grandmother's couch until he is reawakened at 7 a.m. He and his 6-year-old sister later walk to school.

The path to school is filled with risk. In fact, the presence of homeless and drug-abusing adults in the park between his grandmother's house and school requires that he and his sister walk a few extra blocks. Today, they decide to cut through the park to save time. Jordan senses his sister become tense, and he takes her hand as they step around a man who is fast asleep on the ground. He sees a few familiar faces in the group of men who are standing by a tree talking. They are already passing around a bottle in a paper bag. One of the men waves to Jordan and his sister.

The first few hours of the school day are uneventful. Like children everywhere, Jordan and his friends whisper about what they want to do at recess. The teacher warns them to be quiet or face the consequence of staying in the classroom during recess. Jordan can't wait for recess and is the first one on the playground. He quickly finds a friend and asks him about his new Bionicle toy. He is disappointed to learn that his friend has left the toy inside the school. They play tag with some classmates for a bit. Jordan dreads having to return to class and sit still the rest of the day, especially during math.

Later that day Jordan, is surprised when his teacher calls him into the hallway. Jordan's friend is there and is crying and angry. Jordan's friend reports that his Bionicle toy was not in his backpack when he went to retrieve it. He tells his teacher that he is sure that Jordan stole the toy. Jordan becomes very angry about being accused of something he didn't do. He yells and curses and tries to punch his friend. The teacher makes him stay in the hallway while he looks in Jordan's backpack for the toy. He is later invited back to class when the teacher discovers that Jordan did not steal the toy.

Math class is difficult, and Jordan has no idea what the teacher is talking about. He stuffs a homework worksheet into his backpack and lines up to go outside without speaking to anyone. Once outside, Jordan finds his sister, and they walk together to the Bridge Project. His frustration in math class has made him feel helpless.

(continued)

Jordan and his sister walk to the Bridge Project, where they are greeted by their favorite staff member. The counselor immediately finds a snack for everyone and talks to Jordan about his day. Jordan relaxes as he settles into a familiar and comfortable routine. He finishes his writing assignment, and a tutor helps him with a portion of the difficult math assignment. Jordan struggles to understand the content and to fight off tiredness from the early morning start to his day. He later collects his sister and heads down the block toward home. They see activity in the park and choose to take the long way home. Jordan's mother will be home soon, and she will expect him and his sister to have completed their dinner and housekeeping chores. He thinks about getting his very own Bionicle toy but realizes that it may never happen. Besides, he still has that math worksheet to finish.

Theme 1: Assets of the Bridge Project

The theme, *Bridge Project assets*, describes the benefits that children and youth get from participating in program activities. Academic support, positive relationships with peers and staff members, safety, and respect were common elements of this theme. In view of the high percentage of quotes directed at this theme (see Table 6.6), it is important to reiterate that none of the research team members were Bridge Project staff. Further, interviewees were asked about what they liked, and did not like, about the Bridge Project. One limitation of this theme is inherent in the technology team and scholarship participants, as their special statuses may have led to a greater likelihood of finding assets in Bridge Project programs. In this regard it is important to note that the benefits identified by technology team members and scholarship participants align closely with those found among other participant age groups. A brief discussion of the most important elements of the assets theme follows.

Academic Support

Youth in our study samples unanimously viewed the academic supports as a main benefit of the Bridge Project. Respondents identified the specific activities that provide academic support such as informal homework help strategies, relationships with tutors and mentors, and college scholarships; the way in which subjects described these benefits varied by age. For example, one elementary-age interviewee referred to his tutor at the Bridge Project as a role model, someone who it would be good to be like because "...he doesn't say bad words to me...he's happy when I come for tutoring." Middle school interviewees pointed to specific academic supports. One middle school youth uncovers how assistance with math is more than learning math; it also provides an increased sense of personal awareness:

> I can get there even if I learn this topic more slowly than others. A lot of times I don't get like math problems and stuff. So when I went to the Bridge they'd like help me with math and tutoring...so yeah...and it's actually been a big help for school and stuff. So I can learn...like not as fast as everybody...but kind of get there.

Another youth points out how informal reading with a tutor helped her with her English language skills:

> Well yeah like, well since my first language was Spanish...like with my tutor...she help me a lot...like I would read a lot in English and it helped me a lot better to read and how to say stuff better in English because I would confuse it with English and Spanish words.

The high school interviewees reflected on the past years of Bridge Project activities and noted similar positive elements of academic support. They also describe how their current leadership positions involving teaching younger students provide them with new skills and confidence. One focus group participant covers this when he states,

> ...um, I learned them [teaching and youth management skills] from the manager that I used to work with at [name of program site 1]...I couldn't teach...like I was too shy...and it was too hard for me...I couldn't...teaching a class...and then like I would just help and she would run the whole place and then I moved to [name of program site 2] and was the oldest worker...I was kind of a leader...so I got to start helping...so finally I can teach.

Scholarship participants mirror the sentiments of the other youth we interviewed with the by-product of academic programs as preparation for college. For example, one scholarship participant noted that the Bridge academic programs provided support that her parents could not because they had not completed high school:

> ...like my parents they never...they only reached like middle school level. So I never really...like they've always been very supportive, but I've never really had like, Oh let's sit down and let me help you with your homework or this is what you need to do for college and we got that through Bridge, you know?

The parental view about the importance of academic supports at the Bridge Project mirrored that of youth respondents. A majority of the parents noted their great appreciation for the individual tutoring that the Bridge Project affords their children. The following quote is a common sentiment among the parents we interviewed: "They help the kids. The kids are learning a lot from here. The people are real good here...they're learning a lot...they actually...they...so they don't fall behind [in school]." Another parent was more specific when she stated,

> I just see the help...the improvement in my kid's reading, their schoolwork...you know? They're like...you know, they're um...what's the word I'm looking...like their attitude towards learning and stuff like that...is really positive.

More Than Academics

In general, young people in our samples view the Bridge Project as fun and as a positive place to spend time with friends. As one middle school youth stated, "over here...time flies because you're playing with other friends." An elementary school girl noted that her favorite thing about coming to the Bridge Project is

> Ah...cooking...Because when you...if you make the food...when you make the food with the cookers you get to eat it. When we made breakfast last time, we made waffles with the bananas and strawberries. Then we made a smoothie...with milk, bananas, chocolate and strawberries.

At the Bridge Project, the enjoyment of cooking has a latent purpose of teaching healthy nutritional and dietary practices. Testimonials from participants offered support for the social and health-oriented aspects of Bridge Project interventions such as cooking lessons and teen girls groups aimed at discussing sexuality issues. One middle school girl specifically mentioned the importance of the group component because

> I like that we all got to like tell each other how we feel...and we got to like tell each other stuff without everybody else knowing and all we talk about was girls stuff in there.

In another example, from one of the tech team members, a participant talks about learning to play guitar at the Bridge:

> I learned how to play the guitar at the Bridge. I didn't know how to play, but I went there with these two guys they brought their guitar and taught me how to play.

The scholarship participants demonstrated a more sophisticated view of how the Bridge Project provides more than academic supports. The following quote is representative of this:

> If it wasn't for Bridge we would have been wandering around and it wasn't a safe neighborhood...so I think Bridge helped us like I guess waste our time at the Bridge doing good stuff instead of just wandering around and whatever...'Cause they had nothing to do so they were just like at the neighborhood...some did drugs...a 14-year-old girl I think got pregnant...and had she been going to Bridge she would have looked at her future more like schooling and that kind of stuff...

Another scholarship participant reflected on how the Bridge Project has caused her to be tenacious:

> I think that they have really pushed me, because I have always been the type of person that schools like uhhh not the best for me but they have pushed me to go and to believe that I can do it and accomplish things and like other things they do to, all these programs like how they have programs to help you test better or they have programs to know how to invest your money or all these little programs that they have it really helps you become a stronger person.

Some parent participants noted roles of the Bridge Project beyond academic support. For example, there were some parents who noted how hectic their lives are with work and raising children and the relief they felt to know their children were at the Bridge Project during the afterschool hours. A less common sentiment was expressed by a parent who noted what it's like to live in small apartments and how the Bridge helps because her children are there from 3 to 6 each day: "...like every time [the children] get out of school at 3...[they] go over there and stay there till 6 and do a lot of projects...so yeah, it's good."

Relationships and Safety

The learning and skill building that occur in the academic and social components of the Bridge Project are fostered through positive relationships. Many of the participants described the positive relationships they experience at the Bridge Project, particularly with staff members. One of the high school interviewees reminisced about how staff had role-modeled how to talk to younger kids so that she is able to apply it to her tech team leadership role:

> I think I got it from Bridge. 'Cause I came to Bridge when I was really little and I learned how a lot of the staff would talk to us if we ever did something wrong. I guess I just learned from that.

A middle school youth concurred with this reflection when he remarked on his current experience with adults at the Bridge Project: "Like...they're just respectful...and treat you well." Perhaps it is this climate of positive and respectful treatment that influences subjects' perception of staff members as people they feel they can approach for help and support. When one of the middle school interviewees was asked what she does when she faces a challenge, the response was "I'll come at the Bridge...and tell the people who working over here...to help me..." Also, many talked about Bridge Project staff members being willing and able to help. For example, one middle school youth explained the role that the Bridge Project has in the neighborhood:

> Because a lot of kids that live around here come here after school and they get a lot of help...and most always have their homework done...and they...they help a lot in whatever we need.

To further illustrate, one elementary-age youth stated that she has two people she can trust and noted that one of them is, "my big sister mentor [Bridge volunteer]...we go to the movies, to the mall, out to eat, get a little snack, candy...and all kinds of stuff...go to the lake."

A middle school student's statement reflects the most basic function of the afterschool program: "It's really safe here—like a whole bunch of adults are here to watch ya' and stuff." Elementary-age interviewees echoed this view of the atmosphere as an important asset. One student said that he likes the Bridge because "I feel safe here. They respect us and they don't yell at us." Within the context of this safe environment, many participants develop positive peer friendships. For example, several middle school participants talked about peer relationships to describe what they like about the Bridge Project. One participant described how the friendships at the Bridge are different from those at school,

> I see some more of my friends here. I make friends here. At the school sometimes I make enemies or kids hate me for some reason or something. At school sometimes they could tease you.

When asked what she likes the most about the Bridge Project, another middle school youth noted the important role that positive relationships and safety play at the Bridge Project when she stated, "...that we all can get along...without being like unequal." One of the high school participants sums up the manner in which relationships and safety are key when expanding upon her response that the Bridge Project was like family to her, saying,

> Yeah, like cause like I know like everyone...cause like they see me mature...they seen me go through difficult stages...like they just know how to deal with me...cause I'm actually really hard headed...and like they know how to take care of me when I'm hard headed...like to get me back on focus.

A scholarship interviewee mirrors this view of the Bridge Project, noting it was like a second home for her:

> It [the Bridge] was kind of like a second home because all of...all of the people on Tech Team knew each other very well...and umm...I still talk to them all so...we're really close. But also seeing the kids growing up now...like 5 years from now and they're in high school...I'm like "Oh my God I'm getting old."

The scholarship participants also pointed out the important and lasting relationships they formed at the Bridge Project. For example, one of them noted how he is still in contact with his tutor,

> ...I had a tutor...math tutor who umm...he used to help me at the Bridge Project, [names the tutor]...he graduated from DU and moved to New Mexico and he is in medical school right now. I'm in touch with him...he sometimes calls to say hi [and] to see how I am doing.

Parents in our sample also indicated that the Bridge Project provided an important sense of safety for their children. One parent noted how the program provides relief for parents because they knew their children would be doing something positive and that they would not be on the street "smoking marijuana." Another parent summarized this asset by saying,

> I think the Bridge Project...it's a place where the kids come that's safe...where you know responsible adults you know taking care of them...and doing something educational with them.

The life of a typical Bridge Project family is described in Box 6.4.

Box 6.4 AGAINST ALL ODDS: A YOUNG WOMAN'S RESILIENCE

Children and youth who attend the Bridge Project face numerous adversities that place them at later risk for poor behavioral and emotional outcomes. The underlying philosophy of the Bridge Project places great value on the possibility that every child or young person can overcome these obstacles and become healthy and capable adults. Mariana Grant's story is one that illustrates this philosophy. Mariana's family has lived in the neighborhood surrounding the Bridge Project her entire life. Her mother, Sofia, had Mariana when she was very young. Diagnosed with type 1 diabetes when she was just 4 years old, Mariana was placed in foster care as a child due to her family's inability to provide adequate health care. Over time, Mariana's grandmother, Alma, became her primary caregiver and parent.

(continued)

Alma is a strong woman who is devoted to Mariana and the family. She is employed at Denver International Airport where she works 6 days per week as a member of the cleaning staff. Getting to work requires a 3:30 a.m. wake up and two buses. When she arrives back home at 3 p.m., she takes care of her grandchildren, cleans the house, and looks after her husband. In the evening Alma goes to her second job where she cleans offices well into the night.

Mariana expresses an appreciation for the many things her grandmother does for her and notes how she is motivated by her grandmother's hopes for her,

My grandmother is amazing...I have learned so much from having her as a role model...to never let anything or anyone get in the way of your dreams; you can do anything you set your mind to...

Mariana is a junior in high school and a member of the Bridge project technology team. The Bridge Project has been an important part of the family's life since Mariana was 8 years old. Mariana has attended tutoring and homework help sessions since she was in elementary school. She recognizes that life would be different if she did not have the Bridge Project to go to during the afterschool hours. She says that, "...being on the Technology Team has made a huge difference for me...it has pushed me to keep up my grades...and I have learned how to be more responsible."Mariana's physical illness that threatens her health has become a source of inspiration and intellectual interest. She recognizes the incredible role modeling and the devoted care she has received from her grandmother. The odds may be against her, but Mariana's future is now looking very bright. Next year she will apply for a Bridge Project scholarship to attend a local college or university. She says that she wants to work in the medical field and reports that she is studying for the certified nursing assistant exam. Ultimately, she hopes to be a nurse in a children's hospital or a doctor who can help other children. The staff at the Bridge Project believe that her goals will no doubt be met!

Theme 2: Bridge Project Challenges and Problems

The theme, *problems*, refers to participants' reports of negative experiences or to youths' concerns about participating in Bridge Project programs. A segment of our interview protocol asked participants to talk about what they would change about the Bridge Project if they could; most of the quotes addressing this theme were in direct response to this prompt. This range of problems includes: (1) a wish for more of what the Bridge Project has to offer, (2) recommendations made for changing or improving the program, and (3) challenges noted about relationships with peers or staff members.

Provide More!

Youth from elementary school through high school noted a wish for more access to tutoring, academic support activities, and general programming. For example, an elementary-age interviewee stated that he would like there to be greater focus on homework and reading and less time on play-oriented activities. When asked why he would make this change, the child responded: "Because um...kids like they get smarter...like when they're done with their homework...they read books and it helps them." A middle school youth we interviewed had a different take on the need for more of what the Bridge Project has to offer, noting that if the physical space were larger, more youth could be served:

> I would change the certain size of it. 'Cause like the certain number of kids that come now...'cause each year we're increasing in size...I thinking that we would need a bigger location...and more space for these kids and also more volunteers to help tutor...and help clean up...and that would really help the Bridge Project...'cause we're going bigger in size...we're going to need a lot more space.

High school study participants requested extending the hours of operation for the Bridge Project: "I think maybe opening it like on Fridays and Saturdays. Maybe having it on the weekends...more kids would come like there...rather than hanging out." Similar to attracting more youth to attend as the previous quote notes, another high school youth sought to have the program be open to more than the current participants and offered the following statement:

> Um, I might change like trying to get more people from the community involved, like when we do the end of the year things...it's kind of just people who go to Bridge and it could just kind of be like an invitation to bring other people.

Similar quotes are found in the scholarship student data; one young woman who talked about expanding the physical space of the program to meet the growing numbers of youth wanting to access it said:

> I think more people find out about it they know more about Bridge, and they want to volunteer for the program, so, I can see going through years, I can see a lot of new faces, and so I wonder if later on the population of it grows, and you can open up the space bigger, so a lot more, so the community would know more about Bridge and make it bigger.

Another wanted to see the program available to more children:

> ...my recommendation to the Bridge Project is like well right now in the neighborhood we have some kids who are not going to school...if the Bridge Project could encourage some of them...I know they won't listen...the older ones they won't listen...but just encourage them talk to them...Who aren't coming...because some of the kids are not goal oriented...and to reach them...That's probably going to be helpful to them too...

In addition to suggestions that the Bridge Project serve more youth, some of the scholarship students indicated that they would have benefited from more activities geared toward preparation for college. For example, when one young man was asked if he thought the Bridge Project had helped him prepare for college, he responded, "...I think maybe if they would have started earlier...like maybe say Junior year...umm it would have made a difference for me...because I waited till the last minute to do anything...."

Create New Opportunities

An elementary school youth noted what appears to be a wish for more challenge, or perhaps independence, in learning when she noted that she would change the "writing thingy" because "...you don't get to write, you just copy from somebody." Another elementary age child would like opportunities to do more arts. When asked what she would change about the Bridge Project, she stated it would be more fun by "...drawing and painting and music." Also, very typical of elementary-age children, this quote notes the wish to "play all the time and go to the park all of the time." Middle school youth also had suggestions for expanding the programs offered at the Bridge Project such as a chess club, or soccer or football. The following quote is representative of the middle school sentiments:

> Well...I would add like more art and craft stuff...and more adventure stuff for the kids. 'Cause I think like technology's great, we're going to need it obviously...but...most of the time...they forget about going to the mountains or...going fishing...or painting a picture...doing something...they forget all of it...cause of technology...so I think...more arts.

Some high school youth reminisced about the programs that were available at the Bridge Project in the past when they were in a younger age group: "I want the Bridge to have like more field trips. They used to have all these like basketball camps...and stuff like that."

Some scholarship students articulated specific needs that they knew the Bridge Project could meet based on similar services they had seen provided before. For example, one scholarship student wished his cohort met more frequently:

> ...umm I know at the beginning they tried to have more like scholarship meetings...umm and I know at first that would help cause I would see one of my really good friends every time and we would just think a lot of them would be doing good but me and him always understood each other cause he would be doing bad and I would be doing bad and we kind of understood each other. I guess that helped me see that I wasn't the only one struggling. I would say [add] more structure for the scholarship program...even just like meetings so...just to talk. You know see how other people are doing or maybe...if some people have suggestions on like, "oh you know maybe you need to stop partying too much" or maybe just focus more on your education...just things like that you know?

Scholarship participants also echoed the concern raised by the parents we interviewed. Several individuals expressed a wish to have more services available to meet their needs. One service offered only infrequently at the Bridge Project is adult English language classes. One scholarship participant explained that her Arabic-speaking mother wanted to learn English, but that the Bridge Project only offered limited language training opportunities.

Many parents wished for greater parent involvement opportunities through classes offered specifically for adults. For example, one parent wanted to increase her ability to help her own kids do well in life and asked for parent gatherings about:

> how can we better our kids...make kids be there for each other...like you know like the neighborhood watch...you know to get the parents involved. You know and not like leave the parents out or whatever. Just bring them like all together [to help them know] this is what your kids are doing, kind of like school does. Maybe they can offer a class for parents...[such as] how to talk to teens and computer classes.

No One Is Perfect

The previous two sections about problems at the Bridge Project are quite benign and could leave the reader wondering if the study participants were really willing to tell the whole story about their perceptions of the program. The following quotes, however, reveal that participants did have stronger complaints than the minor problems already cited. For example, one young person indicated that some of her non-English-speaking peers do not come to the Bridge Project because there are limited opportunities for children who speak foreign languages. Another youth pointed out the problem of a staff member they didn't like, as the following quote portrays. The interviewer posed the following question after the youth states that he likes everything about Bridge: "You like everything about it? Really?" At this juncture the child states, "...except for the teachers...[names someone]...I don't like her."

The middle school youth we interviewed echo the fact that not all Bridge Project staff and volunteer matches are a perfect fit. For example, one middle school youth talked about problems with his academic tutor that eventually led to being assigned to a different person: "Well, I had one tutor...I forgot his name but...um, it didn't work out that good...so I had another tutor and it worked out good."

Peer dynamics are sometimes challenging for youth when participating in Bridge Project programs. One elementary school student noted difficulty with making friends at the Bridge Project: "I have more friends at school. A lot of people here [at the Bridge] don't really know me that much and don't really talk to me...and at school I have lot of people that I know and they talk to me all the time. 'Cause [at Bridge] they're too busy talking to other people...and when they're done...and they don't really sit by me. I just sit alone." A middle school youth noted that her experience with peers at the Bridge Project is mixed and that sometimes at the Bridge Project "...it's a lot more respectful...but still some kids are rude." Another middle school youth expresses a similar sentiment when she talks about a particular program component that she did not like: "I went to girls group once or twice, but I didn't like it. They mostly talked about gossip...things around like the neighborhood and stuff...I don't know why...I just didn't like it." High school youth in our study sample did not mention negative peer dynamics when participating at the Bridge Project. However, these interviews occurred in focus groups with other peers, which may reflect cohesion within the tech team, or conversely may have prevented them from entering into discussion with content regarding friendships in the program.

Scholarship participants endorsed concerns about interpersonal issues. For example, one participant described a problem in connecting with a staff member:

> What I think they could do better the person who is running the scholarship program right now, doesn't give our calls back or isn't, it's not like it used to be [when] as soon as you call they call you back and everything is said. Like they would be right there right there and now another person is running it and this person never calls you back or you need the books [and] last semester I was going to take two classes but the books weren't listed, only one was so they bought me the first book and when I called to get the second book they couldn't, they never called me back so um I had to drop the class because I couldn't afford the book.

Some of the parents mirrored the youth's sentiments, noting that their children had told them that there are staff members they don't like or that they had problems with other youth calling them names. However, the parents were not sure if any staff members actually knew that the name calling between youth was happening. There was only one parent in the sample who made direct complaints about Bridge Project staff members; these complaints were made in the context of staff changes that had occurred in the past several years. This parent also said she missed certain staff who that she felt were more in tune with her and her children. For example, she stated,

> I've been known [former staff member name] him for years and he's good. He takes his time and he listens to each and every one of everybody's problems and he'd try to figure out a solution.

This parent contrasted this past experience to her current views about the Bridge Project staff as overstepping boundaries, when she noted,

> As to where now…they're too busy and in people's personal business and family business to me…you know things that they're doing now…it's not necessary…to me…they think that they're in a low poverty area…and we're charity cases to them now.

Finally, the same parent summed up her concerns by stating that she wanted staff who are "…older, more mature, more experienced, and that would be assertive and structured." She also expressed disagreement with the way in which Bridge Project staff sometimes disciplined her adolescent. The challenges and rewards of serving youth and families from diverse and multiple cultures are described in Box 6.5.

Box 6.5 WORKING WITH IMMIGRANT FAMILIES AT THE BRIDGE PROJECT

The Bridge Project serves children and families from many racial and ethnic backgrounds. In recent years, the program has helped an increasing number of families who have immigrated to the United States and relocated to Denver. Below we profile two families who emigrated from Somalia and one family who relocated to Denver from Iraq. Each family's story conveys the challenges of adopting the cultural norms and practices of a new country.

SOMALIA: THE TIRI AND FADUMA FAMILIES

A 1991 civil war in Somali has led to an influx of refugees in Denver in the past decade. A number of Somalian families relocated to the public

(continued)

housing neighborhoods served by the Bridge Project. In response, program staff members have worked diligently to adapt interventions and activities to serve children and youth from Somalia. A Bridge Project site director describes the gradual process of gaining trust and working with Somalian families such as the Tiri family:

> The Tiri family came to Denver in 2006. We are lucky enough that they were right across the street...they were our first Somali family, then they got the word out about who we are and what we do and how we can help....The father is very prominent in the Somali community. People really respect him and they trust him so they know we are a safe, good place. This was essential for us because we have so many Somali families in our neighborhood.

The site director also spoke about the importance of connecting with the parents of Somalian children. Reflecting on initial contact with the mother of the Faduma family, she says,

> The mother [Mrs. Faduma] is so inspiring to me. When they first moved into the neighborhood [from another Bridge neighborhood] I made it a point to go over there at least 2 nights a week...she wants to know who is working with her kids and what they are about...She is a strong beautiful woman who speaks incredible English. People come to her for help with accessing resources...She is extremely thankful...She is interested in me, my family, where I'm from...She is definitely the head of the household. This is unusual [for Somalian women]...women are usually more subservient to men...She is extremely strong. Her word is the final word....

The Bridge Project has become an important source of support for families like the Tiri's and the Faduma's. Adjustment to life in the United States is difficult. The site director says that, "the main thing is to make sure they [immigrant families] know who their resources are...and to give them real knowledge and not just do it for them." The staff member provided an example of a case in which her roles at the Bridge Project and in the community intersected with her relationship with Mrs. Faduma:

> The mother [Mrs. Faduma] smacked one of her children across the face at school...It's so important to teach them what is not legal...That [the hitting] was normal in their culture to discipline like that...Social services came to the house...Luckily I had a pretty good relationship with the school social worker. I told her how well I know that mom...

(continued)

The essential challenge of many Somali families concerns a lack of literacy and language skills. As described by a Bridge Project site director,

> They have low reading rates and such newness to America. They struggle in our school system because they are not literate even in their own language... All our paperwork... there is so much paperwork, forms to fill out, they don't know what they say... the most important ones we help them with are for Food Stamps, WIC, milk... any sort of papers... sign up for school... They get these papers and all these words. Junk mail—we teach the family what is important. If it's got pictures of cars in bright colors it's probably not very important. If it's in a white envelope, typed...

Staff members at the Bridge Project are, therefore, focusing efforts on the literacy needs of immigrant children and parents. A site director is especially empathic for immigrants who are adolescents when they arrive:

> The parents have no background because in their culture it is all spoken language. It is very hard to teach the kids to read when they spent their lives so far without literacy. No books were ever read to them. They tell stories. Written language and especially written math are just so difficult.... They come here from Somalia, then Kenya, and straight into high school... I can't imagine how hard it would be... even though they are brilliant... they are... but it makes no sense to them... Our role is to help them... and instill in them that they are smart.

Iraq: The Kahn Family:

> Our life in Iraq was in danger because of Saddam Hussein. We had to leave the country or our dad will be killed... so we ran away from Iraq...

AMAL KHAN, BRIDGE PROJECT SCHOLARSHIP STUDENT

The Khan family first came to the United States in 2000; they secured asylum status and moved into one of the Bridge Project neighborhoods directly from Iraq. Within a few years, the family was referred to the Bridge Project by a teacher in Denver Public Schools. As 19-year-old Amal explains,

> My sister... in elementary school, her teacher told her about... the Bridge Project... 'cause we didn't know about it and our English wasn't so good and we needed help with homework and everything and our parents didn't speak English to help us with our homework... So the teacher told us about the Bridge Project and we all started going there...

Amal's parents valued education, but their life circumstances in Iraq made it difficult for their children to attend or achieve in school. When asked about her life in Iraq, Amal says,

(continued)

Even when we lived in Iraq we had to move to different places and my brothers didn't get to finish schooling...so we would move to a different place in Iraq cause it was dangerous for us to stay in one place...and when we moved here my brothers didn't finish school...my parents always support us to going...they always tell us about how they're suffering and everything and how we should finish school so we don't suffer like that...so they've always told us that since we were little till now...so this is going to stick to our minds on how we should stay on the right path...just go to school...

Today, four of the nine Khan children, including Amal, participate in the Bridge Project. Amal is a college scholarship student, a sister is completing high school, and another sister is a junior in high school. The family also has a son who attends middle school activities at the Bridge Project. Each of the girls has participated in the technology team. In addition, Mrs. Khan works a few hours each night to clean the Bridge Project buildings and has attended adult programs at the agency.

Amal has done well in school. She attributes some of her success to the tutoring and other support she received at the Bridge Project. This is evident when she compares her circumstances to her older siblings. She says,

My sister...the one that is older than me...she didn't go to Bridge and she is having a hard time with a lot of things with schooling and that kind of stuff...but I find it easier for me since I went to Bridge 'cause anything that I need...if I talk to anyone over there they would always help me and I got a scholarship from over there...so I think it's easier for me than her...so I'm always thinking it's probably because of Bridge...I always kind of match her life to my life...stuff is always easier for me than her 'cause...thinking that's probably why too...

Her regard for the positive impact of the Bridge Project on her life is also reflected in her statements about other children growing up in the neighborhood:

'Cause they had nothing to do so they were just like at the neighborhood...some did drugs...a 14-year-old girl I think got pregnant...and had she been going to Bridge she would have looked at her future more like schooling and that kind of stuff...

Families like the Khan's represent unique challenges to programs like the Bridge Project. In this case, success has come in the form of involvement among nearly all family members. Time will tell just how much each of them will accomplish in their lives!

Theme 3: Bridge Project and School

All youth interviewees were prompted with a question about how the Bridge Project experiences were the same or different from what they experienced at school. The theme includes quotes that illustrate a direct comparison between school experiences and Bridge Project activities. As shown in Table 6.6, the actual number of quotes in this theme is low. However, we believe that they offer important insights for understanding the role of the Bridge Project in youth's lives since the program's primary aim is to promote school engagement and academic success.

Most youth reported distinct differences between experiences at school and at the Bridge Project. One youth explained that the proximity of the Bridge Project in comparison with school was different and that most of her friends were at school. Another participant talked about seeing better behavior from peers at the Bridge Project than at school: "Like everybody's mean over there and stuff...at school...[at the Bridge project] they're just respectful and treat you well and so when you're there it's more respectful...and people are just kinder. They don't teach it...it's just I see it every day." In another example, a participant discussed the variety of programs at the Bridge Project: "Bridge is different from school cause um...on Bridge we um do all sort of different programs...and at school we don't have that much." Indicative of the emphasis on peer leadership at the Bridge Project, another participant stated that "there's all little...it's mostly filled up with little kids...we sort of act differently because we start...we try to show the little kids an example of how to behave."

Scholarship participants, who no longer participate directly in afterschool activities, reflected on their involvement as younger students:

> Cause we would go there [to the Bridge] and all the kids were there and we would have good times plus learn. It wasn't just like learning where it gets boring like school and stuff. They divided everything really good...homework time, playing, and computers...whatever...

Only one parent noted a difference between school and the Bridge Project when she stated, "I think over here [the Bridge Project site] they pick up [academic knowledge] more 'cause maybe you know they're not scared...there's like um...I don't know, they're more scared in school."

Themes 4 and 5: Concern for Others and What I Bring

Two additional themes emerge in the data from the technology team interviews: *concern for others* and *what I bring to the kids*. The theme *concern for others* is also present in the scholarship data. *Concern for others* is represented by quotes in which participants express specific concerns for other children. Most of the quotes related to this theme involve a component of caring about the well-being of younger children in community settings and context. For example, the technology team youth shared a concern about younger kids being exposed to antisocial adults who, in turn, have a negative influence on the neighborhood. One youth shared that his worry

> . . . is the drunks and the drug addicts. 'Cause like the kids can tell when they're on a mission, like when they're looking for their drugs, [the kids] can tell like the differences in their personality, 'cause like one minute they'll like say hi to the kids and be like all cool with them and the next, like when they're on their mission they'll be like "beep this, beep that" . . . and it's just like they can tell . . . and like, I just kind of feel bad for the kids 'cause they shouldn't be exposed to that.

Another technology team interviewee stated her worry about the younger children:

> Ah well people, the big people they tell the kids, "You want to buy something?" and then the kids they don't know. They tease the kids so the kids learn that there's a big people there that don't respect each other? So they all care about gangs and stuff . . . about drugs and stuff.

Finally, another participant expressed concern about the safety of children in the neighborhood: " . . . but you could walk around the see broken beer bottles and kids could get hurt anytime like in the playgrounds like in the sand or whatever." Another youth talked about one particular child: " . . . this one kid, he's like 12 years old and already smoking cigarettes and stuff."

In addition to concerns about younger children, high school youth also expressed concern about their younger siblings. For example, one participant worried about his little sister staying on the right path:

> I'm always wondering about my 12-year-old sister. Like if I leave . . . I'm going to leave her in that house . . . and like . . . she's not gonna stay there by herself . . . so like . . . if I leave she'll end up doing some stupid stuff like I did . . . like yeah . . . just like stuff like that.

Another expressed feeling protective of his younger sister:

> I have a sister and like I don't worry about her as much, but I kind of do because she has ADHD and I'm afraid like that kids at school, they treat her almost the same, but some of them see that difference in her and they use it against her and that just pushes me over the edge.

High school participants also expressed a sense of investment in the well-being of the younger children at the Bridge Project. For example, one tech team member shared:

> Yeah, 'cause like sometimes it's anger 'cause you remember like that one kid they were always running around but then again, you think about like oh I like to see the smile on that face when they actually understood it and got it right and they finished this project and they looked at it and it was theirs...I definitely think of the kids...like whenever anybody says Bridge Project...I picture the kids' faces.

In addition to their maturing sense of concern and care for those who are younger, several of the technology team members talked about their approaches and contributions to working with younger children. The theme *what I bring to the kids* captures this quality in the data. This theme is unique to technology team members, since they were discussing their specific role as teachers for the younger children. Quotes that represent this theme are embedded in focus group discussions pertaining to finding effective ways to help and support younger children. Some participants explained how they know to relate to younger kids, such as this quote:

> I know how to like talk to kids I guess and they like understand me. Like there's a lot of times when kids don't like...if you tell them something they won't do it, but then there's sometimes I go and like talk to them and they just do it. So I think I just know how to interact with them.

Several participants described learning these skills by taking care of their younger siblings. For example:

> Yeah like, I'm just like really good with kids 'cause like my parents they're like, they're good parents and all...but I have like to take care of my little sister...so like I know how to deal with kids all different ages...'cause I've been taking care of her since she was really little...since we actually moved, since 3rd grade I've been taking care of her...and so like...I just know how to like deal with kids like...kids respect me and they like...they understand that I mean business...like I'm a disciplinarian at [names a Bridge site].

Another characteristic of this theme pertains to recognizing the importance of having an underlying philosophy or strategy when working with younger children. For example, one high school student discussed how she handles children when they are being difficult: "I like talk to them and switch their minds when they're like refusing to do something. There's some like students that don't give the respect, but all the students give me respect 'cause I give them respect so...and um, they listen to me." Another explained,

Um, how I work with kids is I kind of like stoop down to their level, but then not too much because you still gotta um let them know like the difference between right and wrong...so...yeah...that's how I work with kids...my sister used to be a tech team member here...and that used to be her theory.

Scholarship participants endorsed the theme *concern for others* when they described being worried about the risks younger children are exposed to in the same neighborhoods where they grew up. For example, one participant explained,

Well actually what I'm talking about is the oldest kids that already live in the neighborhood are already a bad influence to the little kids growing up in the neighborhood...that's what I'm talking about. Actually...like if you just go to the park you're going to see those kids standing around smoking and doing all types of things and those little kids are going to watch them and they all doing the same thing. Some don't even go to school they just...They just go around...they just be there. It's just really bad influence to the other kids that come here. So if the other kids just grew up like that watching them...doing the same thing...they might probably end up doing the same thing.

Concern for others extended beyond discussions of the younger children to issues associated with scholarship students' roles in the context of family, peers, and country of origin. For example, one participant described how she sees herself 5 years from now: "I want to get a Master's degree...I want to finish school...and I want to help my parents...and I want to buy a house." Another scholarship student noted that she focuses on college so she can give back to her home country, "...and focus on my dream...and also in my country now they are really short on nurses, doctors, so that's something that really encourage me a lot like I need to be a nurse and go back home and help people there."

In sum, the voices of program participants provide important information about the value and quality of interventions and activities at the Bridge Project. Participant perspectives also help staff members identify unmet client and program needs. Overall, findings from the qualitative interviews and focus groups illustrate the protective function of the Bridge Project in the lives of young people in public housing neighborhoods. Results also describe important elements of PYD at work in the program's intervention components. Implications of these findings are discussed further in the final section of the chapter. Findings relevant to risk and protection and the 5 C's (Lerner et al., 2009) are described next.

Risk and Protection

Risk and protection, key components of the IPEI model, and are used to guide intervention activities at the Bridge Project. Thus, pretest and posttest assessments are conducted annually to identify risk and protective traits that affect children and youth who attend the program. Items from a self-report survey constructed by the research team (Jenson & Anthony, 2003) are used to measure baseline levels of risk and protective factors and to assess change in these factors during the school year. Common risk and protective factors are described in Chapter 1.

Findings from a recent analysis of risk and protection among Bridge Project participants offer a snapshot of the challenges facing children and youth living in the program's four neighborhoods. In this analysis, paired (t-test) comparisons were conducted with a sample of 135 Bridge Project participants in elementary and middle school (Grades 3 to 8) to assess changes in levels of risk and protection between fall and spring. Youth were, on average, 11 years old (SD = 1.8) and in the 5th grade. Fifty-seven percent (N = 77) of subjects were female and 43% (N = 58) were male. Thirty percent (N = 41) of participants were Latino/a, 27% (N = 36) were Asian American, 23% (N = 31) were of mixed race or ethnicity, and 20% (N = 27) were African American.

As shown in Table 6.7, several scales were used to assess participants' perceptions and attitudes of risk and protection. For ease of interpretation, items

Table 6.7 LEVELS OF RISK AND PROTECTION AMONG BRIDGE PROJECT PARTICIPANTS

Risk and Protection Items[a]	Pretest		Posttest		
	M	SD	M	SD	t
Risk Factors					
Friends' antisocial behavior	2.7	(3.4)	2.1	(2.6)	1.14
Relational aggression	1.4	(2.0)	2.6	(0.8)	−2.83*
Attitudes toward antisocial behavior	8.3	(2.8)	8.1	(3.1)	−.36
Community disorganization	8.1	(3.3)	7.8	(2.9)	.45
Family management practices	13.7	(2.3)	14.5	(2.9)	−1.42
Protective Factors					
Commitment to school	11.8	(2.7)	13.8	(3.6)	−2.70**
Belief in the moral order	14.2	(1.9)	14.3	(2.1)	−.06
Family attachment	13.3	(2.7)	12.6	(2.9)	1.36
Self-esteem	11.8	(2.6)	11.5	(2.3)	.77
Rewards for Prosocial Involvement					
Family	13.3	(2.2)	13.4	(1.9)	−.26
School	13.8	(2.8)	14.1	(2.5)	−.49
Opportunities for prosocial involvement					
Family	10.8	(1.8)	10.0	(2.3)	2.09*
School	16.6	(2.7)	17.2	(2.6)	−1.26

Note. N = 135.
[a]Items are from the Risk, Protection, and Antisocial Conduct Inventory (Jenson & Anthony, 2003).
*p < .05, **p < .01.

are coded so that increases in the level of a variable or score indicate an increase in a risk or protective factor, and decreases reveal a decrease in a factor. For example, the risk factor assessing antisocial behavior among peers decreased from an average score of 2.7 ($SD = 3.4$) at pretest to 2.1 ($SD = 2.6$) at posttest. This decrease indicates that participants reported less evidence of antisocial behavior by peers at the end of the academic year compared with the fall.

Findings indicate that most risk factors remain relatively stable across the academic year. In some cases, risk factors such as involvement in relational aggression increased over the course of the academic year as participants grew older. Patterns showing stability or increases in risk are not surprising in light of evidence indicating that risk levels for problems such as aggression tend to increase as children enter their early adolescent years (e.g., Williford, Brisson, Bender, Jenson, & Forrest-Bank, 2011). Subjects in this analysis were in the 5th grade and about to move to middle school, a period in which risk levels are often elevated (Jenson & Fraser, 2011). Thus, the relatively stable patterns of risk reported by participants during the 5th grade may be encouraging given the risky developmental phase in which data collection occurred.

Levels of protection also showed differing patterns. On a promising note, scores for the protective factor of school commitment increased significantly from pretest to posttest. This result is encouraging in view of the inclusion of academic support in nearly all Bridge Project interventions and program activities. Conversely, opportunities for prosocial involvement in the family decreased between fall and spring. This finding may point to a need for additional family-based intervention activities at the Bridge Project. Elements of neighborhood risk and other results are reported in Box 6.6 and Table 6.7.

Box 6.6 DO ANTISOCIAL PEERS INFLUENCE INDIVIDUAL BEHAVIOR?

We were interested in identifying environmental risk factors that may be related to problem behavior and academic achievement among Bridge Project participants. Prior studies indicate that deviant peer networks are strongly related to individual behavior; however, the majority of work in this area examines youths' friends as potential negative influences. Bridge Project participants live in public housing neighborhoods and, as such, neighborhood youth may differentially influence behavior and academic performance. Neighborhood youth may create norms for both prosocial (graduating from high school and finding a job) and antisocial (substance use, violence, and gang involvement) behaviors. Thus, in this analysis we compared the relative influence of deviant friendships with the influence of deviant neighborhood peers on Bridge Project participants' behavioral and academic outcomes.

(continued)

Bridge Project participants in Grades 6–8 (N = 120) completed the *School Success Profile* (SSP) (Bowen & Richman, 2005) at the beginning and end of the academic school year. Two subscales of the SSP were included in analysis; one subscale assessed the youth-reported deviant behavior (i.e., getting in trouble with the police, joining a gang, and using drugs) of the participant's friends, and the other assessed the same youth-reported deviant behaviors of other youth in the participant's neighborhood. In this cross-sectional analysis, linear and logistic regression models (controlling for sociodemographic factors) assessed the associations between deviant friends/deviant neighborhood peers and self-reported behavioral problems in school (i.e., cutting class, physical fights, suspension) and self-reported academic success (ever having earned a failing grade [y/n]).

Deviant neighborhood youth behavior was positively associated with behavioral problems in school (b = −.116, p = .007) but was not significantly related to participants' academic success (b = −.060, p = .830). Friends' deviant behavior was a significant predictor of both behavioral problems in school (b = .201, p = .019) and academic success (b = 1.19, p = .022). When neighborhood youth and friend's behaviors were entered simultaneously to predict problem behavior in school (F (5, 89) = 4.2, p = .002), the relationship between neighborhood peer behavior and school behavior becomes nonsignificant (b = −.08, p = .08) while the relationship between friend behavior and school behavior remains significant (b = .155, p = .02).

Youth who participate in the Bridge Project are living in low-income, high-crime neighborhoods. Our findings confirm that friends' deviant behavior is related to participants' behavioral and academic problems. The findings also suggest that the delinquent behaviors of other youth in the neighborhood are associated with negative outcomes for Bridge participants. Skill-building strategies that provide youth with the ability to select positive peer groups, resist peer pressure, and be effective problem solvers may be one means of combating the negative influence of deviant friends and reducing the negative effects of neighborhood peers. In addition, developing peer contexts for youth that are developmentally appropriate and appealing to their age group, and that also foster a sense of community and acceptance, might be appropriate ways of engaging and retaining youth and promoting positive development. Programming should continue to adapt to address peer risk factors to achieve the aim of improving academic achievement.

The 5 C's of PYD—competence, confidence, connection, character, and caring/ compassion—are core elements of the IPEI framework. These five PYD constructs are critical aspects of Bridge Project intervention components. Thus, evaluating change in PYD constructs among program participants is one of the program's annual evaluation tasks.

To our knowledge, there is no single instrument available to assess the five PYD constructs. Rather, it appears that individual programs use both standardized and informally developed measures to evaluate PYD constructs. To address this limitation, members of the Bridge Project evaluation team developed an instrument that measures each of the 5 C's (Lopez & Jenson, 2011). The instrument, 5 C's of Positive Youth Development-Bridge Project (PYD-Bridge), also yields a total score that is obtained by summing scores from the five individual PYD scales. Developmental processes, scale items and construction, and psychometric properties associated with the instrument are found in Appendix A.

The PYD-Bridge was administered to 99 participants in the fall and spring of the 2010–2011 academic year. The average age of youth in this sample was 10 years (SD = 2.9). Forty-seven percent (N = 47) of respondents were male and 53% (N = 53) were female. Forty-five percent (N = 45) of youth who completed the survey were Latino/a, 22% (N = 22) were African American, and 15% (N = 15) were Asian American. Eighteen percent (N = 18) of participants were Caucasian, American Indian, or of other racial or ethnic background. Findings for overall and individual scale scores on the PYD-Bridge are described below.

Total PYD Scores

The total PYD-Bridge score was calculated by adding the five subscale scores to create an overall PYD score. Paired t-tests were conducted to analyze change in overall scores between fall and spring. As show in Table 6.8, there was a significant increase in total PYD scores among Bridge Project participants between the start and end of the academic year (t = –2.13, p = .037). PYD overall scores increased by an average of 5.4 points between the fall and spring survey surveys. In addition, regression analyses revealed a significant relationship between program participation and PYD overall scores; each hour of Bridge Project participation resulted in a .096 increase in total PYD scores (F = 3.19, p = .045, b = .096). Changes in each of the 5 C subscales are described below.

Table 6.8 POSITIVE YOUTH DEVELOPMENT SCORES AMONG BRIDGE
PROJECT PARTICIPANTS

	Pretest		Posttest		
PYD Scales[a]	M	SD	M	SD	t-value
Competence	23.7	(4.6)	23.9	(3.9)	−.55
Confidence[b]	44.6	(9.6)	46.5	(9.1)	−2.54*
Connection	31.4	(5.6)	31.6	(5.1)	−.81
Character	32.2	(8.1)	33.8	(5.7)	−1.65
Caring and Compassion	16.7	(4.5)	17.6	(3.2)	−1.63
Overall PYD score	148.8	(25.6)	154.2	(19.6)	−2.13*

[a]PYD scales of competence, connection, character, and caring and compassion are from Lopez and Jenson (2011). See Appendix A.
[b]The confidence scale is from the Piers-Harris Self-Concept Scale
(Piers & Herzberg, 2002). $N = 99$. * p < .05.

Competence

The PYD construct *competence* is a nine-item scale that asks youth to reflect on their ability to be successful in academic settings. There was a moderate, though not statistically significant, increase in competence scores among Bridge Project participants in the past academic year. However, each hour of participation in technology training was related to a .065 increase in competence scores ($F = 5.14$, $p = .006$, $b = .065$). Additional measures of competence are reported in the academic outcomes section of this chapter.

Confidence

The PYD construct of *confidence* was assessed with the Piers-Harris Self-Concept Scale (Piers & Herzberg, 2002). This 60-item survey evaluates young people's self-perceptions across domains of behavior, intellect, physical appearance, popularity, anxiety, and happiness/satisfaction. The scale was administered to Bridge Project participants in the fall and spring. Psychometric properties of the Piers-Harris Self-Concept Scale are found in Appendix A.

Youth demonstrated a significant and positive change on the total Piers-Harris scale score between the beginning and end of the school year ($t = 2.54$, $p = .012$). Participants' scores on the physical appearance ($t = -2.48$, $p = .015$) and happiness/satisfaction ($t = -2.43$, $p = .022$) subscales improved significantly between fall and spring semesters. Scores on the behavior, intellect, popularity, and anxiety scales improved during the school year.

However, as shown in Table 6.8, changes in these scales were not statistically significant.

Connection and Character

The PYD scales of *connection* and *character* revealed modest improvements during the academic year. In each case, scale scores increased between fall and spring; these changes, however, were not statistically significant. Each hour of participation in Bridge Project skills training activities, controlling for age, resulted in a .200 increase in character scores ($F = 4.73$, $p = .011$, $b = .200$).

Caring and Compassion

Caring and *compassion* were measured by a seven-item scale that asked youth to evaluate their perceptions of concern for others and community. As shown in Table 6.8, no significant differences were found in levels of caring and compassion between fall and spring. Involvement in skills training activities at the Bridge Project, however, was associated with a .217 increase in caring and compassion scores for all participants.

Qualitative results reported in the themes of *concern for others* and *what I bring to the kids* also reflect PYD constructs of caring and compassion. As described earlier, the theme *concern for others* is represented by young people's expressed concern for their peers, particularly for children who are younger in age. This sentiment was common among technology team members and among scholarship students. The theme of concern for younger children is one that appears to emerge among Bridge Project during the late middle school and high school years. Finally, some youth noted the importance of the skills and attributes they bring to younger children at the Bridge Project. This theme was also strong among the technology team participants. Illustrations that represent this theme are found in focus group discussions pertaining to finding effective ways to help and support younger children that were described in an earlier section of this chapter.

Academic performance reflects the final set of outcomes specified in the IPEI model. Results from assessments of reading skills, standardized test scores, grades, and school attendance are described below.

Academic Outcomes

Reading Skills

Reading skills are instrumental to children's success at school. Unfortunately, many participants at the Bridge Project begin school with lower than average reading abilities. Thus, literacy programs are a primary component of afterschool programming at the Bridge Project. Literacy programs are used to implement several evidence-based programs, including Read Well for Grades K-2 (Wahl, 2007) and Reading Plus for Grades 3–6 (Taylor & Associates, 2009). Literacy programs are taught by professional educators with teaching degrees and certifications trained in the use of these curricula.

Recent evaluation efforts aimed at assessing reading skills have examined changes in reading ability over the course of the academic year. We have also investigated whether exposure frequency and type of programming are associated with reading ability. The Developmental Reading Assessment (DRA) (DRA, 2009; Beaver & Carter, 2003), a standardized measure of youths' reading abilities, was used to assess reading level at pretest and posttest. The DRA assessed reading level, including accuracy, fluency, and comprehension through individual reading conferences in which students read selected texts with the onsite educator.

A pretest–posttest design was used to assess changes in reading ability from the beginning to the end of the academic year among 150 Bridge Project participants in Grades K–8 (N = 145). Subjects averaged 9 years old (SD = 2.3). Fifty-three percent (N = 77) of participants were male and 47% (N = 68) were female. Forty-six percent (N = 67) of youth who completed reading assessments were Latino/a, 23% (N = 33) were African American, and 12% (N = 17) were Asian American. Nineteen percent (N = 28) of participants were Caucasian, American Indian, or of other racial or ethnic background.

Youth revealed a significant improvement in reading levels from the fall pretest to the spring posttest (t = –14.66, p < .001). Change scores on the

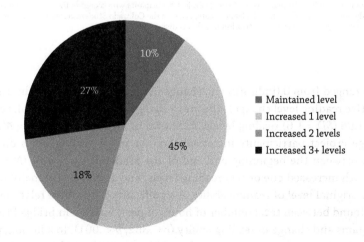

Figure 6.1
Changes in Reading Levels Among Bridge Project Participants Between Fall and Spring, 2010–2011

Table 6.9 *COLORADO STUDENT ASSESSMENT PROFILE* (CSAP) SCORES FOR
BRIDGE PROJECT PARTICIPANTS BY PROFICIENCY LEVEL AND AGE, 2010

	CSAP Proficiency Profile Scores		
	Reading	Math	Writing
All Youth			
Unsatisfactory	50%	49%	26%
Partially proficient	23%	35%	62%
Proficient	27%	12%	10%
Advanced	N/A	4%	1%
Elementary (Grades 3–5)			
Unsatisfactory	45%	39%	27%
Partially proficient	29%	47%	64%
Proficient	26%	6%	7%
Advanced	n/a	9%	2%
Middle (Grades 6–8)			
Unsatisfactory	46%	57%	17%
Partially proficient	27%	31%	69%
Proficient	27%	10%	14%
Advanced	n/a	2%	0%
High School (Grades 9–12)			
Unsatisfactory	65%	70%	39%
Partially proficient	8%	17%	52%
Proficient	26%	13%	9%
Advanced	n/a	0%	0%

Note. Numbers reflect the percentage of Bridge Project participants who scored in the unsatisfactory, partially proficient, proficient, and advanced categories on the Colorado Student Assessment Profile in 2010. Data are compiled by the Denver Public Schools district. $N = 172$.

DRA ranged from 0 (indicating no change in reading level) to 7 (indicating a positive reading level change). The mean change score in ability for all youth was 1.96 ($SD = 1.6$) reading levels. As shown in Figure 6.1, 27% ($N = 42$) of Bridge Project participants increased three or more reading levels on the DRA between the beginning and end of the academic year; 62% ($N = 93$) of youth increased one or two reading levels, and 10% ($N = 15$) maintained their original level of reading ability. A significant and positive relationship was found between total number of hours of participation in Bridge Project programs and change in reading ability ($r = .362$, $p < .001$). In addition, participation in literacy programming ($r = .369$, $p < .001$) and homework help ($r = .181$, $p < .05$) sessions were positively related to improvements in reading. Finally, a subset of participants ($N = 35$) attended a summer literacy program aimed at maintaining reading improvements shown during the school year, and these youths demonstrated significant improvement in reading skills between May and August.

Standardized Test Scores and Academic Grades

Colorado State Assessment Profile (CSAP) scores from 2010 were analyzed for a sample of 172 Bridge Project participants. Fifty percent ($N = 86$) of all youth scored at the partially proficient and proficient levels in 2010. Forty-seven percent ($N = 81$) and 72% ($N = 124$) of participants obtained scores of partially proficient and proficient on the 2010 math and writing tests, respectively. The percentage of youth who scored at advanced, proficient, partially proficient, and satisfactory levels on CSAP tests are shown for the complete sample, and by age, in Table 6.9.

School grades and factors associated with academic performance were analyzed using items from the Morgan-Jinks Student Efficacy Scale (MJSES) (Jinks & Morgan, 1999). Academic grades in math, science, reading, and social studies were used in these analyses. A total of 128 youth completed pretest and posttest assessments of the MJSES. The average age of youth in this analysis was 11 years old ($SD = 2.4$). Fifty-two percent ($N = 67$) of participants were male and 48% ($N = 61$) were female. Forty-two percent ($N = 54$) of youth who completed reading assessments were Latino/a, 26% ($N = 33$) were African American, and 15% ($N = 19$) were Asian American. Seventeen percent ($N = 22$) of participants were Caucasian, American Indian, or of other racial or ethnic background.

Individual responses to the four academic areas were ranked $(5) = A$, $(4) = B$, $(3) = C$, $(2) = D$, and $(1) = F$ and then summed to create an aggregate score. The aggregated score for the sample was 15.9 ($SD = 3.25$), or approximately a B–/C+ average across the four subject areas. Summed self-reports of grades in math, science, reading, and social studies were regressed on participants' total MJSES scores at posttest to assess the relationship among self-efficacy, program exposure, and academic performance. Age and gender were also included in the analyses. Levels of program participation and self-efficacy, controlling for age and gender, accounted for 42% of the variance in academic grades among participants in the sample.

School Attendance

Data from Denver public schools are used routinely to assess school attendance among Bridge Project participants; records were obtained for 293 students in 2010–2011. Students missed an average of 19.5 ($SD = 18.5$) days.

There was a significant negative correlation between number of days missed and total hours of exposure to Bridge Project interventions (-.447, p <.001). Program exposure was a significant predictor of the number of days missed ($t = -7.623$, p < .001), with each hour of program exposure predicting a decrease in days missed by .045. Participation in Bridge Project programs accounted for 20% of the variance in days absent from school. Participation in homework help (-.455, <.001) and tutoring (-.386, p <. 001) were significantly related to fewer missed days of school.

PROGRAM AND PRACTICE IMPLICATIONS

Evaluation activities are critical aspects of developing and sustaining a community-based youth service agency. In this chapter, we described findings from the evaluation strategies used to understand and assess the effects of Bridge Project program activities on staff members, community professionals, and child, youth, and parent participants. We believe that comprehensive evaluations of this nature are critical to improving the integrity of a program over time. What can be learned from community and mixed-methods evaluation studies at the Bridge Project? How can experiences in one urban afterschool program be used to generate new ideas for other community-based youth service agencies?

First, the results of the community study reinforce the need to work collaboratively with other organizations and professionals. The Bridge Project relies on a host of other organizations to deliver key intervention activities. For example, staff members depend heavily on a core set of collaborative organizations to deliver education services. The program also relies on distinct groups of organizations to provide important support services to children and families. Personal accounts from key Bridge Project staff and volunteers noted that the program could not survive, much less flourish, without the material and moral support from the larger Denver community. Findings from the community sample confirm the importance of personal, professional, and reciprocal relationships in delivering interventions to youth in community-based programs.

Results from qualitative interviews and focus groups with Bridge Project participants provide important insights about the presence and scope of risk and protection in the lives of children and youth living in public housing communities. Living in conditions of poverty is challenging to even the most well-adjusted child. Supports are often limited or simply do not exist. Parent's resources are constrained by inadequate income and are exacerbated frequently by limited education, cultural and language barriers, and scarce employment opportunities.

Responses to our qualitative interviews and focus groups suggest that the Bridge Project is an important source of support and protection for young people. Many respondents noted the importance of a safe place to go during the afterschool hours. Our findings suggest that embedding afterschool activities in the neighborhoods they serve is essential in the context of public housing. Respondents also highlighted the importance of talking to staff members about school problems or other personal matters. We believe that the integration of social work and educational services is the single most important factor in increasing the efficacy of afterschool programs like the Bridge Project. Finally, respondents reported that the structure and consistency of intervention activities were important program elements. Participants clearly value the educational support services and the supportive environment of the Bridge Project. In fact, many children, youth, and parents wished the program could do more to help them reduce the risk and adverse influences they experience on an almost daily basis.

Results from the analysis of risk and protective traits confirm the presence of both adversity and resilience in the lives of participants. For example, children at the Bridge Project report significant individual protective traits in the form of self-confidence and self-efficacy. Protective factors are also evident in participants' perceptions of their school environment. However, it appears that some youth, particularly younger children, have strong perceptions about the lack of parent and family support for homework and academic activities. In addition, several parents noted the desire for additional support to raise their children in the midst of neighborhood-level risk factors. Thus, enhancing family involvement in Bridge Project activities may be an important future direction.

Quantitative indicators of PYD constructs (5 C's) at the Bridge Project reveal modest to significant improvements during the academic year. Scores on the overall PYD measure increased significantly between fall and spring, suggesting that Bridge Project participants are making positive developmental strides between the beginning and end of the school year. Self-esteem and academic self-efficacy also increased significantly between fall and spring. Levels of academic self-efficacy among youth were, in turn, positively related to academic grades.

A significant percentage of young people at the Bridge Project improved their reading skills during the academic year. Further, findings from an analysis of a subsample of youth who participated in summer intervention activities revealed that many youth maintain reading improvements over the summer months. Reading gains are particularly important in the context of interpersonal, social, and environmental risk. We view improvement in academic skills, particularly in basic skills such as reading, to be one of the most important keys to escaping poverty and reducing the effects of adverse community influences. Evidence from Bridge Project evaluation studies supports the importance of emphasizing academic instruction and skill development during the afterschool hours.

SUMMARY

Findings from recent mixed-methodology evaluations conducted at the Denver Bridge Project demonstrate the complexity of assessing the effects of community-based interventions for at-risk children and youth. Community programs operate in a world of uncertainty, characterized by rapid changes in funding, fluctuations in client participation, and real-life evaluation constraints. Conducting meaningful evaluation activities in such an environment is a challenge to even the most stable community-based program. To minimize this complexity, assessment activities at the Bridge Project are guided by an agency evaluation plan and by the processes and goals specified in the IPEI model. These two important tools provide the blueprint for all evaluation tasks conducted at the Bridge Project. Our experience suggests that an evaluation plan grounded in theory—the IPEI model in the case of the Bridge Project—is the key to identifying program challenges and to determining the effects of interventions on the lives of children and families. The evaluation tasks and results reported in this chapter, while still a work in progress, illustrate many of the steps necessary to improve the lives of young people living in disadvantaged neighborhoods and communities. We hope the strategies and experiences of the Bridge Project will be used by other community-based programs to improve the efficacy of interventions for children and youth. Recommendations for advancing policy, practice, and research in afterschool and community-based programs for youth are identified in the final chapter.

CHAPTER 7

Where Do We Go from Here?

Advancing Community-Based Programs for
Children and Youth

The chapters in this book emphasize the importance of using theory to pre-vent or reduce child and adolescent problems. We have also emphasized the need to integrate principles of leadership, organizational change, and evaluation in the design and implementation of community-based programs for children and youth. We applied these elements to the Bridge Project After-School Program to illustrate how a theoretically based intervention developed and evolved over time. In this chapter, we identify critical aspects in improving outcomes and ensuring the healthy development of children and youth who participate in com-munity-based afterschool programs. Recommendations for practice, policy, and research in community-based programming for at-risk youth are noted.

REDUCING RISK AND PROMOTING POSITIVE YOUTH DEVELOPMENT

Young people are confronted by a number of individual, social, and environmen-tal risks as they navigate the road to young adulthood (Jenson & Fraser, 2011). Some children experience interpersonal problems caused by inadequate parenting practices. Many adolescents fall victim to illicit drugs, alcohol, or premature preg-nancy, or participate in other risky or illegal behaviors in the community. In some cases, children and youth fail to thrive at school and suffer serious educational and career setbacks that block their path to a promising future.

On a more positive note, prior research and our own experience at the Denver Bridge Project suggest that many youth successfully avoid deviant behavior, excel in school, and find happiness as adults. The accounts of Bridge Project participants illustrated in earlier chapters—corroborated by evaluation data—confirm the existence of resilience among young people. As described throughout this book, many Bridge Project participants make significant and positive strides and avoid involvement in problem behavior despite the presence of risk and adversity.

Still, it is important to recognize that "growing up" has become much more complicated than it was in the past. Today, children and youth are exposed to rapid changes in technology and social media on a daily basis. The world, too, has become a much smaller place in which ideas and social trends are created and exchanged quickly and spontaneously. Few would argue with the proposition that today's young people encounter considerably greater social, economic, and environmental complexity than was the case several decades ago.

EDUCATIONAL AND ECONOMIC DISPARITIES AFFECTING CHILDREN AND YOUTH

Two of the most significant challenges facing children and youth are embedded in the social context of education and economics. For example, studies indicate that access to public education and success in school are affected greatly by a student's race, ethnicity, and income level (e.g., Frey, Walker, & Perry, 2011). Differences in academic achievement have long been noted between youth of color and Caucasian youth. Six percent of the nation's 16-to-19-year-old youth dropped out of school in 2009 (Annie E. Casey Foundation, 2011b). Particularly troubling, however, is evidence indicating that youth of color drop out of school at considerably higher rates than Caucasian students. In 2009, 10% of Latino/a, 13% of American Indian, and 8% of African American students dropped out of school compared with only 4% of Caucasian youth (Annie E. Casey Foundation, 2011b).

Variations in academic achievement between youth of color from low-income families and Caucasian youth have been discussed extensively in policy and practice circles. Jencks and Phillips (1998) reviewed studies of the *Black–White* achievement gap and concluded that differences in parenting practices between underprivileged African American and Caucasian families contributed greatly to discrepancies in childhood academic performance. In addition, it appeared that the gap in academic achievement began before children started kindergarten, further raising the question of the relationship between home environment and children's cognitive abilities. In a subsequent study, Lareau (2003) found that underprivileged and minority children were more likely than Caucasian youth to be raised in environments that did not promote adequate vocabulary development or positive attitudes toward school and learning. The absence of essential reading skills, in turn, was related to poor academic performance for many of these children and youth (Lareau, 2003).

The sad truth is that, for some children, the race to the top begins before they ever reach the starting line. The gap in educational achievement by income, race, and ethnicity illustrates this fact all too well; many children of color living in impoverished neighborhoods start school with a distinct disadvantage to their peers (Tough, 2009). The disparity in academic achievement points to a need to teach reading, math, and other cognitive skills to at-risk children at a very young age. The acquisition of skills, coupled with sustained academic support from parents, may well be the most promising and powerful avenue to a successful future for young people (Tough, 2009).

Why is the ability to read and understand math so important to a child's future? Simply put, the nature of the economy has changed dramatically since the 1990s. In today's global economy, *skills* have become more important than hard work, family background, or other factors that used to account for a successful life. In fact, recent studies indicate that cognitive skills associated with reading and math now trump ethnicity and poverty as the most powerful determinant of success in life (e.g., Tough, 2009). In short, children with strong literacy and math skills are more likely than other young people to finish school, complete college, and compete successfully for good jobs.

Economic divisions between disadvantaged and middle- and upper-class children and families exacerbate the educational deficits found among many at-risk youth. In 2009, 20% of all American children under 18 years old lived in conditions of poverty (Annie E. Casey Foundation, 2011a). Years of accumulated research indicate that underprivileged children suffer serious individual and social setbacks that leave them vulnerable to a range of adverse outcomes as adolescents and young adults (Mayer, 1997; Tough, 2009; Wilson, 1987). Yet, despite concentrated efforts to reduce poverty, the gap between underprivileged and other children has widened significantly in recent years (Tough, 2009).

Many of today's economic policies are aimed at identifying and analyzing the influence of global markets and macrolevel economic conditions on people's lives (e.g., Ehrenberg & Smith, 2011). Such analysis is important; few people would disagree with the need to understand the effects of underlying economic factors on people's lives. Further, finding new solutions that increase economic opportunities for all families should be part of an overall strategy to narrow the economic gap. However, such analysis should not come at the cost of reducing or eliminating funding for basic education policy or supporting educational strategies like afterschool programs.

We believe that adequately funded public education, including the provision of extended educational opportunities and support services like the Bridge Project, is *the* key to decreasing income disparities that develop during early childhood and adolescence. Education policy and practice at the national, state, and local levels should include afterschool programs like the Bridge Project as part of a strategy to promote educational achievement and, thereby, reduce the economic gap experienced by disadvantaged children and families. The emphasis on extended education strategies needs to be innovative, consistent, and sustained. Unfortunately, this has not been the case in recent years. Rather, in the past decade, periods of economic instability have led to swift and significant reductions in funding for education and other social programs (Frey et al., 2011). History suggests that these types of funding cuts often provide only short-term solutions and lead frequently to unintended and negative consequences for underprivileged children and youth (Bernard, 1992; Jenson & Fraser, 2011; Jenson & Howard, 1998).

There are disadvantaged children in every town and city who do not succeed in school. In many cases, a child's poor school performance is not due to her or his lack of ability or motivation. Rather, the risks and burdens that many children carry are often so overwhelming and traumatizing that they have little desire or energy for learning. These children may appear lethargic and uninterested in school because they have not had the opportunity to learn or practice the cognitive skills that are necessary to perform routine academic and social demands. In addition, children may feel disenfranchised because they are often well aware of the inadequacies of their educational experience and background (Fine, Burns, Payne, & Torre 2004). Meanwhile, national and state policies stipulate that funding for education should be reduced and that underachieving schools should be closed. Ironically, these schools are the very institutions that need additional financial resources to train teachers and implement effective curricula.

Individual accounts of resilience expressed by Bridge Project participants suggest that there are likely to be thousands of disadvantaged children living in public housing communities who have the potential to become poets, artists, pharmacists, doctors, nurses, engineers, and business owners. The individual and social costs associated with ignoring these children are beyond calculation, but real nonetheless. Community-based afterschool programs like the Bridge Project must be part of a comprehensive approach to eliminating achievement and income gaps among children and youth. We outline steps necessary to advance afterschool programs in the next section.

ADVANCING EDUCATIONAL POLICY AND SOCIAL WORK PRACTICE IN AFTERSCHOOL PROGRAMS

In this book, we have constructed a program and organizational model for community-based programs that can be adopted by any locality in the country. As we noted in earlier chapters, effective community-based programs for children and youth are a product of many factors. First, theoretical suppositions about childhood and adolescent development and knowledge of evidence-based interventions are necessary to provide important building blocks for programs aimed at vulnerable children and youth. Second, an effective organizational structure is needed to support the intervention. Third, evaluation strategies are needed to determine program effectiveness. Finally, dissemination strategies and policy efforts are necessary to ensure the longevity of community-based programs and intervention approaches.

Reducing economic disparities and enhancing educational achievement requires communities to construct a careful continuum of services for children and youth. We believe that community-based support services such as the Bridge Project are a critical part of this continuum. The integrated prevention and early intervention model (IPEI) described in Chapter 4 provides a model that communities can use to assess problems, design or adopt programs, and test the effects of interventions on child and youth participants. In this book, the IPEI is applied to afterschool interventions for young people. However, we believe that the IPEI framework may be adapted and used in different settings. In this context, we offer suggestions for creating effective university–community partnerships in Box 7.1. Program, policy, and research recommendations aimed at improving afterschool programs for youth in community settings are described below.

Box 7.1 A TOOLBOX FOR DEVELOPING AND SUSTAINING UNIVERSITY–COMMUNITY PARTNERSHIPS

The Denver Bridge Project is an example of what reciprocity can accomplish when a university works collaboratively with a community partner. The program, located in the Graduate School of Social Work (GSSW) at the University of Denver, benefits from the shared expertise of faculty and students in numerous ways. Faculty and students bring tested and innovative intervention ideas to Bridge Project staff members. Master of Social Work students complete structured internships at the four program sites. Doctoral students from GSSW provide invaluable research and evaluation support to Bridge Project staff.

The University of Denver and GSSW also benefit greatly from this unique collaboration. The Bridge Project offers a natural training environment for students interested in at-risk youth and clinical or community practice. It also fulfills an important part of the university's broader mission of serving the public good as evidenced by the Foreword to this book by Governor John Hickenlooper. Finally, by reaching out to children and youth in four of Denver's most troubled neighborhoods, GSSW students, faculty, and volunteers are rewarded by knowing successful Bridge Project participants, and their motivation deepens because they see the positive outcomes of their time and energy.

What does it take to create and sustain an effective university–community program and research collaboration? The answer to this question

(continued)

is far from simple. Our experience at the University of Denver's Bridge Project suggests that several key elements are necessary to forge and maintain a successful university–community relationship. Effective and long-lasting university–community partnerships are characterized by the following attributes:

- The identification of a serious social problem that can only be addressed effectively by collaborative action
- A high level of energy that emerges from passion and commitment
- Leadership in both the university and community that is dedicated, politically skillful, and willing to provide the necessary resources for start-up
- An active, committed, and informed board of directors composed of both community and university members
- Goals and objectives that are clear and measurable
- Diverse skills and strengths among the community members, faculty, and volunteers
- Mutual respect among all members
- Roles and responsibilities of all members that are clearly delineated
- Shared decision making between the university and community
- An organizational and administrative structure that is compatible with the interests and values of both parties
- Continual process and outcome evaluations that are routinely shared among all members
- Persistent outreach within the university and in the community and that unearths new members to renew and enrich the collaboration

The partnership between the University of Denver and the Bridge Project has adhered to these principles during most of the past 20 years. The partnership benefits from a shared passion for helping children and youth, an organizational structure that clearly identifies roles and responsibilities, mutual respect among members, shared decision making, and a committed external board of directors. GSSW provides an organizational home for the Bridge Project and the University of Denver offers institutional support and infrastructure assistance through technology and other forms of assistance. *Above all, both the university and community benefit directly from the Bridge Project.* In our experience, these are among the keys to creating and sustaining an effective university–community partnership. Readers who are interested in learning more about university–community collaborations may wish to consult these additional sources (Alter, 2009; Soska & Johnson Butterfield, 2004; Yale Center for Clinical Investigation, 2011).

A theoretical orientation and organizing framework is essential to any community-based afterschool program. Practitioners and researchers agree that theories informing youth programs must consider the influence of individual characteristics and social and environmental factors on behavior (Durlak, Mahoney, Bohnert, & Parente, 2010a; Jenson & Fraser, 2011). Further, there is wide consensus that theories should specify change mechanisms by linking etiological factors to program services and intervention elements (Catalano, Hawkins, Berglund, Pollard, & Arthur, 2002; Fraser, Richman, Galinsky, & Day, 2009).

The IPEI integrates elements of risk and resilience and positive youth development in a single framework that offers specific guidelines for intervention. As shown in Chapter 4, the IPEI accounts for individual, social, and environmental levels of risk and protection (Jenson & Fraser, 2011). However, the model extends commonly accepted and empirically supported principles of risk and resilience by also including positive youth development constructs (Vazsonyi, 2005). Together, risk and resilience and principles of positive youth development provide an integrated and seamless basis for selecting and monitoring interventions implemented at the Bridge Project. The IPEI also incorporates a useful organizational framework for any community-based youth service program interested in improving academic performance and preventing childhood and adolescent problem behavior.

Recommendations. Many community-based afterschool programs for children and youth lack a theoretical base to guide program development, implementation, and evaluation activities (Anthony, Alter, & Jenson, 2009; Gottfredson, Cross, & Soule, 2007). In the absence of theory, programs are unable to adapt to rapid changes in social, political, and economic conditions that threaten the stability and sustenance of program services over time. To address these limitations:

1. Practitioners and administrators should identify and select an empirically supported theory to guide program and intervention efforts.
2. The identified theory should be linked closely to specific program goals, activities and intervention elements, and intended short- and long-term outcomes.
3. The ability of a selected theory to adapt to changes in patterns of childhood and adolescent behavior and to fluctuations in social and political priorities should be monitored consistently over time.

Intervention and Evaluation Elements

Many intervention approaches are used by practitioners and administrators in afterschool program settings. Indeed, reviews of the afterschool literature reveal considerable variation in program types, approaches, and structures (Durlak et al., 2010a; Durlak, Weissberg, & Pachan, 2010b; Gottfredson et al., 2007). For example, some programs include intervention components that focus on social and cultural activities while others concentrate solely on academic activities such as tutoring, homework help, and technology training. Few programs integrate social and academic program elements in a systematic or theoretically informed manner (Durlak et al., 2010a).

Leadership and collaboration elements are often given inconsistent attention in afterschool programs (Alter, 2009; Alter & Hage, 1993; Larson & Walker, 2010). We described a model of interorganizational collaboration in Chapter 3 that addresses many of the deficiencies inherent in collaboration. To be effective, we believe that afterschool programs must integrate child and youth interventions with well-designed collaboration principles and practices. Such integration should be intentional and be monitored consistently by administrative and evaluation staff. The Bridge Project is a unique collaboration between a private university and a community-based program located in four of Denver's most disadvantaged neighborhoods. The partnership was developed, and has been strengthened, by adhering to the principles of collaboration and organizational structure noted in Chapter 3.

Evaluating community-based afterschool programs is challenging. As noted in Chapter 5, many programs lack the skills or resources to conduct rigorous evaluation studies. Further, ethical problems associated with conducting randomized studies that require withholding intervention services from some children pose unique challenges to afterschool programs. Findings from well-conducted and rigorous evaluations are necessary to identify, disseminate, and implement evidence-based policies and practices in community-based youth service programs. Therefore, finding ways to use rigorous study designs while not compromising young people's exposure to essential services is an important next step in evaluation research related to afterschool programs for children and youth (Bender, Brisson, Jenson, Forrest-Bank, Lopez, & Yoder, 2011; Jenson, 2010).

Recommendations. Community-based afterschool interventions display considerable variation in program design, structure, and intended outcomes (Gottfredson et al., 2007). Equally important, interorganizational and collaborative elements specified by program theory and intervention elements are absent or given only limited attention by practitioners and stakeholders (Alter, 2009; Larson & Walker, 2010). Finally, evaluation designs are seldom incorporated in a program's logic model or theory of change. To address these limitations:

1. Afterschool programs should be structured and be designed to offer well-planned and empirically supported program activities. Selected intervention elements should be implemented with consistency and fidelity.

2. Afterschool interventions for children and youth should emphasize educational components such as tutoring, homework help, and technology training. To increase effectiveness, programs should also include skill training that promotes social, emotional, behavioral, and cognitive skills among participants.
3. Intervention elements should be culturally relevant and tailored to meet the diverse needs of child, youth, and adult participants. Intervention specialists and professional staff members must be cognizant of cultural influences and racial and ethnic differences among child, youth, and family participants. Staff members should be encouraged to model principles of inclusivity and acceptance.
4. Adult education, family support, and counseling interventions should be available or provided routinely to program participants.
5. Afterschool programs in high-risk neighborhoods should be located in safe and accessible sites. Programs should be within walking distance from school and home. Parents should be assured that their children are in a safe and secure environment in the hours following release from school.
6. Administrative and program staff members should develop, implement, and consistently monitor elements of interorganizational collaboration. Effective collaboration elements should be identified and implemented consistently by program stakeholders.
7. Afterschool programs should be linked closely to local schools. Strategies that promote effective and frequent communication among afterschool program staff, teachers, students, and parents should be developed, implemented, and monitored in afterschool programs.
8. Community-based afterschool providers should increase their efforts to design and conduct evaluation studies. Programs should seek evaluation expertise through established evaluation organizations, colleges, and universities.
9. University and community partnerships should be promoted as a means of developing and implementing community-based programs, including afterschool interventions, for children and youth.

Policy Elements

The federal government allocates nearly $1.2 billion in annual funding to afterschool activities through the 21st Century Community Learning Centers (21st CCLC) initiative (Anderson-Butcher, 2004; U.S. Department of Education, 2009). While this is a significant amount of money, the popularity and proliferation of afterschool programs across the country place a tremendous strain on 21st CCLC funds. Consequently, the number of afterschool programs far exceeds available funding in most large cities. Further, in 2002, the federal government transferred the administration of grants from the 21st CCLC from the Department of Education to individual states. Thus, there is currently no national office or federal mechanism to represent or monitor the activities of afterschool programs.

Despite the struggle for funding, programs like the Bridge Project are now an integral part of educational services for children and families in many communities. A majority of afterschool interventions are single-agency programs that were created with financial support from private donors and local government sources. On a positive note, there has been at least one large-scale afterschool initiative in the past decade. Holleman and colleagues (Holleman, Sundis, & Bruns, 2010) describe a comprehensive plan developed by the city of Baltimore to create a coordinated set of afterschool programs. The final plan provides a community process and a citywide blueprint that should be helpful to other municipalities interested in creating a network of afterschool programs. Additional large-scale efforts modeled after the initiative in Baltimore are needed.

Prevention systems aimed at helping communities identify and understand child and adolescent problems are a second source of potential support for afterschool programs. Systems such as Communities that Care (Hawkins, Catalano, Arthur, & Egan, 2008) and *Promoting School, Community, and University Partnerships to Enhance Resiliency* (PROSPER) (Spoth & Greenberg, 2011) use a structured planning and implementation process to help community leaders identify prevalent youth problems and select intervention approaches and programs to target these problems. Tests of the two approaches have yielded positive outcomes in reducing problems such as delinquency and drug use (Hawkins, Oesterle, Brown, & Arthur, 2009; Spoth et al., 2011). Afterschool programs represent a viable program site for prevention efforts and should be included more frequently in tests of CTC and PROSPER.

The location of afterschool programs for children and youth is another important policy consideration. Evidence presented in Chapter 6 suggests that public housing communities are appropriate sites for afterschool interventions. Access to vulnerable and at-risk youth is relatively easy in public housing communities, and the need for additional educational support services is generally quite high (Anthony et al., 2009).

Recommendations. Federal funding streams and national policy pertaining to community-based afterschool interventions are limited primarily to the 21st CCLC initiative. This single source lacks the resources and organizational structure to impact and monitor the quality and effectiveness of afterschool interventions. In addition, few large or systematic efforts have been undertaken to develop, test, and disseminate information about efficacious afterschool interventions. To address these limitations:

1. Federal legislation to provide appropriate funding, allocation, and monitoring mechanisms for community-based afterschool programs should be

developed and enacted. States should play an important coordinating role in the implementation of federal legislation.

2. Systemic prevention processes should be used to assess needs, identify and select evidence-based intervention components, and implement activities in afterschool programs. Priority should be given to programs located in high-risk neighborhoods and communities with elevated levels of risk and problem behavior.

3. Afterschool interventions should be implemented widely in high-risk neighborhoods. Priority should be placed on locating programs in local, state, or federally sponsored public housing communities.

Research Elements

Program evaluations and longitudinal studies of community-based afterschool programs have produced mixed results. On the one hand, investigations indicate that afterschool program participants show significant and positive changes in academic achievement and in school engagement (Durlak et al., 2010a; Harvard Family Research Project, 2003; Shernoff, 2010). These results are similar to the improvements in reading scores, school attendance, and standardized test scores among Bridge Project participants that are described in the previous chapter. In addition, evaluations have reported significant reductions or delays in the onset of antisocial conduct among afterschool participants when compared with other youth (e.g., Durlak & Weissberg, 2007).

Studies have also examined the characteristics of effective and ineffective afterschool programs (e.g., Gottfredson et al., 2007). Findings from these reviews provide important insights into intervention and program components that are associated with effectiveness. For example, the degree of structure in afterschool programs appears to be an important moderator of program effectiveness (Gottfredson et al., 2007). Highly structured programs that use evidence-based strategies have produced the most positive outcomes among children and youth who receive afterschool services. Conversely, loosely structured programs with little or no systematic educational intervention elements have often shown few or no positive effects (Dynarski et al., 2004; Osgood, Anderson, & Shaffer, 2005).

The inclusion of skills training curricula in afterschool programs is an important moderator of effectiveness. Theoretically based and manualized curricula designed to teach young people social, cognitive, and behavioral skills have been shown to be more effective than "homegrown" skills training interventions (Durlak & Weissberg, 2007). Finally, size of afterschool programs and staff composition are also associated with program success. Smaller programs and a higher percentage of male staff members are related to positive outcomes in several studies (Gottfredson et al., 2007).

Participation, measured by the frequency of attendance or amount of exposure to afterschool program activities, is positively related to prosocial behavior and academic performance in several investigations (Anthony et al., 2009; Lauer et al., 2006; Simpkins, Little, & Weiss, 2004). However, findings from at least two studies have yielded nonsignificant relationships between level of participation and selected outcomes. The mixed evidence regarding the relationship between program exposure suggests a need for additional research in this area (Roth, Malone, & Brooks-Gunn, 2010; Sheldon, Arbreton, Hopkins, & Grossman, 2010).

Recommendations. Limited research has been conducted to examine the characteristics of effective afterschool programs. In many cases, existing studies have suffered from biased sampling strategies and relatively weak research designs. These methodological deficits limit the integrity of findings and reduce the generalizability of program effects reported by investigators. To address these limitations:

1. Efficacy trials using randomized designs should be conducted to test the effects of afterschool programs on selected academic and behavioral outcomes.
2. The effects of intervention activities such as tutoring, homework help, skills training, and topical classes and groups (e.g., a support group for middle school girls or a job-training class for high school students) on academic performance and behavior should be tested separately and in combination using rigorously designed investigations.
3. Effective afterschool program models should be replicated, disseminated, and made available to community leaders, practitioners, and school district personnel.

SUMMARY

Community afterschool programs like the Denver Bridge Project provide important educational, interpersonal, and social support for children, youth, and parents. The Bridge Project is based on the IPEI, a theoretical model that integrates elements of risk and resilience, positive youth development, and interorganizational collaboration. The IPEI framework offers a practical way for practitioners, administrators, and researchers to plan, implement, and test the effects of afterschool interventions.

Programs like the Bridge Project are found in nearly every American town and city. What makes the Bridge Project unique? How has the program persevered in the context of constantly changing and limited resources? The Bridge Project—its staff, volunteers, and participants—is nothing if not resilient.

To sustain programming, the program has relied time and time again on the elements described in the IPEI model to guide critical decision making. As described throughout this book, these elements include a well-supported theoretical base, intervention activities that are informed by theory and empirical evidence, a commitment to program evaluation, and a strong inter-organizational collaboration model. In short, the Bridge Project program has survived financial difficulties, personnel turnover, and program relocations by embracing a commitment to rational program planning and a well-specified implementation process. We hope our experiences at the Bridge Project, and the process outlined in the IPEI model, give community leaders and practitioners the tools necessary to create, enhance, or sustain effective afterschool programs for children and youth. If so, the hard work and determination of countless individuals at the Denver Bridge Project will have been well worth the effort.

APPENDIX A
Study Procedures

A mixed-methodology approach was used at the Bridge Project to conduct: (1) a community study of the program's network members and staff, and (2) an investigation of program participants and program effects. Methods used in each investigation are described below.

THE COMMUNITY STUDY

A study of the Bridge Project and its relationship to the broader Denver community was conducted to examine the scope of services offered by the network of organizations in which the Bridge Project is embedded. The study aimed to identify and assess the mechanisms used by the program to coordinate and integrate its activities with the other organizations in its network. Bridge Project personnel were asked to reflect on their views of the effectiveness of this network.

Procedures and Methods

By definition, the unit of study in interorganizational research is the community: in this case, the community of organizations that includes the Bridge Project. In this context, we wanted to know more about the characteristics of this community network: its size, the mix of services and resources available, and the intensity of interaction between the members. This type of study shifts the focus from individual children and youth to the organizational level in order to understand the types of linkages that the Bridge Project has with its network partners and the degree to which staff believe this work is effective.

Sample

Sixteen Bridge Project staff members were providing services to children and families at the time of data collection; all personnel were interviewed for the study. Staff members included an executive director, three site directors, a development director, an operation and budget director, a volunteer coordinator, an education coordinator, two education specialists, a youth counselor, a cultural enrichment coordinator, a health care coordinator, a scout liaison, and two administrative assistants. Thus, Bridge Project staff members who participated in the interviews included four administrators, four program coordinators, and eight staff members. Eighty-eight percent ($N = 14$) of respondents were female. Staff members were comparatively young; the average age of respondents was 34 ($SD = 5.6$) years old. Respondents were employed an average of 3.8 years ($SD = 1.8$) at the time of data collection. Of the 16 employees, 50% ($N = 8$) had master's degrees (three with MAs, five with MSWs), 31% ($N = 5$) had a bachelor's degree, and 19% ($N = 3$) were high school graduates.

Measures

Data were collected using an interview schedule and questionnaire that assessed three aspects of interorganizational research: (1) network configuration, (2) coordination and integration, and (3) program effectiveness. To assess network configuration, Bridge Project staff members were asked to list the names of all organizations to which they make requests or have interactions and from which they receive requests or have interactions in the course of a month. These data provided the information needed to map the actual network in Denver that serves at-risk children and youth living in public housing. Coordination and integration were evaluated by asking staff members to estimate the percent of interorganizational interactions in which they rely on the coordination mechanisms of friendship, exchange, informal agreements, and formal agreements. Staff members were also asked to estimate the percentage of all their interorganizational relationships that can be characterized by mechanisms of sequential, reciprocal, and collective integration. Finally, program effectiveness was assessed using a method that focuses on measures of network performance rather than the performance of the Bridge Project per se. We define effectiveness as a perception among administrators and workers that their network is achieving what it was intended to achieve, that it works smoothly, and that its level of production meets community standards. This orientation is based on the premise that organizational performance is always relative to resources (Goodman & Pennings, 1977); that is, a staff can be doing the best job that is humanly possible, but without adequate resources its practice cannot attain what we call "best practice." Thus, the item we developed is perceptual and allows staff to compare the actual performance of their network with an idealized model that has all necessary resources for best practices. This item yields a performance "gap score" that reflects the difference between the current situation and the idealized standard if all necessary resources were available.

Protocols and questionnaires used in the community study are found in Appendix B.

Analysis Strategies

Data analysis was completed in three parts. First, responses concerning number and type of interactions and requests between Bridge Project staff and other organizations were used to construct a two-way matrix. The matrix was used to construct a facsimile of the interorganizational network of the Bridge Project. The resulting map yielded information regarding the size, shape, and functioning of the network as well as the number of core members and the intensity of their interactions with the program. Second, responses to quantitative items concerning the types of relationships between organizational members of the network were subjected to analysis of variance tests. This output provides information about the degree to which the Bridge Project staff as a whole uses different types of coordination and integration as methods of acquiring resources needed by the program. Finally, responses on the effectiveness item were subjected to "gap analysis"; that is, the responses to five items regarding actual performance were subtracted from the responses regarding best possible practice. The resulting 18 scores were then analyzed to determine whether the staff's position and role within the Bridge Project affected their perceptions of the program's overall effectiveness.

MIXED-METHOD STUDY OF BRIDGE PROJECT
PARTICIPANTS AND PROGRAMS

A. Focus Group and Qualitative Interview Procedures: Voices and Perspectives of Children, Youth, and Parents

Samples

Thirty child and youth participants and 10 parents completed qualitative interviews and focus groups during the 2009–2010 academic year. A random sample of 20 elementary and middle school students between Grades 3 and 8 was selected to complete semistructured interviews with members of the evaluation team. The sample averaged 12 years old and included 12 girls and 8 boys; 70% (N = 14) of the sample was Latino/a, 20% (N = 4) was African American, 5% (N = 1) was Asian American, and 5% (N = 1) was American Indian.

At least one parent of each child and youth in the randomly selected youth sample was then asked to complete interviews with the research team. Ten parents agreed to be interviewed in a one-to-one setting. Eight of the parents who completed interviews resided in one of the four Bridge Project public housing neighborhoods; two parents lived in nearby neighborhoods. Sixty percent ($N = 6$) of parents was Latina, 30% ($N = 3$) was African American, and 10% ($N = 1$) was Asian American.

A purposive sample of 10 technology team participants was selected to participate in two separate focus groups. As described in Chapter 4, technology team members are high school students who teach computing and other technology skills to younger children at the Bridge Project. Technology team students who attended the focus groups were between 14 and 18 years old; six girls and four boys participated in the groups. Forty percent ($N = 4$) of technology team participants was Latino/a, 30% ($N = 3$) was African American, and 30% ($N = 3$) was White. Finally, seven randomly selected scholarship students were interviewed individually by a research team member. Scholarship students are college students whose tuition is partially or fully paid by donations to the Bridge Project. Chapter 4 describes this program in detail. Two of the scholarship students were male, and five were female; 40% ($N = 3$) of students was Asian American, 30% ($N = 2$) was Latino/a, 15% ($N = 1$) was African American, and 15% ($N = 1$) was of Middle Eastern ethnic background. The average age of scholarship students was 20 years. Three of the participants were freshman in college, one was a sophomore, one was a junior, and two were seniors.

Measures

A semistructured interview was used to guide interviews with child and youth samples. Interview questions were developed to cover a scope of content that would allow for the theoretical constructs of risk and protection and the 5 C's to be evaluated. Content addressed: (1) neighborhood, school, and family context; (2) interpersonal relationships; and (3) intrapersonal or internal psychoemotional factors. After responding to questions asking for some demographic information, what school they were to attend in the fall, and how many siblings they had, participants were asked to describe what they liked or disliked in their neighborhoods and what kinds of challenges they faced in their communities. The participants were then asked to tell a story about how they managed to overcome a challenge in their lives and probed to describe what they do to maintain their physical, spiritual, and mental health. Participants next were asked to describe how they and other people manage to be healthy despite the challenges faced in their lives and neighborhoods. All participants also responded to questions that asked about their perceptions of both positive and negative experiences at the Bridge Project.

Focus group interviews with technology team members included additional questions about what they learned when they were younger that they were able to apply in their current work with Bridge Project elementary and middle school children. They were also asked to reflect on future aspirations. Scholarship students were asked additional questions relevant to their age and development. They were asked to talk about their role models and aspirations as children and how they changed as they became adults. Scholarship students were further queried about positive and negative choices that they made and the relationships in their lives that have been important supports for them. They were also asked questions about their academic pursuits as college students and goals for the future. Lastly, they were asked what advice they would give to young Bridge Project participants.

The parent interview protocol was slightly more prescribed than the youth interview. Similar to the youth interviews, the research team used a questionnaire that included questions about neighborhood context. Parents were also asked to reflect on their experiences with the Bridge Project, both positive and negative. Two of the 10 interviews were conducted through a translator because the parent interviewees were recent immigrants who did not speak English.

Protocols and questionnaires used in the qualitative interviews and focus groups are found in Appendix B.

Qualitative Analysis Strategies

All interviews were audio recorded and transcribed for analysis in ATLAS.ti (Scientific Software Development, 2009). Constant comparative methods were used in conjunction with content analysis. The first round of analysis employed a content analysis based on protocol coding (Saldana, 2009) in which a priori categories developed from the theories that inform the previously described IPEI model were applied to the data. In this regard, the frame for a priori categories was based on theories of risk and resilience (Jenson & Fraser, 2011) and positive youth development (PYD) (Lerner, Lerner, & Phelps, 2009). For example, risk and resilience theory signaled a search of the data for qualities and transactions of risk and protection within the context of Bridge Project interventions. PYD framed the search of the data for context qualities and transactions that promoted the 5 C's.

The second round of data analysis applied constant comparative strategies (Lincoln & Guba, 1985) to ensure that observations from the protocol coding remained grounded in the voices of the participants. In other words, the research team members met and reviewed the codes developed from the protocol coding to confirm their consistency with the verbatim quotations in the data. During this process codes were refined and added as the analysis progressed and the data from the different participant groups were analyzed. These steps resulted in a codebook that includes descriptions of the codes as well as specific parameters for applying them to the data. The final step in the constant comparison phase involved magnitude coding (Saldana, 2009), which allowed us to examine the presence of each theme within and across the participant groups. The magnitude of each code is reported in Chapter 6.

B.Survey and School District Data: Risk, Protection, Positive Youth Development, and Academic Performance

Samples

Bridge Project participants complete pretest and posttest interviews and standardized instruments each academic year. Each youth is assigned a unique identification number at the time of registration and is subsequently tracked for participation and exposure to each intervention component. Outcomes from constructs identified in the IPEI model form the basis for outcome evaluation efforts at the Bridge Project. Specific evaluation tasks focus on assessing baseline and posttest levels of risk and protection, the 5 C's of PYD (Lerner et al., 2009), and academic performance.

Participation in Bridge Project program components (e.g., tutoring, homework help, technology training, etc.) varies by age and by the individual and developmental needs of children and youth. Consequently, sample sizes pertaining to evaluation questions differ considerably by study purpose. Therefore, sample characteristics relevant to each reported evaluation outcome are reported in the results section of Chapter 6.

Measures

Self-report and official record indicators are used to assess risk and protective factors, the 5 C's of PYD, and academic performance at the Bridge Project.

1. Risk and Protection

Risk and protective factors associated with academic achievement and other child and adolescent behaviors are assessed annually using a self-report survey constructed by the research team. The Bridge Project Risk, Protection, and Antisocial Conduct Interview (Jenson & Anthony, 2003) was used to assess risk factors of antisocial behavior by peers, involvement in relational aggression, attitudes toward antisocial conduct, community disorganization, and perceived family management practices. Protective factors included school commitment, values and beliefs, family attachment, self-esteem, and perceived opportunities and rewards for prosocial involvement at school and in the family. Alpha reliabilities for the scales reported in Table 6.7 ranged from .74 to .92.

2. The 5 C's of PYD

We found no single instrument in the published literature that comprehensively evaluates the core constructs of PYD. These constructs are commonly referred to as the 5 C's of competence, confidence, connection, character, and caring/compassion (Lerner et al., 2009). To increase the overall efficiency of data collection and to better assess changes in PYD constructs over time, members of the Bridge Project team developed an instrument that measures each of the 5 C's specified in PYD and IPEI frameworks (Lopez & Jenson, 2011). The instrument, 5 C's of Positive Youth Development-Bridge Project (PYD-Bridge), yields a total score that is obtained by summing scores from the five individual PYD scales.

PYD-Bridge scale development. Items from several existing instruments were selected or adapted to develop PYD scales that measured each of the 5 C's. The PYD construct *competence* is a nine-item scale that asks participants to reflect on their ability to be successful in academic settings. *Connection* is measured using a nine-item scale that asks subjects to reflect on the quality of their relationships with adults. *Character* is a ten-item scale that examines how children and youth respond to antisocial influences and behavior. Several questions in this scale also assess participants' hope for the future. *Caring* and *compassion* is a seven-item scale that assesses subjects' ability to take the perspective of others and to feel empathy for peers. The Piers-Harris Self-Concept Scale (Piers & Herzberg, 2002), a 60-item survey used to assess young people's perceptions of self across domains of behavior, intellect, physical appearance, popularity, anxiety, and happiness/satisfaction, was used to measure the PYD construct of *confidence*.

Individual items used to construct the competence, connection, character, and caring and compassion scales are shown Table A.1. Additional item and scale properties for the Piers-Harris Self-Concept Scale are described in a later section.

The PYD-Bridge was first administered to 135 Bridge Project participants in fall, 2010. Item response theory (IRT) was used to analyze the scale (van der Linden & Hambleton, 1996). This step led to the removal of six inappropriate survey questions. Following removal of these items, IRT statistics demonstrated an adequate fit (infit = 1.04; zstd = .00). The person separation reliability, a measure analogous to Cronbach's alpha, was

Table A.1 ITEMS AND ITEM SOURCES FOR THE POSITIVE YOUTH
DEVELOPMENT CONSTRUCTS OF COMPETENCE, CONNECTION, CHARACTER,
AND CARING/COMPASSION: PYD-BRIDGE PROJECT SURVEY

PYD Construct and Items	Item Source
Competence	
I could get the best grades if I tried.	Morgan-Jinks Student Efficacy Scale[a]
I think assignments are easy.	Morgan-Jinks Student Efficacy Scale[a]
I am one of the best students.	Morgan-Jinks Student Efficacy Scale[a]
My teacher thinks I am smart.	Elementary School Success Profile[b]
I am good at reading.	Morgan-Jinks Student Efficacy Scale[a]
I am good at math.	Morgan-Jinks Student Efficacy Scale[a]
I am smart.	Morgan-Jinks Student Efficacy Scale[a]
I work hard in school.	Morgan-Jinks Student Efficacy Scale[a]
I get good grades.	Morgan-Jinks Student Efficacy Scale[a]
Connection	
Adults are nice to me.	Elementary School Success Profile[b]
There are adults available if I need to talk.	School Success Profile[c]
Adults tell me to do a good job.	Elementary School Success Profile[b]
Adults in my life know what is	Elementary School Success Profile[b]
important to me.	School Success Profile[c]
	Elementary School Success Profile[b]
I can ask adults for help.	School Success Profile[c]
I get along with my teacher.	Elementary School Success Profile[b]
	Elementary School Success Profile[b]
My teacher listens to me.	School Success Profile[c]
My teacher cares about my school work.	Elementary School Success Profile[b]
If I don't understand, my teacher will help me.	Elementary School Success Profile[b]
Character	
I fight with other kids.	Social Development Research Group[d]
I am mean to other kids.	Social Development Research Group[d]
I help other kids.	Bryant Empathy Scale[e]
I help adults.	Bryant Empathy Scale[e]
I follow the rules.	Elementary School Success Profile[b]
My friends follow the rules.	Social Development Research Group[d]
My friends listen to adults.	Social Development Research Group[d]
It is important to plan for the future.	Bridge Project staff
If I do not do well at something, I will try again.	Bridge Project staff
If I set a goal, I will complete it.	Bridge Project staff
Caring and Compassion	
If I am upset, my friends help me.	Elementary School Success Profile[b]
My friends listen to me.	School Success Profile[c]
My friends are happy for me.	School Success Profile[c]
My friends and I have fun together.	Elementary School Success Profile[b]
My friends are on my side.	School Success Profile[c]
I'm sad to see a kid with no one to play with.	Bryant Empathy Scale[e]
If a kid does not have something, I will share.	Bryant Empathy Scale[e]

[a]Jinks & Morgan, 1999.
[b]Bowen, 2006.
[c]Bowen & Richman, 2005.[d]Social Development Research Group (2011).[e]Bryant (1982).

.97. A subsequent residual analysis explained 59% of the variance and indicated the presence of a one-dimensional scale. The overall PYD-Bridge scale yielded a reliability of .92. Reliability coefficients for individual scales were .79 for competence, .84 for connection, .88 for character, and .88 for caring and compassion.

A second administration of the PYD-Bridge was conducted with 153 youth in spring, 2011. As shown in Table A.2, an exploratory factor analysis (EFA) using a principal component procedure yielded four unique factors that were consistent with the PYD constructs of competence, connection, character, and caring/compassion. Factor loadings of .50 or above were used to identify items relevant to the four factors representing each of the PYD constructs. This model explained 50% of the overall variance; correlations between PYD constructs ranged from .30 to .50 and were all statistically significant. As noted above, the fifth PYD construct—confidence—was measured with the Piers-Harris Self-Concept Scale (Piers & Herzberg, 2002).

Properties of the Piers-Harris Self-Concept Scale. An exploratory factor analysis of the Piers-Harris Self-Concept Scale revealed strong support for each of the instrument's subscales. Results of the factor analysis are shown in Table A.3. Factor loadings in bold text are those items reported in Piers & Herzberg (2002). To be consistent with the authors' published scales, several items cross-loaded in two domains. The alpha reliability for the overall score on the Piers-Harris was .89. Reliabilities for the six individual domains were .81 for anxiety, .67 for intellect, .76 for behavior, .72 for physical appearance, .71 for popularity, and .54 for happiness.

3. Academic Performance

The Developmental Reading Assessment (DRA) (Beaver, 2006; DRA, 2009), a standardized measure of reading abilities, was used to assess academic competence at pretest and posttest. The DRA evaluates accuracy, fluency, and comprehension through individual reading conferences in which students read selected texts with onsite educators. Colorado State Assessment Profile (CSAP) scores (Colorado State Department of Education, 2011), a statewide standardized achievement test, are obtained annually from Denver Public Schools. Official indicators reflecting academic grades and attendance are accessed through the school district database twice each academic year. Self-reported grades and measures of academic efficacy were also collected using the Morgan-Jinks Student Efficacy Scale (MJSES) (Jinks & Morgan, 1999).

Table A.2 EXPLORATORY FACTOR ANALYSIS OF 5 C'S OF PYD-BRIDGE SURVEY

Item	Factor 1 Competence	Factor 2 Connection	Factor 3 Character	Factor 4 Caring and Compassion
I could get the best grades if I tried.	.006	.150	−.005	**.670**
I think assignments are easy.	.312	−.143	.084	.303
I am one of the best students.	.205	.202	−.058	**.535**
My teacher thinks I am smart.	.085	.201	.082	**.748**
I am good at reading.	−.003	.067	.069	**.603**
I am good at math.	.449	−.058	−.031	.378
I am smart.	.166	.029	−.030	**.695**
I work hard in school.	.264	.272	−.083	**.536**
I get good grades.	−.033	.301	.234	**.614**
Adults are nice to me.	.094	**.641**	.033	.125
There are adults available if I need to talk.	.120	**.698**	−.096	.170
Adults tell me to do a good job.	.051	**.629**	.074	.109
Adults in my life know what is important to me.	.094	**.747**	.194	.160
I can ask adults for help.	.073	**.568**	.157	.039
I get along with my teacher.	.296	**.520**	.236	.278
My teacher listens to me.	.368	**.597**	.059	.081
My teacher cares about my schoolwork.	.217	**.613**	.134	.064
If I don't understand, my teacher will help me.	−.019	**.521**	.257	.245
I fight with other kids.	**.703**	−.038	.077	.060
I am mean to other kids.	**.724**	.075	.142	.045
I help other kids.	**.659**	.282	.283	.201
I help adults.	**.525**	.438	.098	.069
I follow the rules.	**.614**	.247	.239	.203
My friends follow the rules.	**.492**	.230	.367	.254
My friends listen to adults.	**.528**	.234	.306	.076
It is important to plan for the future.	**.518**	.298	.313	.047
If I do not do well at something, I will try again.	**.544**	.149	.296	.081
If I set a goal, I will complete it.	**.694**	.229	.210	.123

(continued)

Item	Factor 1 Competence	Factor 2 Connection	Factor 3 Character	Factor 4 Caring and Compassion
If I am upset, my friends help me.	.180	.206	**.772**	.048
My friends listen to me.	.232	.155	**.786**	.053
My friends are happy for me.	.148	.177	**.810**	−.029
My friends and I have fun together.	.386	.019	**.651**	−.089
My friends are on my side.	.227	−.052	**.812**	.157

Note. Four factors of PYD—competence, connection, character, and caring and compassion—are shown here. Factor loadings of .50 or above were used to identify items relevant to the four factors representing competence, connection, character, and caring and compassion. The fifth C, confidence, was assessed using the Piers-Harris Self-Concept Scale (Jinks & Morgan, 1999). *N* = 153.

Table A.3 EXPLORATORY FACTOR ANALYSIS OF THE PIERS-HARRIS SELF-CONCEPT SCALE

	Piers-Harris Scales					
	Anxiety	Intellect	Behavior	Physical	Popularity	Happiness
My classmates make fun of me.	**.516**	.138	.265	.060	.032	.262
I am a happy person.	.086	.094	.119	−.059	.056	**.588**
It is hard for me to make friends.	**.527**	.176	.247	.133	−.211	.154
I am often sad.	**.505**	−.047	.016	.065	.086	.294
I am smart.	.026	**.469**	.001	.221	.272	.031
I am shy.	**.361**	.046	−.071	**.393**	.100	−.076
I get nervous when the teacher calls on me.	**.497**	.066	−.100	.045	.233	−.180
My looks bother me.	**.463**	.190	.167	.073	.164	−.205
I am a leader in games and sports.	.132	.029	.086	**.381**	.117	−.407
I get worried when we have tests in school.	**.322**	.200	−.133	−.031	.250	−.332
I am unpopular.	**.538**	−.097	−.116	.254	.020	.090
I am well behaved in school.	−.152	**.339**	.183	−.210	−.011	.137
It is usually my fault when something goes wrong.	.189	**.578**	.040	−.097	.084	−.051

(continued)

Table A.3 (CONTINUED)

Piers-Harris Scales

	Anxiety	Intellect	Behavior	Physical	Popularity	Happiness
I cause trouble to my family.	.314	**.549**	−.070	.179	−.088	.036
I am strong.	.128	.137	.139	**.406**	−.058	−.345
I am an important member of my family.	.079	−.049	−.040	.001	.238	**.391**
I give up easily.	**.309**	**.371**	**.368**	−.021	−.004	.133
I am good in my schoolwork.	−.076	.319	.236	.013	**.643**	−.049
I do many bad things.	.167	**.364**	**.398**	−.033	−.052	.294
I behave badly at home.	.277	**.622**	.057	.177	−.023	−.186
I am slow in finishing my schoolwork.	.176	**.495**	−.098	.054	.254	−.117
I am an important member of my class.	−.138	.005	.051	.276	**.464**	.025
I am nervous.	**.497**	.085	−.119	.299	.214	−.169
I can give a good report in front of the class.	.066	−.035	.326	.207	**.438**	−.290
In school I am a dreamer.	.210	.042	.196	−.284	.035	.121
My friends like my ideas.	.181	−.073	**.563**	.094	.298	−.160
I often get into trouble.	.137	**.564**	.066	.083	.073	.108
I am lucky.	.092	−.015	.000	.223	.222	.115
I worry a lot.	**.638**	.119	.141	.193	−.106	−.143
My parents expect too much of me.	**.318**	.340	−.105	.062	−.063	.099
I like being the way I am.	.009	−.053	.150	.069	**.333**	.119
I feel left out of things.	**.549**	.262	.227	.060	−.090	−.129
I have nice hair.	.020	.277	.051	**.433**	.238	.178
I often volunteer in school.	−.087	−.118	**.487**	.210	.170	−.185
I wish I were different.	**.535**	.175	.242	−.205	−.044	−.043
I hate school.	.080	.107	**.406**	−.039	−.008	.085
I am among the last to be chosen for games and sports.	**.575**	.308	−.042	−.094	.033	.051
I am often mean to others.	−.122	**.426**	**.544**	−.089	−.121	−.023
My classmates think I have good ideas.	.149	.017	**.655**	.276	.250	−.237
I am unhappy.	**.455**	.397	.445	.153	−.103	.139
I have many friends.	.277	−.068	.417	.088	.126	.166

(continued)

Table A.3 (CONTINUED)

	Anxiety	Intellect	Behavior	Physical	Popularity	Happiness
I am cheerful.	−.215	.084	.152	**.392**	.288	.295
I am dumb about most things.	**.365**	**.346**	−.065	−.201	.260	.127
I am good looking.	−.092	.130	−.002	**.576**	.179	−.025

Piers-Harris Scales

	Anxiety	Intellect	Behavior	Physical	Popularity	Happiness
I get into a lot of fights.	.158	**.465**	.094	−.287	.033	−.005
I am popular with the boys.	.308	−.022	.070	**.504**	−.042	−.148
People pick on me.	**.527**	.106	.080	−.135	.105	.192
My family is disappointed in me.	.086	**.473**	.031	.095	.005	.112
I have a pleasant face.	−.018	.162	.254	**.518**	−.076	.163
When I grow up, I will be an important person.	−.014	.151	.028	**.218**	.044	.372
In games and sports, I watch instead of play.	**.501**	−.104	.197	.049	−.259	−.178
I forget what I learn.	.281	.142	.054	−.067	**.514**	−.021
I am easy to get along with.	.004	.142	**.466**	.097	.226	.226
I am popular with girls.	.040	−.028	.119	**.498**	.062	.030
I am a good reader.	−.056	.059	.035	.034	**.618**	.112
I am often afraid.	**.556**	.314	.017	.199	.137	−.125
I am different from other people.	**.338**	.045	−.003	−.091	−.066	.070
I think bad thoughts.	.289	**.346**	.209	−.016	.080	.131
I cry easily.	**.469**	.206	.174	−.158	.005	−.106
I am a good person.	−.109	**.531**	.183	.172	.006	−.140

Note. Factor loadings in bold text are consistent with items on the Piers-Harris Self-Concept Scale (Piers & Herzberg, 2002). $N = 99$.

Quantitative Analysis Strategies

A pretest–posttest design based on the academic school calendar (August to May) was used to assess changes in risk, protection, the 5 C's, and academic performance over time. Paired comparisons (*t*-tests) assessing levels of change between fall and spring were used as a primary analytic approach. Ordinary least squares regression was used to assess the relationship between program participation and selected IPEI outcomes.

Instruments Created for This Study

Community Study Questionnaire
Interview Protocol for Youth Participants
Interview Protocol for Parent Participants
Interview Protocol for Scholarship Students
The 5 C's of Positive Youth Development
Risk, Protection, and Antisocial Conduct Interview

BRIDGE PROJECT

Community Study Questionnaire

Questionnaire Completed by. _____

Job Title: _____

Bridge Location: _____

Phone Number: _____

E-mail address: _____

Years Employed at the Bridge Project: _____

Gender: _____ Male _____ Female

Age: _____

Highest academic degree earned: _____ Major Field of Study: _____

Thank you for agreeing to do this interview. I'd like to begin by asking you several questions about your role at the Bridge Project.

1. In your opinion, what is the goal(s) of the Bridge Project?
2. What is your part in helping the Bridge Project reach this/these goal(s)? Please describe your job at the Bridge Project.
3. In what part of your job are you most successful in helping Bridge Project participants? Why?
4. In what part of your job are you least successful in helping Bridge Project participants? Why?
5. What part of the Bridge Project is the most successful?
6. What are the biggest challenges facing the Bridge Project?

Agency staff members sometimes find that they can't provide all that their clients need from resources available within their organizations and they must then reach out to others. This next section asks about the work you perform on behalf of Bridge Project participants outside the program.

7. Do you ever interact with other organizations, agencies, or institutions in order to obtain resources needed by Bridge Project participants?
   Yes _____ No _____

8. If yes, please check all of the following resources that you access on behalf of Bridge Project participants in the course of your work.

Concrete Resources	Health Care
_____Food	_____Medical Preventive Care
_____Clothing	_____Medical Specialized Treatment
_____Financial Aid	_____Mental Health Care
_____Books/School Supplies	_____Dental
_____Sport Equipment	_____Ophthalmology/Eye Care
_____Hobby/Craft Supplies	_____Hearing
_____Toys, Puzzles, Games	_____Ears, Nose, and Throat
_____Transportation	_____Health/Wellness Education
_____Other	_____Other
_____Other	_____Other

Enrichment Resources	Educational Resources
_____Music	_____Technical Training
_____Art	_____Tutoring
_____Dance	_____Specialized Tutoring
_____Drama	_____Group Educational Experiences
_____Cultural Experiences	_____College Preparation
_____Other	_____Other
_____Other	_____Other

Consultative Resources	Family Resources
_____Consultation Time With Teachers	_____Food, Clothing, Housing
_____Consultation Time With Other	_____Financial Aid
Professionals	_____Medical/Health
_____Other	_____Employment
_____Other	_____Other

9. This section asks for the names of the organizations from which you seek resources for children and youth at the Bridge Project.

    a. Name of organization: _____

    b. Your principal contact: _____

    c. Approximately how many requests do you make to this organization in a month?

    d. What type of help or assistance do you request from this organization?

    e. Approximately how many requests does this organization make to you in a month?

    f. What type of help or assistance is requested by this organization?

10. What are the biggest challenges you face in accessing resources for Bridge Project children and youth?

* * * * * * * *

The next section asks how you obtain resources for participants from sources outside of the Bridge Project. For example, the **basis** upon which you can ask and can have some assurance your request will be fulfilled are as follows:

Friendship
You can ask someone outside Bridge to provide something to Bridge participants, and they will comply because you are friends.

Exchange
You can ask someone outside Bridge to provide something to Bridge participants, and they will comply because you provide something in return (tit for tat).

Informal Agreements
You can ask someone outside Bridge to provide something to Bridge participants because your respective organizations have a history of close working relationships.

Formal Agreements
You can ask someone outside Bridge to provide something to Bridge participants because Bridge has a formal agreement (a signed document) that stipulates certain areas of cooperation and exchange.

11. Please think about all of the times you have sought resources outside of the Bridge Project. Estimate below the percent of your requests that fall into each of these categories:

Friendship	_____	%
Exchange	_____	%
Informal Agreements	_____	%
Formal Agreements	_____	%
Total for all requests	100	%

This section asks you to describe the nature of the relationship that exists between the Bridge Project and the organizations you named in the last question. Please look at the diagrams you have been handed and decide, of *all* the organizations with which you work, what percentage of them can be characterized as based on these three types of relationships:

Sequential Relationships	_____	%
Reciprocal Relationships	_____	%
Collective Relationship	_____	%
Total	100	%

This last question has to do with the effectiveness of your work with all of the organizations you have named above. Because the Bridge Project cannot achieve all of its goals by itself, it relies on a network of organizations to provide resources. However, seldom are networks of organizations as effective as they can be in serving a group of clients. Usually forces beyond the control of workers prevent networks from being as effective as they could be, i.e., resource scarcity, inhibiting rules, etc.

This question is constructed to identify any **gaps** between how effective your network of organizations is in actual practice and how effective it could be (the best practice that is potentially possible).

12. Please indicate on the 6-point scale below the extent to which each of the following statements applies to the network of organizations that serve children and youth at the Bridge Project (1 = No agreement......6 = Very high agreement).

	In Actual Practice	Best Practice
Goals of the Bridge Project are achieved,	1 2 3 4 5 6	1 2 3 4 5 6
Bridge, working with its networks of organizations, can generate adequate resources.	1 2 3 4 5 6	1 2 3 4 5 6
The network works smoothly.	1 2 3 4 5 6	1 2 3 4 5 6
The network is productive.	1 2 3 4 5 6	1 2 3 4 5 6
The network is effective.	1 2 3 4 5 6	1 2 3 4 5 6
Overall, I am satisfied with the performance of this organizational network.	1 2 3 4 5 6	1 2 3 4 5 6

BRIDGE PROJECT

Interview Protocol for Youth Participants

Thank you for agreeing to complete this interview. In the next 30 to 45 minutes, I plan to ask you a number of questions about what it is like to live in your neighborhood. I will also be asking you about your experiences at the Bridge Project. I'm part of a research team from the University of Denver that is interested in finding the best ways to help children and families. Your honest answers to these questions will help us know how programs like the Bridge Project can best help young people and their parents.

I'd like to begin by asking a few questions about you.

- How old are you? What racial or ethnic group do you belong to?
- What grade will you be in when you go back to school this fall? What school do you plan to attend?
- Do you live with one or both of your parents?
- How many brothers and sisters do you have?
- Which neighborhood do you live in, and how long have you lived in your neighborhood?

Tell me what it is like to live in your neighborhood.[1]

- What are the good things about living in your neighborhood? What are the things you like the least?
- What kinds of things are most challenging for you growing up in your neighborhood?
- Can you share a story about how you have managed to overcome challenges you face personally, in your family, or outside your home in your school or community?
- What would I need to grow up well in your neighborhood?
- What does being healthy mean to you and others in your family and community?
- What do you and others do to keep healthy—mentally, physically, emotionally, and spiritually?
- How do you describe people who grow up well in your neighborhood despite the problems you face?
- What do you do when you face difficulties in your life?

Next, I'd like to ask you a few general questions about the Bridge Project.

- How long have you been coming to the Bridge Project? How did you first find out about it?
- What programs at Bridge do you participate in? How many days a week do you come to Bridge? What happens on the days when you don't get to come to Bridge?

---

[1] Neighborhood items adapted from Ungar & Liebenberg (2005).

- Do you have older or younger siblings that come to Bridge?
- Tell me what it's like to attend the Bridge Project. What do you like about it? What would change about it?
- Is there anything that you do or that happens at Bridge that helps you in school?
- How is the Bridge Project different than school?
- Do your parents ever come to the Bridge Project programs or events?

Now I'd like to talk to you about people who support you in your life.
- When you need someone to talk to, when you need help—who is there for you?
- When you think about growing up, who do you know that you would most want to be like?
- What about that person do you want to be like? What are you already doing that will help you be like that on when you grow up?

Also ask tech team youth:
- What did you learn when you were younger and at the Bridge Project that helps you work with the kids now?
- What have you learned from your family that helps you to work with children at the Bridge Project?
- Do your parents ever come to the Bridge Project programs or events?
- What did you want to be or do when you were 10 (or some age) and how is it different now? If different, what made you change your mind or ideas about this?

BRIDGE PROJECT

Interview Protocol for Parent Participants

Thank you for agreeing to complete this interview. In the next 45–60 minutes, I plan to ask you a number of questions about what it is like to live in your neighborhood and raise children here. I will also be asking you about your (and your child's) experiences at the Bridge Project. I'm part of a research team from the University of Denver that is interested in finding the best ways to help children and families. Your honest answers to these questions will help us determine how programs like the Bridge Project can best help young people and their parents.

I'd like to begin by asking a few questions about you.
- What racial or ethnic group do you belong to?
- How many children do you have?
- Who else lives in your home?
- Which neighborhood do you live in, and how long have you lived in this neighborhood?

Now I would like to ask some more specific questions about your experience in your neighborhood. Please respond to each of the following items by indicating the likelihood that the condition exists or the circumstance would happen in your neighborhood (interviewer: circle one).[2]

(1) If a group of neighborhood children were skipping school and hanging out on a street corner, how likely is it that your neighbors would do something like call the school or parents?	very likely	likely	unlikely	very unlikely
(2) If some children were spray-painting graffiti on a local building, how likely is it that your neighbors would do something about it?	very likely	likely	unlikely	very unlikely
(3) If a child was showing disrespect to an adult, how likely is it that people in your neighborhood would scold that child or tell the child's parents?	very likely	likely	unlikely	very unlikely
(4) How easy is it for you to pick out people who are outsiders or who obviously don't live in this area?	very easy	some- what easy	some- what difficult	very difficult

---

[2] Items 1–16: Anthony & Nicotera, 2008; Sampson, Raudenbush, & Earls, 1997; Seidman et al. 1995; Sheidow, Gorman-Smith, Tolan, & Henry, 2001.

For the next questions, please respond to each of the following by indicating whether you 1 = strongly disagree, 2 = disagree, 3 = neutral, 4 = agree, or 5 = strongly agree with the statement (interviewer: circle one).

People around here are willing to help their neighbors.	strongly disagree	disagree	neutral	agree	strongly agree
This is a close-knit neighborhood.	strongly disagree	disagree	neutral	agree	strongly agree
People in this neighborhood can be trusted.	strongly disagree	disagree	neutral	agree	strongly agree
People in this neighborhood generally don't get along with each other.	strongly disagree	disagree	neutral	agree	strongly agree
People in this neighborhood do not share the same values.	strongly disagree	disagree	neutral	agree	strongly agree
I can get the groceries I need in my neighborhood.	strongly disagree	disagree	neutral	agree	strongly agree
I can get health care services for myself and my children in or near my neighborhood.	strongly disagree	disagree	neutral	agree	strongly agree
I can find employment in or near my neighborhood.	strongly disagree	disagree	neutral	agree	strongly agree
Public transportation is available in walking distance of my home.	strongly disagree	disagree	neutral	agree	strongly agree
I can find financial (e.g., bank) and legal services in or near my neighborhood.	strongly disagree	disagree	neutral	agree	strongly agree
My children can get to and from school safely in my neighborhood.	strongly disagree	disagree	neutral	agree	strongly agree
My children can get a decent education in my neighborhood.	strongly disagree	disagree	neutral	agree	strongly agree

Now I would like to ask you about your experiences raising your children in your neighborhood and with the Bridge Project.

- How long have your children been coming to the Bridge Project?
- Do you participate in any activities at the Bridge Project (such as parenting groups, family fun nights, etc.)?

- How did you first find out about the Bridge Project?
- Please describe your experience living in this neighborhood. What is it like to live here? What is it like to raise children here?
- What/who in this neighborhood helps you in your efforts to raise healthy children? (If parent mentions Bridge, explore response in more detail—for example, what specifically about Bridge helps? Staff? Programs? What about what Bridge has to offer, etc.? Connections between school and other resources?)
- What/who in this neighborhood restricts or limits your efforts to raise healthy children?
- If Bridge is not mentioned in above questions, ask about the role of Bridge in their lives, specific to raising their children.
- What (programs, site computers, etc.) and who (staff, interns, other kids, mentors/tutors, other volunteers, etc.) at Bridge supports your efforts to raise their children to be healthy adults? How does this occur?

BRIDGE PROJECT

Interview Protocol for Scholarship Students

Thank you for agreeing to complete this interview. In the next 30 to 45 minutes, I plan to ask you a number of questions about what it is like to be a scholarship student at the Bridge Project. I will also be asking you to reflect on neighborhood experiences and to discuss ways in which the Bridge Proect has affected your life. I'm part of a research team from the University of Denver that is interested in finding the best ways to help children and families. Your honest answers to these questions will help us determine how programs like the Bridge Project can best help young people and their parents.

Age:

Grade:

Ethnicity:

1. How long did you go to the Bridge Project?
2. How did you first find out about it?
3. What programs at the Bridge Project did/do you participate in?
4. How many days a week did you come to the Bridge Project?
5. Do you have older or younger siblings who also attend/ed the Bridge?
6. Tell me what it was like to attend the Bridge Project. What did you like about it? What would you change about it? (Probe for the Bridge components.) What role did it have in your life?
7. Did the Bridge Project help you in school? In what ways?
8. Did your parents ever come to the Bridge Project programs or events?
9. What was it like growing up in your neighborhood? What were the best/worst things about it?
10. When you needed support during your school-age years, who was there for you? (Probe for the Bridge Project components, family members, peers, neighbors, others.)
11. When you were growing up, who were your role models?
12. What did you want to be when you grew up? How are things the same/different now? What made them change?
13. Do you remember choices you had to make when you were younger that helped you get where you are today? Were there times when you wanted to make a choice that would not have helped you get where you are today? Do you remember making any bad choices that you had to work through? How did you do it?

14. Of all the people you have relationships with, when things are falling apart, when nothing's going right, who is there for you? How does that help you? How does it help you get unstuck? Do those same people come to you for help?

15. If you were called upon to help someone younger than you, what relationships in your life help you know how to help that person?

16. What experiences do you draw on when someone comes to you for help?

17. When you do or accomplish something you are proud of or happy about, whom do you want to tell?

18. What do you think you might have learned about college/vocational school and learning after high school from being at the Bridge project (e.g., bridging social capital, exposure to professors, researchers, folks with college degrees)?

19. Can you list the top three things that helped you get through tough times? (Examples are family, school, friends, Bridge.)

20. Tell me what you are doing in school now. What are you studying? How did you decide to pursue the major you selected?

21. Looking back, how do you think the Bridge Project contributed to the things (your studies) you are doing today?

22. Looking back, what do you think has been the single most important thing that has contributed to your success as a college/university student?

23. What are your future goals (education, career, and personal)?

24. What do you see yourself doing in 5 years?

25. If you could tell today's young people at the Bridge Project one or two things to keep them on the right path, what would you tell them?

BRIDGE PROJECT

The 5 C's of Positive Youth Development

Name: _____   Bridge ID #:_____

Directions:_____

Mark (the big) No! (N) if you think the statement is **definitely** not true for you.
Mark (the little) no (n) if you think the statement is not true for you.
Mark (the little) yes (y) if you think the statement is true for you.
Mark (the big) YES! (Y) if you think the statement is **definitely** true for you.

Competence				
Question	NO! ☹	no 😖	yes 😊	YES! ☺
1. I could get the best grades if I tried.				
2. I think assignments are easy when others think they are hard.				
3. I am one of the best students in my class.				
4. My teacher thinks I am smart.				
5. I am good at reading.				
6. I am good at math.				
7. I am smart.				
8. I work hard in school.				
9. I get good grades when I try.				
Connection				
Question	NO! ☹	no 😖	yes 😊	YES! ☺
1. Adults are nice to me.				
2. If I need to talk, there are adults who listen to me.				
3. Adults tell me to do a good job.				
4. There are adults who know what is important to me.				
5. I can ask adults for help.				
6. My teacher and I get along well.				
7. My teacher listens to me.				
8. My teacher lets me know she cares about my work.				
9. If I don't understand something, my teacher helps me.				

Character				
Question	**NO!** ☹	**no** 😦	**yes** 🙂	**YES!** ☺
1. I fight with other kids.				
2. I am mean to other kids.				
3. I help other kids.				
4. I help adults.				
5. I follow the rules.				
6. My friends follow the rules.				
7. My friends listen to adults.				
8. It is important to plan for the future.				
9. If I do not do well at something, I will try again.				
10. If I set a goal, I will complete it.				
Caring & Compassion				
Question	**NO!** ☹	**no** 😦	**yes** 🙂	**YES!** ☺
1. If I am upset, friends help me.				
2. My friends listen to me.				
3. My friends are happy when something good happens to me.				
4. My friends and I have fun together.				
5. My friends are on my side.				
6. It makes me sad when I see a kid who does not have anyone to play with.				
7. If I notice that someone does not have something (like food or school supplies), I will share with them.				

Risk, Protection, and Antisocial Conduct Interview

Instructions:
- This is not a test. There are no right or wrong answers.
- All your answers are confidential. This means that your answers will only be seen by the research team and not read by anyone connected to the Bridge Project.
- I'll read each question out loud and give you time to decide which answer to give.
- Please answer each question as truthfully as you can.

Part I: Questions About You
The first section asks some general questions about you.

1. How old are you?

2. What is your birth date?

3. What grade are you in?

4. What best describes your racial/ethnic background?

    1 = Caucasian
    2 = Latino/Hispanic
    3 = African American
    4 = American Indian
    5 = Asian
    6 = Pacific Islander
    7 = Other (please specify)

5. What is the name of the school you currently attend?

6. a. Have you changed schools in the *past year*?

    1 = yes
    2 = no

    b. Have you changed teachers in the *past year*?

    1 = yes
    2 = no

7. How many times have you changed schools since *kindergarten*?
    _____ Indicate actual number of times

8. How often do you attend religious services or activities?

    1 = never
    2 = rarely
    3 = sometimes
    4 = often
    5 = almost always or always
    8 = don't know
    9 = refused

Part II: School Experiences

The next section is about your experiences at school.
Please answer BIG YES!, little yes, little no, or BIG NO! for the following statements and questions about the school that you currently attend.

	YES!	yes	no	NO!
9. In my school, students have lots of chances to help decide things like class activities and rules.	Y	y	n	N
10. Teachers ask me to work on special classroom projects.	Y	y	n	N
11. My teacher(s) notice when I am doing a good job and let me know about it.	Y	y	n	N
12. There are lots of chances for students in my school to get involved in sports, clubs, or other school activities outside of class.	Y	y	n	N
13. There are lots of chances for students in my school to talk with a teacher one on one.	Y	y	n	N
14. I feel safe at my school.	Y	y	n	N
15. The school lets my parents know when I have done something well.	Y	y	n	N
16. My teachers praise me (tell me I'm doing well) when I work hard in school.	Y	y	n	N
17. I have lots of chances to be part of class discussions or activities.	Y	y	n	N
18. Are your school grades better than the grades of most students in your class?	Y	y	n	N

19. Think back over the *past month* in school, how often did you....

	Almost always	Often	Sometimes	Rarely	Never
A. Enjoy being in school?	A	B	C	D	E
B. Hate being in school?	A	B	C	D	E
C. Try to do your best work in school?	A	B	C	D	E
D. Look forward to going to school?	A	B	C	D	E
E. Take part in sports, clubs, organizations, or other activities at school?	A	B	C	D	E

Part III. Your Family

The next questions ask about the family that you have lived with the most since you began kindergarten.

Please answer BIG YES!, little yes, little no, or BIG NO! to the following statements about this (your) family.

	YES!	yes	no	NO!
20. Do you feel very close to your mother?	Y	y	n	N
21. Do you share your thoughts and feelings with your mother?	Y	y	n	N
22. Do you enjoy spending time with your mother?	Y	y	n	N
23. Do you feel very close to your father?	Y	y	n	N
24. Do you share your thoughts and feelings with your father?	Y	y	n	N
25. Do you enjoy spending time with your father?	Y	y	n	N
26. My parents ask me what I think before most family decisions affecting me are made.	Y	y	n	N
27. If I had a personal problem, I could ask my mom or dad for help.	Y	y	n	N
28. My parents give me lots of chances to do fun things with them.	Y	y	n	N
29. My parents ask if I've gotten my homework done.	Y	y	n	N
30. My parents would know if I did not come home on time.	Y	y	n	N
31. The rules in my family are clear.	Y	y	n	N
32. When I am not at home, one of my parents knows where I am and who I am with.	Y	y	n	N
33. My parents want me to call if I'm going to be late getting home.	Y	y	n	N
34. My family has clear rules about alcohol and drug use.	Y	y	n	N

35. How often do your parents notice when you are doing a good job and let you know about it?
    1 = never or almost never
    2 = sometimes
    3 = often
    4 = all of the time

36. How often do your parents tell you they're proud of you for something you've done?
    1 = never or almost never
    2 = sometimes
    3 = often
    4 = all of the time

Part IV. Your Neighborhood
Please answer the following questions about the neighborhood and community where you live.

		YES!	yes	no	NO!
37.	How much does each of the following statements describe your neighborhood?				
	A. There is lots of graffiti.	Y	y	n	N
	B. There are fights.	Y	y	n	N
	C. There is crime and/or drug selling.	Y	y	n	N
38.	There are lots of adults in my neighborhood I could talk to about something important.	Y	y	n	N
39.	There are people in my neighborhood who are proud of me when I do something well.	Y	y	n	N
40.	There are people in my neighborhood who encourage me to do my best.	Y	y	n	N
41.	My neighbors notice when I am doing a good job and let me know about it.	Y	y	n	N
42.	In my neighborhood, kids can help decide which activities are provided or how they are run.	Y	y	n	N
43.	In my neighborhood, adults pay attention to what kids have to say.	Y	y	n	N

Part V. Your Friends and Experiences
For this next set of questions, think of your four best friends (the friends you feel closest to). These questions will ask about things that have happened in the past year.

44. In the *past year* (12 months), how many of your *best friends* have…	**None of my friends**	**1 of my friends**	**2 of my friends**	**3 of my friends**	**4 of my friends**
A. Tried to do well in school?	0	1	2	3	4
B. Been involved in sports, clubs, organizations, or other activities at school?	0	1	2	3	4
C. Been suspended from school?	0	1	2	3	4
D. Stolen something worth more than $5?	0	1	2	3	4
E. Been in trouble with the police?	0	1	2	3	4
F. Smoked cigarettes?	0	1	2	3	4

Now we'd like to ask you about some things that you may or may not have done.

45. Have you *ever*:	**No, never**	**Yes, but not in the last year**	**Yes, 1 or 2 times in the last year**	**Yes, 3 or more times in the last year**
A. Gotten back at another student by not letting them be in your group?	A	B	C	D
B. Told lies or started rumors about other students to make other kids not like them?	A	B	C	D
C. Been in trouble with your teachers for something you did at school?	A	B	C	D
D. Stolen something worth more than $5?	A	B	C	D

E.	Been suspended from school?	A	B	C	D
F.	Been in trouble with the police?	A	B	C	D
G.	Damaged or broken other people's property?	A	B	C	D

46. Have you been bullied recently (teased or called names; had rumors spread about you; been deliberately left out of things, threatened physically, or actually hurt)?

A. No

B. Yes, less than once a week

C. Yes, about once a week

D. Yes, most days

47. How many times have you done the following things?

	Never	I've done it, but not in the past year	Less than once a month	About once a month	2 or 3 times a month	Once a week or more
A. Done what feels good no matter what.	A	B	C	D	E	F
B. Done something dangerous because someone dared you to do it.	A	B	C	D	E	F
C. Done crazy things even if they are a little dangerous.	A	B	C	D	E	F

Think about the following statements and give the answer that is best for you.

	YES!	yes	no	NO!
48. I ignore rules that get in my way.	Y	y	n	N
49. It is all right to beat up people if they start the fight.	Y	y	n	N
50. It is important to be honest with your parents, even if they become upset or you get punished.	Y	y	n	N

51. I do the opposite of what people tell me, just to get them mad.	Y	y	n	N
52. I think it is okay to take something without asking if you can get away with it.	Y	y	n	N
53. I think sometimes it's okay to cheat at school.	Y	y	n	N
54. It's important to think before you act.	Y	y	n	N

Part VI. Your Feelings
Please indicate how true each of the following statements has been for you during the past 30 days.

55. In the *past 30 days* (1 month)...	True	Sometimes true	Not true
A. I felt miserable or unhappy.	A	B	C
B. I felt that there are a number of good things about me.	A	B	C
C. I didn't enjoy anything at all.	A	B	C
D. I was very restless (couldn't sit still or quiet).	A	B	C
E. I felt so tired I just sat around and did nothing.	A	B	C
F. I felt I was no good anymore.	A	B	C
G. I was able to do things as well as most people.	A	B	C
H. I cried a lot.	A	B	C
I. I found it hard to pay attention or focus.	A	B	C
J. I hated myself.	A	B	C
K. I was a bad person.	A	B	C
L. I took a positive attitude towards myself.	A	B	C
M. I felt lonely.	A	B	C
N. I thought nobody really loved me.	A	B	C
O. I generally felt satisfied with myself.	A	B	C
P. I thought I could never be as good as other kids.	A	B	C
Q. I did everything wrong.	A	B	C
R. I felt I am a person of worth, as good as others.	A	B	C

REFERENCES

Addams, J. (1912). *Twenty years at Hull-House, with autobiographical notes*. New York: MacMillan.

Agnew, R. (2001). Building on the foundation of general strain theory: Specifying the types of strain most likely to lead to crime and delinquency. *Journal of Research in Crime and Delinquency, 38,* 319–352.

Agranoff, R. (1991). Human services integration: Past and present challenges in public administration. *Public Administration Review, 6,* 212–225.

Agranoff, R., & Pattakos, A. (1979). *Dimensions of services integration: Service delivery, program linkages, policy, management, and organizational structure*. Washington, DC: Human Service Monograph Series Project Share, Government Printing Office.

Akers, R. L. (1977). *Deviant behavior: A social learning approach*. Belmont, MA: Wadsworth Press.

Alter, C. (2008). Building community partnerships and networks. In R. J. Patti (Ed.), *Handbook of human services management* (2nd ed., pp. 435–454). Thousand Oaks, CA: Sage Publications, Inc.

Alter, C. (2009). Creating community partnerships and networks. In R. Patti (Ed.), *Handbook of social welfare management* (2nd ed., pp. 203–302). Beverly Hills, CA: Sage.

Alter, C., & Hage, J. (1993). *Organizations working together*. Beverly Hills, CA: Sage.

Anderson-Butcher, D. (2004). Transforming schools in to 21st Century Community Learning Centers. *Children and Schools, 26,* 248–252.

Andrews, D. W., Soberman, L. H., & Dishion, T J. (1995). The Adolescent Transitions program for high-risk teens and their parents: Toward a school-based intervention. *Education and Treatment of Children, 18,* 478–498.

Annie E. Casey Foundation. (2011a). *Children in poverty 2009*. Retrieved on June 22, 2011 from *Kids Count* data center, http://www.aecf.org/MajorInitiatives/KIDSCOUNT.aspx

Annie E. Casey Foundation. (2011b). *Teen ages 16 to 19 not in school and not high school graduates 2009*. Retrieved on June 22, 2011 from *Kids Count* data center, http://datacenter.kidscount.org/data/acrossstates/Rankings.aspx?ind=73

Annie E. Casey Foundation. (2011c). Retrieved February 10, 2011 from http://www.aecf.org/MajorInitiatives.aspx

Anthony, E. J. (1987). Risk, vulnerability, and resistance. In E. J. Anthony & B. J. Choler (Eds.), *The invulnerable child* (pp. 3–48). New York: Guilford.

Anthony, E. K., Alter, C. F., & Jenson, J. M. (2009). Development of a risk and resilience-based out-of-school program for children and youth. *Social Work, 54,* 45–55.

Anthony, E., & Nicotera, N. (2008). Youth's perceptions of neighborhood hassles and resources: A mixed methods analysis. *Children and Youth Services Review, 30,* 1246–1255.

Anthony, E. K., & Stone, S. I. (2010). Individual and contextual correlates of adolescent health and well-being. *Families in Society, 91,* 225–233.

Argyris, C. (2002). Organizational learning and management information systems. *Accounting, Organizations and Society, 2,* 113–123.

Argyis, C., & and Schon, D. A. (1974). *Theory in practice.* San Francisco: Jossey-Bass.

Aspy, C. B., Oman, R. F., Vesely, S. K., McLeroy, K., Rodine, S., & Marshall, L. (2004). Adolescent violence: The protective effects of Youth Assets. *Journal of Counseling and Development, 82,* 269–277.

Atkins, L. A., Oman, R. F., & Vesely, S. K. (2002). Adolescent tobacco use: The protective effects of developmental assets. *American Journal of Health Promotion, 16,* 198–205.

Austin, M. J. (2004). *Changing welfare services: Case studies of local welfare reform programs.* New York: Haworth Press.

Austin, M. J., & Solomon, J. R. (2008). Managing the planning process. In R. J. Patti (Ed.), *Handbook of human services management* (2nd ed., pp. 321–338). Thousand Oaks, CA: Sage Publications, Inc.

Baltes, P. B. (1987). Theoretical propositions of life-span developmental psychology: On the dynamics between growth and decline. *Developmental Psychology, 23,* 611–626.

Baltes, P. B., Lindenberger, U., & Staudinger, U. M. (1998). Life-span theory in developmental psychology. In R. M. Lerner (Ed.) & W. Damon (Series Ed.), *Handbook of child psychology: Vol. 1. Theoretical models of human development* (5th ed., pp. 1029–1144). New York: Wiley.

Baltes, P. B., Staudinger, U. M., & Lindenberger, U. (1999). Lifespan psychology: Theory and application to intellectual functioning. In J. T. Spence, J. M. Darley, & D. J. Foss (Eds.), *Annual review of psychology* (Vol. 50, pp. 471–507). Palo Alto, CA: Annual Reviews.

Bandura, A. (1989). Human agency in social cognitive theory. *American Psychologist, 14,* 1175–1184.

Bangert-Drowns, R. L. (1988). The effects of school-based substance abuse education: A meta-analysis. *Journal of Drug Education, 18,* 243–264.

Barton, W. H. (2011). Juvenile justice policies and programs. In J. M. Jenson & M. W. Fraser (Eds.), *Social policies for children and families. A risk and resilience perspective* (pp. 306–352). Thousand Oaks, CA: Sage.

Beaver, J. M. (2006). *Teacher guide: Developmental reading assessment, grades K– 3* (2nd ed.). Parsippany, NJ: Pearson Education, Inc.

Beaver, J. M., & Carter, M. A. (2003). *Teacher guide: Developmental Reading Assessment, Grades 4–8* (2nd ed.). Parsippany, NJ: Pearson Education, Inc.

Beder, H. (1984). *Realizing the potential of interorganizational cooperation.* San Francisco: Jossey-Bass.

Belknap, J., & Holsinger, K. (2006). The gendered nature of risk factors for delinquency. *Feminist Criminology, 1,* 48–71.

Bender, K. A., Brisson, D., Jenson, J. M., Forrest-Bank, S. S., Lopez, A., & Yoder, J. (2011). Challenges and strategies for conducting program-based research in after-school settings. *Child and Adolescent Social Work Journal, 28,* 319–334.

Benson, J. (1975). The interorganizational network as a political economy. *Administrative Science Quarterly, 20,* 229–249.

Benson, P. L. (1997). *All kids are our kids: What communities must do to raise caring and responsible children and adolescents*. San Francisco: Jossey-Bass.

Benson, P. L. (2003). Developmental assets and asset-building community: Conceptual and empirical foundations. In R. M. Lerner & P. L. Benson (Eds.), *Developmental assets and asset-building communities: Implications for research, policy, and practice* (pp. 19–43). Norwell, MA: Kluwer.

Benson, P. L., Leffert, N., Scales, P. C., & Blyth, D. A. (1998). Beyond the "village" rhetoric: Creating healthy communities for children and adolescents. *Applied Developmental Science, 2*, 138–159.

Berleman, W. C. (1980). *Juvenile delinquency prevention experiments: A review and analysis*. Washington, DC: U.S. Department of Justice, Law Enforcement Assistance Administration, Office of Juvenile Justice and Delinquency Prevention.

Bernard, T. J. (1992). *The cycle of juvenile justice*. New York: Oxford University Press.

Biglan, A., Brennan, P. A., Foster, S. L., & Holden, H. D. (2004). *Helping adolescents at risk. Prevention of multiple problem behaviors*. New York: The Guilford Press.

Bodilly, S., & Beckett, M. K. (2005). *Making out of school time matter: Evidence for an action agenda*. Santa Monica, CA: RAND Corporation.

Borland, M., Hill, M., Laybourn, A., & Stafford, A. (2001). *Improving consultation with children and young people in relevant aspects of policy-making and legislation in Scotland*. Edinburgh, UK: The Scottish Parliament.

Botvin, G. J., & Griffin, K. W. (2003). Drug abuse curricula in schools. In Z. Sloboda & W. J. Bukoski (Eds.), *Handbook of drug abuse prevention: Theory, science, and practice* (pp. 45–69). New York: Kluwer Academic.

Bowen, N. K. (2006). Psychometric properties of the *Elementary School Success Profile* for children. *Social Work Research, 301*, 51–63.

Bowen, G. L., & Richman, J. M. (2005). *School Success Profile*. Chapel Hill, NC: Jordan Institute for Families, School of Social Work, University of North Carolina at Chapel Hill.

The Bridgespan Group. (2011). *Promise neighborhoods*. Retrieved on June 15, 2011 from http://www.bridgespan.org/promise-neighborhoods.aspx

Bronfenbrenner, U. (1979). *The ecology of human development: Experiments by nature and design*. Cambridge, MA: Harvard University Press.

Bronfenbrenner, U. (1986). Ecology of the family as a context to human development: Research perspectives. *Development Psychology, 22*, 723–742.

Bronfenbrenner, U., & Morris, P. A. (1998). The ecology of developmental process. In R. M. Lerner (Ed.) & W. Damon (Series Ed.), *Handbook of child psychology: Vol. 1. Theoretical models of human development* (5th ed., pp. 993–1028). New York: Wiley.

Bryant, B. K. (1982). An index of empathy for children and adolescents. *Child Development, 53*, 413–425.

Bryson, J. M. (1995). *Strategic planning for public and nonprofit organizations*. New York: Wiley.

Buckley, P., Barry, M., Schoales, V., Levy, S., & Montague, L. (2008). *Access to quality public schools in Denver. An analysis of where low-income students live in proximity to quality schools*. Denver, CO: The Piton Foundation.

Bursik, R. J. (1984). Urban dynamics and ecological studies of delinquency. *Social Forces, 63*, 393–413.

Butler, M., Kane, R. L., McAlpine, D., Kathol, R. G., Fu, S. S., Hagedorn, H., et al. (2008). *Integration of mental health/substance abuse and primary care* (Publication No. 09-E003). Rockville, MD: Agency for Healthcare Research and Quality.

Cairns, R. B. (1998). The making of developmental psychology. In R. M. Lerner (Ed.) & W. Damon (Series Ed.), *Handbook of child psychology: Vol 1. Theoretical models of human development* (5th ed., pp. 419–448). New York: Wiley.

Carlson, M., & Donohoe, M. (2003). *The executive director's survival guide: Thriving as a nonprofit leader*. San Francisco: Jossey-Bass.

Catalano, R. F. (2007). Prevention is a sound public and private investment. *Criminology and Public Policy, 6*, 377–398.

Catalano, R. F., Arthur, M. W., Hawkins, J. D., Berglund, L., & Olson, J. J. (1998). Comprehensive community and school based interventions to prevent antisocial behavior. In R. Loeber & D. P. Farrington (Eds.), *Serious and violent juvenile offenders: Risk factors and successful interventions* (pp. 248–283). Thousand Oaks, CA: Sage.

Catalano, R. F., Berglund, M. L., Ryan, J. A. M., Lonczak, H. S., & Hawkins, J. D. (1998). *Positive youth development in the United States: Research findings on evaluations of positive youth development programs*. Washington, DC: U.S. Department of Health and Human Services, Office of the Assistant Secretary for Planning and Evaluation and National Institute for Child Health and Human Development.

Catalano, R. F., Berglund, M. L., Ryan, J. A. M., Lonczak, H. S., & Hawkins, J. D. (2004). Positive youth development in the United States: Research findings on evaluations of positive youth development programs. *The Annals of the American Academy of Political and Social Science, 591*, 98–124.

Catalano, R. F., Gavin, L. E., & Markham, C. M. (2010). Future directions for Positive Youth Development as a strategy to promote adolescent sexual and reproductive health. *Journal of Adolescent Health, 46*, S92–S96.

Catalano, R. F., & Hawkins, J. D. (1996). The social development model: A theory of antisocial behavior. In J. D. Hawkins (Ed.), *Delinquency and crime: Current theories* (pp. 149–197). New York: Cambridge University Press.

Catalano, R. F., Hawkins, J. D., Berglund, M. L., Pollard, J. A., & Arthur, M. W. (2002). Prevention science and positive youth development: Competitive or cooperative frameworks? *Journal of Adolescent Health, 31*, 230–239.

Catalano, R. F., Loeber, R., & McKinney, K. (1999). School and community interventions to prevent serious and violent offending. *Juvenile Justice Bulletin* (October). Washington, DC: Office of Juvenile Justice and Delinquency Prevention.

Centers for Disease Control and Prevention. (2011). *The public health approach to violence prevention*. Retrieved on June 29, 2011 from http://www.cdc.gov/ncipc/dvp/PublicHealthApproachTo_ViolencePrevention.htm

Cicchetti, D., Rappaport, J., Sandler, L., & Weissberg, R. P. (Eds.). (2000). *The promotion of wellness in children and adolescents*. Washington, DC: Child Welfare League of America.

Cloward, R. A., & Ohlin, L. B. (1960). *Delinquency and opportunity*. New York: Free Press.

Coie, J. D., Watt, N. F., West, S. G., Hawkins, J. D., Asarnow, J. R., Markman, H. J., et al. (1993). The science of prevention: A conceptual framework and some directions for a national research program. *American Psychologist, 48*, 1013–1022.

Colorado State Department of Education. (2011). *Colorado State Assessment Profile Scores, 2010*. Denver, CO: Author.

Community Plan to Prevent and End Homelessness in Dane County. (2011). Retrieved on May 15, 2011 from http://www.cityofmadison.com/cdbg/docs/community_plan_to_end_homelessness_final.pdf

Contractor, F. J., & Lorange, P. (Eds.). (2002). *Cooperative strategies and alliances*. Amsterdam, Boston: Elsevier Science.

Creswell, J., & Plano Clark, V. (2011). *Designing and conducting mixed methods research.* Thousand Oaks, CA: Sage.

Damon, W. (2004). What is positive youth development? *The Annals of the American Academy, 591,* 13–24.

Das, T. K., & Teng, B. S. (2002). Social exchange theory of strategic alliances. In F. J. Contractor & P. Lorange (Eds.), *Cooperative strategies and alliances* (pp. 439–460). Amsterdam, Boston: Elsevier Science.

Denver Bridge Project. (2011). *The Denver Bridge Project.* Retrieved on March 31, 2011 from http://www.du.edu/bridgeproject/

Denver Piton Foundation. (1991). Improving public education in Denver. Retrieved on March 31, 2011 from http://www.piton.org/Documents/educationreport.pdf

Denver's Road Home. (2011). Retrieved on May 6, 2011 from http://www.denversroadhome.org/

Developmental Reading Assessment (DRA). (2009). *DRA 2 K-8 Technical manual* (2nd ed.). Upper Saddle River, NJ: Pearson Education.

Durlak, J. A., Mahoney, J. L., Bohnert, A. M., & Parente, M. E. (2010a). Developing and improving after-school programs to enhance youth's personal growth and adjustment: A special issue of AJCP. *American Journal of Community Psychology, 45,* 285–293.

Durlak, J. A., & Weissberg, R. P. (2007). *The impact of after-school programs that promote personal and social skills.* Chicago: Collaborative for Academic, Social, and Emotional Learning.

Durlak, J. A., Weissberg, R. P., & Pachan, M. (2010b). A meta-analysis of after-school programs that seek to promote personal and social skills in children and adolescents. *American Journal of Community Psychology, 45,* 294–309.

Dryfoos, J. D. (1991). *Adolescents at risk: Prevalence and prevention.* Oxford, UK: Oxford University Press.

Dubois, D. L., Holloway, B. E., Valentine, J. C., & Cooper, H. (2002). Effectiveness of mentoring programs for youth. A meta-analytical review. *Journal of Community Psychology, 30,* 157–197.

Dynarski, M., James-Birdumy, S., Moore, M., Rosenberg, L., Deke, J., & Mansfield, W. (2004). *When schools stay open late: The national evaluation of the 21st Century Community Learning Centers Program.* U.S. Department of Education, National Center for Education Evaluation and Regional Assistance. Washington, DC: U.S. Government Printing Office.

Edwards, O. W., Mumford, V. E., & Serra-Roldan, R. (2007). A positive youth development model for students considered at-risk. *School Psychology International, 28,* 29–45.

Ehrenberg, R. G., & Smith, R. S. (2011). *Modern labor economics: Theory and public policy* (11th ed.). Upper Saddle River, NJ: Prentice Hall.

Elliott, D. S., Huizinga, D., & Menard, S. W. (1989). *Multiple problem youth: Delinquency, substance use, and mental health problems.* New York: Springer-Verlag.

Elliott, D. S., Wilson, W. J., Huizinga, D., Sampson, R. J., Elliott, A., & Rankin, B. (1996). The effects of neighborhood disadvantage on adolescent development. *Journal of Research in Crime and Delinquency, 33,* 389–426.

Empey, L. T., Stafford, M. C., & Hay, C. H. (1999). *American delinquency: Its meaning and construction* (4th ed.). Belmont, MA: Wadsworth Publishing.

Farah, M. J., Noble, K. G., & Hurt, H. (2006). Poverty, privilege, and brain development: Empirical findings and ethical implications. In Judith Iles (Ed.), *Neuroethics: Defining the issues in theory, practice and policy* (pp. 45–87). New York: Oxford University Press.

Farber, B. A., & Azar, S. T. (1999). Blaming the helpers: The marginalization of teachers and parents of the urban poor. *American Journal of Orthopsychology, 69,* 515–528.

Festinger, T. (1984). *No one ever asked us: A postscript to the foster care system.* New York: Columbia University Press.

Fine, M., Burns, A., Payne, Y., & Torre, M. (2004). Civics lessons: The color and class of betrayal. *Teachers College Record, 106,* 2193–2223.

Foxcroft, D. R., Ireland, D., Lister-Sharp, D. J., Lowe, G., & Breen, R. (2003). Longer term primary prevention for alcohol misuse in young people: A systematic review. *Addiction, 98,* 397–411.

Fraser, M. W., Kirby, L. D., & Smokowski, P. R. (2004). Risk and resilience in childhood. In M. W. Fraser (Ed.), *Risk and resilience in childhood: An ecological perspective* (2nd ed., pp. 13–66). Washington, DC: NASW Press.

Fraser, M. W., Richman, J. M., & Galinsky, M. J. (1999). Risk, protection, and resilience: Towards a conceptual framework for social work practice. *Social Work Research, 23,* 131–144.

Fraser, M. W., Richman, J. M., Galinsky, M. J., & Day, S. H. (2009). *Intervention research. Developing social programs.* New York: Oxford University Press.

Freud, A. M. (1969). Adolescence as a developmental disturbance. In G. Caplan & S. Lebovici (Eds.), *Adolescence* (pp. 5–10). New York: Basic Books.

Frey, A. J., Walker, H. M., & Perry, A. R. (2011). Education policy for children, youth, and families. In J. M. Jenson & M. W. Fraser (Eds.), *Social policy for children and families: A risk and resilience perspective* (2nd ed, pp. 113–145). Thousand Oaks, CA: Sage Publications.

Gambrill, E. (2007). Transparency as the route to evidence-informed professional education. *Research on Social Work Practice, 17,* 553–560.

Garmezy, N. (1985). Vulnerability research and the issue of primary prevention. *American Journal of Orthopsychiatry, 41,* 101–116.

Germain, C. B. (1991). *Human behavior in the social environment: An ecological view.* New York: Columbia University Press.

Gilbody, S., Fletcher, J., & Richards, D. (2006). Collaborative care for depression: A cumulative meta-analysis and review of longer-term outcomes. *Archive of Internal Medicine, 166,* 2314–2321.

Glisson, C. (2009). Organizational climate and culture and performance in the human services. In R. J. Patti (Ed.), *Handbook of human services management* (2nd ed., pp. 119–142). Thousand Oaks, CA: Sage Publications, Inc.

Goodman, P. S., & Pennings, J. M. (1977). *New Perspectives on Organizational Effectiveness.* San Francisco: Jossey-Bass.

Gottfredson, D. C., Cross, A., & Soule, D. A. (2007). Distinguishing characteristics of effective and ineffective after-school programs to prevent delinquency and victimization. *Criminology and Public Policy, 6,* 289–318.

Gottfredson, D. C., Gerstenblith, S. A., Soule, D. A., Womer, S. C., & Lu, S. (2004). Do after-school programs reduce delinquency? *Prevention Science, 5,* 253–266.

Gottfredson, D. C., & Wilson, D. B. (2003). Characteristics of effective school-based substance abuse prevention. *Prevention Science, 4,* 27–38.

Gould, S. J. (1996). *The mismeasure of man.* New York: W.W. Norton and Company.

Greenberg, G., & Rosenheck, R. (2010). An evaluation of an initiative to improve coordination and service delivery of homeless services networks. *Journal of Behavioral Health Services & Research, 37,* 184–196.

Grinnell, R. M., Gabor, P. A., & Unrau, Y. A. (2009). *Program evaluation for social workers: Foundations of evidence-based programs* (5th ed.). New York: Oxford University Press.

Grunwald, H. E., Lockwood, B., Harris, P. W., & Mennis, J. (2010). Influences of neighborhood context, individual history, and parenting behavior on recidivism among juvenile offenders. *Journal of Youth and Adolescence, 39,* 1067–1079.

Gulati, R. (2007). *Managing network resources: Alliances, affiliations, and other relational assets.* New York: Oxford University Press.

Hahn, R., Fuqua-Whitley, D., Wethington, H., Lowy, J., Crosby, A., Fullilove, M., et al. (2007). Effectiveness of universal school-based programs to prevent violent and aggressive behavior. *American Journal Preventive Medicine, 33,* S114–S129.

Hallinan, M. T. (2008). Teacher influences on students' attachment to school. *Sociology of Education, 81,* 271–283.

Hansen, W. B., Malotte, C. K., & Fileding, J. E. (1988). Evaluation of a tobacco and alcohol abuse prevention curriculum for adolescents. Special Issue: The role of the schools in implementing the nation's health objectives for the 1990's. *Health Education Quarterly, 15,* 93–114.

Hage, J. (2005). *Communication and organizational control: Cybernetics in health and welfare organizations.* New York: John Wiley.

Hart, R. (2002). *Children's participation: The theory and practice of involving young citizens in community development and environmental care.* London: Earthscan.

Hart, B., & Risley, T. R. (1995). *Meaningful differences in the everyday experience of young American children.* Baltimore: P. H. Brookes.

Harvard Family Research Project. (2003). *A review of out-of-school time program quasi-experimental and experimental evaluation results.* Cambridge, MA: Harvard Family Research Project.

Hawkins, J. D. (2006). Science, social work, prevention: Finding the intersection. *Social Work Research, 30,* 137–152.

Hawkins, J. D., Catalano, R. F., & Arthur, M. W. (2002). Promoting science-based prevention in communities. *Addictive Behaviors, 27,* 951–976.

Hawkins, J. D., Catalano, R. F., Arthur, M. W., & Egan, E. (2008). Testing Communities that Care: The rationale, design and behavioral baseline equivalence of the Community Youth Development Study. *Prevention Science, 9,* 178–190.

Hawkins, J. D., Catalano, R. F., Kosterman, R., Abbott, R., & Hill, K. G. (1999). Preventing adolescent health-risk behaviors by strengthening protection during childhood. *Archives of Pediatrics and Adolescent Medicine, 153,* 226–234.

Hawkins, J. D., Catalano, R. F., & Miller, J. Y. (1992). Risk and protective factors for alcohol and other drug problems in adolescence and early adulthood: Implications for substance abuse prevention. *Psychological Bulletin, 112,* 64–105.

Hawkins, J. D., Herrenkohl, T., Farrington, D. P., Brewer, D. D., Catalano, R. F., & Harachi, T. W. (1998). A review of predictors of youth violence. In R. Loeber & D. P. Farrington (Eds.), *Serious and violent juvenile offenders: Risk factors and successful interventions* (pp. 106–146). Thousand Oaks, CA: Sage.

Hawkins, J. D., Jenson, J. M., Catalano, R. F., & Lishner, D. L. (1988). Delinquency and drug abuse: Implications for social services. *Social Service Review, 62,* 258–284.

Hawkins, J. D., Oesterle, S., Brown, E. C., & Arthur, M. W. (2009). Results of a type 2 translational research trial to prevent adolescent drug use and delinquency: A test of Communities that Care. *Archives of Pediatrics and Adolescent Medicine, 163,* 789–798.

Herrera, C., Grossman, J. B., Kauh, T. J., Feldman, A. F., McMaken, J., & Jucovy, L. J. (2007). *Making a difference in schools: The Big Brothers Big Sisters School-Based Mentoring Impact Study.* Philadelphia: Public/Private Ventures.

Hill, M. (2006). Children's voices on ways of having a voice: Children's and young people's perspectives on methods used in research and consultation. *Childhood, 1,* 69–89.

Hirschi, T. (1969). *Causes of delinquency*. Berkeley, CA: University of California Press.

Hoffman, H. L., Castro-Dolan, C. A., Johnson, V. M., & Church, D. R. (2004). The Massachusetts HIV, hepatitis and addiction services integration (HHASI) experience: Responding to the community needs of individuals with co-occurring risks and conditions. *Public Health Reports, 119*, 25–31.

Hogg Foundation. (2006). Retrieved on May 5, 2011 from http://www.hogg.utexas.edu/detail/18/ihc_grantees_selected.html

Holleman, M. A., Sundis, M. J., & Bruns, E. J. (2010). Building opportunity: Developing city systems to expand and improve after school programs. *American Journal of Community Psychology, 45*, 405–416.

Hood, D., & Cassaro, D. (2002). Feminist evaluation and the inclusion of difference. *New Directions for Evaluation, 96*, 27–40.

Howard, M. O., Allen-Meares, P., & Ruffolo, M. C. (2007). Teaching evidence-based practice: Strategic and pedagogical recommendations for schools of social work. *Research on Social Work Practice, 17*, 561–568.

Hudson, B. (1987). Collaboration in social welfare: A framework for analysis. *Policy and Politics, 15*, 175–182.

Israel, B., Schulz, A., & Becker, A. (1998). Review of community-based research: Assessing partnership approaches to improving public health. *Annual Review of Public Health, 19*, 173–202.

Jencks, C., & Phillips, M. (1998). *The black-white test score gap*. Washington, DC: Brookings Institution Press.

Jenson, J. M. (2005). Connecting science to intervention: Advances, challenges, and the promise of evidence-based practice. *Social Work Research, 29*, 131–135.

Jenson, J. M. (2006). Advances and challenges in preventing childhood and adolescent problem behavior. *Social Work Research, 30*, 131–134.

Jenson, J. M. (2010). Advances in preventing childhood and adolescent problem behavior. *Research on Social Work Practice, 20*, 701–713.

Jenson, J. M., & Anthony, E. K. (2003). *Risk, Protection, and Antisocial Conduct Inventory*. Denver, CO: Graduate School of Social Work, University of Denver.

Jenson, J. M., & Dieterich, W.A. (2007). Effects of a skills-based prevention program on bullying and bully victimization among elementary school children. *Prevention Science, 8*, 285–296.

Jenson, J. M., & Fraser, M. W. (Eds.). (2011). *Social policy for children and families: A risk and resilience perspective* (2nd ed.). Thousand Oaks, CA: Sage Publications, Inc.

Jenson, J. M., & Howard, M. O. (1998). Youth crime, public policy, and practice in the juvenile justice system: Recent trends and needed reforms. *Social Work, 43*, 324–334.

Jenson, J. M., & Howard, M. O. (1999). *Youth violence. Current research and recent practice innovations*. Washington, DC: NASW Press.

Jenson, J. M., & Howard, M. O. (2001). Causes and prevention of youth violence. *Denver University Law Review, 77*, 629–660.

Jenson, J. M., & Lopez, A. (2010). *Bridge Project annual report, 2009–2010*. Denver, CO: Graduate School of Social Work, University of Denver.

Jenson, J. M., Powell, A., & Forrest-Bank, S. S. (2011). Effective violence prevention approaches in school, family, and community settings. In T. I. Herrenkohl, E. Aisenberg, J. H. Williams, & J. M. Jenson (Eds.), *Violence in context: Current evidence on risk, protection, and resilience* (pp. 130–167). New York: Oxford University Press.

Jinks, J., & Morgan, V. L. (1996). Students' sense of academic efficacy and achievement in science: A useful direction for research regarding scientific literacy? *Electronic Journal of Science Education, 1*, 2–8.

Jinks, J., & Morgan, V. (1999). Children's perceived academic self-efficacy: An inventory scale. *The Clearing House, 72,* 224–230.

Kelly, M. S., Raines, J. C., Stone, S., & Frey, A. (2010). *School social work: An evidence-informed framework for practice.* New York: Oxford University Press.

Kibel, B. (1999). *Success stories as hard data: An introduction to results mapping.* New York: Pluwer Academic/Plenum Publishers.

King, P. E., Dowling, E. M., Mueller, R. A., White, K., Schultz, W., Osborn, P., et al. (2005). Thriving in adolescence: The voices of youth-serving practitioners, parents, and early and late adolescents. *The Journal of Early Adolescence, 25,* 94–112.

Kirst-Ashman, K. K., & Hull, G. H. (2009). *Understanding generalist practice.* Belmont, CA: Brooks/Cole.

Klofas, J., & Duffee, D. (1981). The change grid and the active client. *Criminal Justice and Behavior, 8,* 95–118.

Knight, G. P., Roosa, M. W., & Umana-Taylor, A. J. (2009). Studying ethnic minority and economically disadvantaged populations: Methodological challenges and best practices. Washington, DC: American Psychological Association.

Krisberg, B., & Austin, J. F. (1993). *Reinventing juvenile justice.* Thousand Oaks, CA: Sage.

Kuperminc, G. P., Emshoff, J. G., Reiner, M. M., Secrest, L. A., Niolon, P. H., & Foster, J. D. (2005). Integration of mentoring with other programs and services. In D. L. Dubois & M. J. Karcher (Eds.), *Handbook of youth mentoring* (pp. 314–334). Thousand Oaks, CA: Sage Publications.

Kusserow, R. (1991). *Services integration: A twenty-year retrospective* (Publication No. OEI-01-00580). Washington, DC: U.S. Department of Health and Human Services, Office of Inspector General.

Lareau, A. (2003). *Unequal childhoods: Class, race, and family life.* Berkeley, CA: University of California Press.

Larson, R. W., & Walker, K. C. (2010). Dilemmas of practice: Challenges to quality encountered by youth program leaders. *American Journal of Community Psychology, 45,* 338–349.

Lattimore, P., and Visher, C. (2009). *The multi-site evaluation of SVORI: Summary & synthesis.* Newark, DE: The Urban Institute and RTI International. Retrieved on May 22, 2011 from http://www.urban.org/uploadedpdf/412075_evaluation_svori.pdf

Lauer, P. A., Akiba, M., Wilkerson, S. B., Apthorp, H. S., Snow, D., & Martin-Green, M. (2006). Out-of-school time programs: A meta-analysis of effects for at-risk students. *Review of Educational Research, 76,* 275–313.

Lefton, M., & Rosengren, W. (1968). Organizations and clients: Lateral and longitudinal dimensions. *American Sociological Review, 31,* 802–810.

Lerner, R. M. (1998). Theories of human development: Contemporary perspectives. In R. M. Lerner (Ed.). *Handbook of child psychology: Vol. 1. Theoretical models of human development* (5th ed., pp. 1–24). New York: Wiley.

Lerner, R. M. (2005, September). *Promoting positive youth development: Theoretical and empirical bases.* White paper prepared for Workshop on the Science of Adolescent Health and Development, National Research Council/Institute of Medicine, Washington, DC. Washington, DC: National Academy of Sciences.

Lerner, R. M., Almerigi, J. B., Theokas, C., & Lerner, J. V. (2005). Positive youth development: A view of the issues. *The Journal of Early Adolescence, 25,* 10–16.

Lerner, R. M., Dowling, E. M., & Anderson, P. M. (2003). Positive youth development: Thriving as the basis of personhood and civil society. *Applied Developmental Science, 7,* 172–180.

Lerner, R. M., Fisher, C. B., & Weinberg, R. A. (2000). Toward a science for and of the people: Promoting civil society through the application of developmental science. *Child Development, 71,* 11–20.

Lerner, R. M., Lerner, J. V., & Phelps, E. (2009). *Waves of the future: The first five years of the 4-H study of positive youth development.* Medford, MA: Tufts University, Institute for Applied Research in Youth Development.

Limbos, M. A., Chan, L. S., Warf, C., Schneir, A., Iverson, E., Shekelle, P., et al. (2007). Effectiveness of interventions to prevent youth violence. A systematic review. *American Journal of Preventive Medicine, 33,* 65–74.

Lincoln, Y., & Guba, E. (1985). *Naturalistic inquiry.* London: Sage.

Loeber, R., & Farrington, D. P. (Eds.). (1998). *Serious and violent juvenile offenders: Risk factors and successful interventions.* Thousand Oaks, CA: Sage.

Loeber, R., Farrington, D. P., Stouthamer-Loeber, M., & Van Kammen, W. B. (1998). *Antisocial behavior and mental health problems.* Mahwah, NJ: Lawrence Erlbaum.

Longoria, R. A. (2005). *Is inter-organizational collaboration always a good thing?* Retrieved on May 15, 2011 from http://www.thefreelibrary.com/

Lopez, A., & Jenson, J. M. (2011). *The 5 C's of Positive Youth Development: An evaluation tool.* Denver, CO: Graduate School of Social Work, University of Denver.

Lopez, A., & Yoder, J. (2011). *Parent involvement in their children's education: A qualitative study.* Denver, CO: Graduate School of Social Work, University of Denver.

Luthar, S. S. (2003). *Resilience and vulnerability: Adaptation in the context of childhood adversities.* Cambridge, UK: Cambridge University Press.

Maierhofer, N., Kabanoff, B., & Griffen, M. (2002). The influence of values in organizations: Linking values and outcomes at multiple levels of analysis. In C. Cooper & I. Robertson (Eds.), *International review of industrial and organizational psychology* (Vol. 17, pp. 163–217). New York; Chichester, UK: Wiley.

March, J. G., & Simon, H. A. (1958). *Organizations.* New York: John Wiley.

Marlatt, G. A., & Gordon, J. R. (Eds.). (1985). *Relapse prevention strategies in the treatment of addictive behaviors.* New York: Guilford Press.

Masten, A. S. (2001). Ordinary magic: Resilience processes in development. *American Psychologist, 56,* 227–238.

Masten, A. S., & Powell, J. L. (2003). A resiliency framework for research, policy and practice. In S. Luthar (Ed.), *Resiliency and vulnerability: Adaptation in the context of childhood adversity* (pp. 1–29). Cambridge, UK: Cambridge University Press.

Mathiessen, T. (1971). *Across the boundaries of organizations.* Berkeley, CA: Flendessary Press.

Matsueda, R. L. (1982). Testing control theory and differential association: A causal modeling approach. *American Sociological Review, 47,* 489–504.

Mayer, S. E. (1997). *What money can't buy: Family income and children's life chances.* Cambridge, MA: Harvard University Press.

Merton, R. K. (1957). *Social theory and social structure.* New York: Free Press.

Moffitt, T. E. (1997). Adolescent-limited and life-course persistent offending: A complementary pair of developmental theories. In T. P. Thornberry (Ed.), *Developmental theories of crime and delinquency: Advances in criminological theory* (pp. 11–54). Piscataway, NJ: Transaction Publishers.

National 4-H Youth Development Organization (2010). About 4-H. Retrieved January 13, 2011 from www.4-h.org/about

Nicotera, N. (2007). Measuring neighborhood: A conundrum for human services researchers and practitioners. *American Journal of Community Psychology, 40,* 26–51.

Nicotera, N. (2008). Building skills for civic engagement: Children as agents of neighborhood change. *Journal of Community Practice, 16*, 221–242.

Nicotera, N. (2011). *Life in public housing neighborhoods: Views of young people.* Unpublished manuscript, Graduate School of Social Work, University of Denver. Denver, CO.

Nicotera, N., Altschul, I., Munoz, A., & Webman, B. (2010). Conceptual and analytic development of a civic engagement scale for pre-adolescents. In J. Keshen, B. Moely, & B. Holland (Eds.), *Advances in Service-Learning Research, Vol. 10: Research for what? Making engaged scholarship matter* (pp. 71–89). Charlotte, NC: Information Age Publishing.

Nicotera, N., & Matera, D. (2010, January). *Building civic leadership through neighborhood-based afterschool programming.* Paper presented at the Society for Social Work and Research Conference, San Francisco.

Olsson, C. A., Bond, L., Burns, J. M., Vella-Brodrick, D. A., & Sawyer, S. M. (2003). Adolescent resilience: A concept analysis. *Journal of Adolescence, 26*, 1–11.

Osgood, D. W., Anderson, A. L., & Shaffer, J. N. (2005). Unstructured leisure in the after-school hours. In J. L. Mahoney, R. W. Larson, & J. S. Eccles (Eds.), *Organized activities as contexts of development: Extracurricular activities, after-school, and community programs.* Mahwah, NJ: Lawrence Erlbaum.

Ouwens, M., Wollersheim, H., Hermens, R., Hulscher, M., & Grol, R. (2005). Integrated care programmes for chronically ill patients: A review of systematic reviews. *International Journal for Quality in Health Care, 17*, 141–146.

Packard, T. (2008). Leadership and performance in human services organizations. In R. J. Patti (Ed.), *Handbook of human services management* (2nd ed., pp. 143–164). Thousand Oaks, CA: Sage Publications, Inc.

Padgett, D. K. (2008). *Qualitative methods in social work research* (2nd ed.). Los Angeles: Sage.

Park, S. H. (1996). Managing an interagency network: A framework of the institutional mechanism for network control. *Organizational Studies, 17*, 795–824.

Patterson, G. R. (1982). *A social learning approach: Coercive family process* (Vol. 3). Eugene, OR: Castalia.

Patton, M. Q. (2002). *Qualitative evaluation and research methods* (3rd ed.). Beverly Hills, CA: Sage Publications, Inc.

Pecora, P. J., & Harrison-Jackson, M. (2011). Child welfare policies and programs. In J. M. Jenson & M. W. Fraser (Eds.), *Social policy for children and families. A risk and resilience perspective* (2nd ed., pp. 57–112). Thousand Oaks, CA: Sage.

Pepper, S. C. (1942). *World hypotheses.* Berkeley, CA: University of California Press.

Phelps, E., Balsano, A., Fay, K., Peltz, J., Zimmerman, S., Lerner, R., M., et al. (2007). Nuances in early adolescent development trajectories of positive and of problematic/risk behaviors: Findings from The 4-H Study of Positive Youth Development. *Child and Adolescent Clinics of North America, 16*, 473–496.

Piers, E. V., & Herzberg, D. S. (2002). *Piers-Harris 2: Piers-Harris Children's Self-Concept Scale* (2nd ed.). Los Angeles: Western Psychological Services.

Pittman, K. (1992, September/October). *Let's make youth work a field.* Washington, DC: The Forum for Youth Investment.

Platt, A. M. (1969). *The child savers. The invention of delinquency.* Chicago: University of Chicago Press.

Polansky, N. (1986). There is nothing so practical as a good theory. *Child Welfare, 65*, 3–5.

Polanyi, M. (1983). *The tacit dimension.* Gloucester, MA: Peter Smith.

Pollard, J. A., Hawkins, J. D., & Arthur, M. W. (1999). Risk and protection: Are both necessary to understand diverse behavioral outcomes in adolescence? *Social Work Research, 23,* 145–158.

Potter, S., & McKinlay, J. (2005). From a relationship to encounter: An examination of longitudinal and lateral dimensions in the doctor-patient relationship. *Social Science & Medicine, 61,* 465–479.

Prout, A. (2000). Foreword. In P. Christensen & A. James (Eds.), *Research with children: Perspectives and practices* (pp. xi–xii). New York: Falmer Press.

Rhodes, J. E. (2002). *Stand by me: The risks and rewards of mentoring today's youth.* Cambridge, MA: Harvard University Press.

Richmond, M. E. (1917). *Social diagnosis.* New York: Russell Sage Foundation.

Rodriquez, A., Pereira, J. A., & Brodnax, S. (2004). Latino nonprofits: The role of intermediaries in organizational capacity building. In D. Maurrasse & C. Jones, *A future for everyone: Innovative social responsibility and community partnerships* (pp. 79–100). New York: Routledge.

Rossa, M. W. (2002). Some thoughts about resilience versus positive development, main effects, versus interaction effects and the value of resilience. *Child Development, 71,* 567–569.

Roth, J. L., Brooks-Gunn, J., Murray, L., & Foster, W. (1998). Promoting healthy adolescents: Synthesis of youth development program evaluations. *Journal of Research on Adolescence, 8,* 423–459.

Roth, J. L., Malone, L. M., & Brooks-Gunn, J. (2010). Does the amount of participation in afterschool programs relate to developmental outcomes? A review of the literature. *American Journal of Community Psychology, 45,* 310–324.

Rounds, K. A., Huitron, G. V., & Ormsby, T. C. (2011). Health policy for children and youth. In J. M. Jenson & M. W. Fraser, *Social policy for children and families: A risk and resilience perspective* (2nd ed., pp. 195–235). Thousand Oaks, CA: Sage Publications.

Royse, D., Thyer, B. A., & Padgett, D. K. (2010). *Program evaluation: An introduction* (5th ed.). New York: Brooks-Cole.

Rutter, M. (1987). Psychosocial resilience and protective mechanisms. *American Journal of Orthopsychiatry, 57,* 316–331.

Rutter, M. (1979). Protective factors in children's responses to stress and disadvantage. In M. W. Kent & J. E. Rolf (Eds.), *Primary prevention of psychopathology: Vol. 3, Social competence in children.* (pp. 49–74). Hanover, NH: University Press of New England.

Rutter, M. (2001). Psychosocial adversity: Risk, resilience, and recovery. In J. M. Richman & M. W. Fraser (Eds.), *The context of youth violence: Resilience, risk, and protection* (pp. 13–41). Westport, CT: Praeger Publishers.

Sackett, D. L., Rosenberg, W., Gray, J. A. M., Haynes, R. B., & Richardson, W. S. (1996). Evidence-based medicine: What it is and what it isn't. *British Medical Journal, 312,* 71–72.

Sackett, D. L., Straus, S. E., Richardson, W. S., Rosenberg, W., & Haynes, R. B. (2000). *Evidence-based medicine: How to practice and teach EBM* (2nd ed.). New York: Churchill Livingstone.

Salamon, L. M. (1999). *America's nonprofit sector: A Primer.* New York: The Foundation Center.

Salamon, L. M. (2002). *The state of nonprofit America.* Washington, DC: Brookings Institution Press.

Salamon, L. M., Musselwhite, J. C., & Abramson, A. J. (1987). Voluntary organizations and the crisis of the welfare state. *The New England Journal of Human Services, 4,* 25–36.

Saldana, J. (2009). *The coding manual for qualitative researchers*. Thousand Oaks, CA: Sage.

Sameroff, A. J. (1999). Ecological perspectives on developmental risk. In J. D. Osofsky & H. E. Fitzgerald (Eds.), *WAIMH handbook of infant mental health: Vol. 4. Infant mental health groups at risk* (pp. 223–248). New York: Wiley.

Sameroff, A. J., Bartko, W. T., Baldwin, A., Baldwin, C., & Siefer, R. (1999). Family and social influences on the development of child competence. In M. Lewis & C. Feiring (Eds.), *Families, risk, and competence* (pp. 161–186). Mahwah, NJ: Lawrence Erlbaum.

Sameroff, A. J., & Fiese, B. H. (2000). Transactional regulation: The developmental ecology of early intervention. In J. P. Shonkoff & S. J. Meisels (Eds.), *Handbook of early childhood intervention* (2nd ed., pp.135–159). New York: Cambridge University Press.

Sameroff, A. J., & Gutman, L. M. (2004). Contributions of risk research to the design of successful interventions. In P. Allen-Meares & M. W. Fraser (Eds.), *Intervention with children and adolescents: An interdisciplinary approach* (pp. 9–26). Boston: Allyn & Bacon.

Sampson, R. J., Raudenbush, S. W., & Earls, F. (1997). Neighborhoods and violent crime: A multilevel study of collective efficacy. *Science, 277*, 918–924.

Scales, P. C., & Leffert, N. (1999). *Developmental assets: A synthesis of the scientific research on adolescent development*. Minneapolis, MN: Search Institute.

Schaps, E., Bartolo, R. D., Moskowitz, J., Palley, C. S., & Churgin, S. (1981). A review of 127 drug abuse prevention program evaluations. *Journal of Drug Issues, 11*, 17–43.

Scheier, L. M., & Botvin, G. J. (1998). Relations of social skills, personal competence, and adolescent drug use: A developmental exploratory study. *Journal of Early Adolescence, 18*, 77–114.

Schein, E. H. (1992). *Organizational culture and leadership*. San Francisco: Jossey-Bass.

Schmid, H. (2008). Agency-environment relations: Understanding external and natural environments. In R. J. Patti (Ed.), *Handbook of human services management* (2nd ed., pp. 411–434). Thousand Oaks, CA: Sage Publications, Inc.

Scientific Software Development. (2009). *Atlas-ti (version 6.2.23)*. Berlin: Gmbh.

Search Institute. (2006). *40 developmental assets for middle childhood (ages 8–12)*. Minneapolis, MN: Search Institute.

Sears, R. R. (1975). Your ancients revisited: A history of child development. In E. M. Hetherington (Ed.), *Review of child development research* (Vol. 6., pp. 1–73). Chicago: University of Chicago Press.

Seidman, E., Allen, L., Aber, J. L., Mitchell, C., Feinman, J., Yoshikawa, H., et al. (1995). Development and validation of adolescent-perceived microsystem scales: Social support, daily hassles, and involvement. *American Journal of Community Psychology, 23*, 355–388.

Shaw, C. F., & McKay, H. D. (1942). *Juvenile delinquency in urban areas*. Chicago: University of Chicago Press.

Sheidow, A. J., Gorman-Smith, D., Tolan, P., & Henry, D. B. (2001). Family and community characteristics: Risk factors for violence exposure in inner-city youth. *Journal of Community Psychology, 29*, 345–360.

Sheldon, J., Arbreton, A., Hopkins, L., & Grossman, J. B. (2010). Investing in success: Key strategies for building quality in after-school programs. *American Journal of Community Psychology, 45*, 394–404.

Shernoff, D. J. (2010). Engagement in after-school programs as a predictor of social competence and academic performance. *American Journal of Community Psychology, 45*, 325–337.

Simpkins, S., Little, P., & Weiss, H. (2004). *Understanding and measuring attendance in out-of-school time programs*. Cambridge, MA: Harvard Family Research Project.

Social Development Research Group. (2011). *Communities that Care Survey*. Seattle, WA: Author, School of Social Work, University of Washington.

Solansky, S. T., & Beck, T. E. (2009). Enhancing community safety and security through understanding interagency collaboration in cyber terrorism exercises. *Administration and Society, 40,* 852–875.

Soska, T. M., & Butterfield Johnson, A. K. (Eds.). (2004). *University-community partnerships. Universities in civic engagement*. London: Taylor and Francis/Haworth Press.

Spencer, R., & Rhodes, J. E. (2005). A counseling and psychotherapy perspective on mentoring relationships. In D. L. Dubois & M. J. Karcher (Eds.), *Handbook of youth mentoring* (pp. 118–132). Thousand Oaks, CA: Sage Publications.

Spoth, R., & Greenberg, M. (2011). Impact challenges in community science with practice: Lessons from PROSPER on transformative practitioner-scientist partnerships and infrastructure development. *American Journal of Community Psychology, 48,* 106–119.

Spoth, R., Redmond, C., Clair, S., Shin, C. Greenberg, M., & Feinberg, M. (2011). Preventing substance misuse through community-university partnerships. Randomized controlled outcomes 4.5 years past baseline. *American Journal of Preventive Medicine, 40,* 440–447.

Stabell, D. B., & Fjeldstad, O. D. (1998). Configuring value for competitive advantage: On chains, shops and networks. *Strategic Management Journal, 19,* 413–437.

Sutherland, E. H. (1939). *Principles of criminology*. Philadelphia: J.B. Lippincott.

Sutherland, E. H. (1973). Development of the theory [Private paper published posthumously]. In K. Schuessler (Ed.), *Edwin Sutherland on analyzing crime*. Chicago: University of Chicago Press.

Swift, M. C., Roeger, L., Walmsley, C., Howard, S., Furber, G., & Allison, S. (2009). Rural children referred for conduct problems: Evaluation of a collaborative program. *Australian Journal of Primary Health, 15,* 335–340.

Taylor & Associates. (2009). *Reading Plus research, rational, & results: A report on the research basis and effectiveness of Reading Plus*. Retrieved on May 15, 2011 from http://www.readingplus.com/index.php/download_file/-/view_inline/55

Terra, J. C., & Angeloni, T. (2005). Understanding the difference between information management and knowledge management. In L. Morel-Guimaraes, T. Khalil, & Y. Hosni (Eds.), *Management of technology: Key success factors for innovation and sustainable development* (pp. 3–4). Amsterdam, Boston: Elsevier Science.

Theokas, C., Almerigi, J. B., Lerner, R. M., Dowling, E. M., Benson, P. L., Scales, P. C., et al. (2005). Conceptualizing and modeling individual and ecological asset components of thriving in early adolescence. *The Journal of Early Adolescence, 25,* 113–143.

Thompson, J. (1967). *Organizations in action: Social science bases of administration theory*. New Brunswick, NJ: Transaction Publishers.

Thornberry, T. P. (1998). Membership in youth gangs and involvement in serious and violent offending. In R. Loeber & D. P. Farrington (Eds.), *Serious & violent juvenile offenders. Risk factors and successful interventions* (pp. 147–166). New York: Sage.

Thornberry, T. P., & Krohn, M. D. (Eds.). (2003). *Taking stock of delinquency: An overview of findings from contemporary longitudinal studies*. New York: Kluwer Academic/Plenum Publishers.

Tierney, J. P., Grossman, J. B, with Resch, N. L. (1995). *Making a difference: An impact study of Big Brothers/Big Sisters*. Philadelphia: Public/Private Ventures.

Tobler, N. S. (1986). Meta-analysis of 143 adolescent drug prevention programs: Quantitative outcome results of program participants compared to a control comparison group. *Journal of Drug Issues, 16,* 537–567.

Tough, P. (2009). *Whatever it takes. Geoffrey Canada's quest to change Harlem and America.* Boston, New York: Houghton Mifflin Harcourt.

Turvey, M. T. (1990). Coordination. *American Psychologist, 45,* 938–953.

21st Century Community Learning Centers. (2011). Retrieved on May 15, 2011 from http://www2.ed.gov/programs/21stcclc/guidance2003.pdf

Ungar, M. (2011). The social ecology of resilience. Addressing contextual and cultural ambiguity of a nascent construct. *American Journal of Orthopsychiatry, 81,* 1–17.

Ungar, M., & Liebenberg, L. (2005). The International Resilience Project: A mixed-methods approach to the study of resilience across cultures. In M. Ungar (Ed.), *Handbook of working with children and youth: Pathways to resilience across cultures and contexts* (pp. 211–226). Thousand Oaks, CA: Sage.

University of Denver. (2011). Public good at the University of Denver. Retrieved on April 3, 2011 from http://www.du.edu/ccesl/publicgood.html

U.S. Department of Education, (2009). *21st Century community learning centers.* Retrieved on June 30, 2011 from http://www2.ed.gov/programs/21stcclc/index.html

Vandell, D., & Posner, J. (1999). Conceptualization and measurement of children's after-school environments. In S. Freidman & T. Wachs (Eds.), *Measuring environment across the life span: Emerging methods and concepts* (pp. 167–196). Washington, DC: American Psychological Association.

van der Linden, W. J., & Hambleton, R. K. (1996). *The theory and practice of item response theory.* New York: Springer.

Vazsonyi, A. T. (2005). Commentary: The PYD perspective and the five Cs. *Journal of Early Adolescence, 25,* 5–9.

Vervest, P. (2005). *Smart business networks.* New York: Springer Publishing.

Vigil, J. D. (1990). Cholos and gangs: Culture change and street youth in Los Angeles. In R. Huff (Ed.), *Gangs in America: Diffusion, diversity, and public policy* (pp. 142–162). Thousand Oaks, CA: Sage.

Wahl, M. (2007). Florida Center for Reading Research. Read Well. Tallahassee, FL: Florida Center for Reading Research. Retrieved on May 15, 2011 from http://www.fcrr.org/fcrrreports/PDF/read_well_report.pdf

Wang, C. (2006). Youth particpation in photovoice as a strategy for community change. *Journal of Community Practice, 14,* 147–161.

Wang, C., Morrel-Samuels, S., Hutchison, P., Bell. L., & Pestronk, R. (2004). Flint photovoice: Community building among youths, adults, and policy makers. *American Journal of Public Health, 94,* 911–913.

Webster-Stratton, C., Reid, M. J., & Hammond, M. (2004). Treating children with early-onset conduct problems: Intervention outcomes for parent, child, and teacher training. *Journal of Clinical Child and Adolescent Psychology, 33,* 105–124.

Weissman, H. H. (1969). *Community development in the mobilization for youth experience.* New York: Association Press.

Werner, E. E., & Smith, R. S. (1982). *Vulnerable but invincible: A longitudinal study of resilient children and youth.* New York: Adams, Bannister, and Cox.

Werner, E. E., & Smith, R. S. (1992). *Overcoming the odds: High risk children from birth to adulthood.* New York: Cornell University Press.

Wholey, J. S., Hatry, H. P., & Newcomer, K. E. (2010). *Handbook of practical program evaluation.* New York: Jossey-Bass.

Williams, J. H., Ayers, C. D., Van Dorn, R. A., & Arthur, M. W. (2004). Risk and protective factors in the development of delinquency and conduct disorder. In M. W. Fraser (Ed.), *Risk and resiliency in childhood: An ecological perspective* (2nd Ed., pp. 209–249). Washington, DC: NASW Press.

Williford, A. P., Brisson, D., Bender, K. A., Jenson, J. M., & Forrest-Bank, S. (2011). A longitudinal investigation of the stability in bullying and victimization from middle childhood to early adolescence using latent variable modeling. *Journal of Youth and Adolescence, 40,* 644–655.

Wilson, W. J. (1987). *The truly disadvantaged: The inner city, the underclass, and public policy.* Chicago: University of Chicago Press.

Wilson, S. J., & Lipsey, M. W. (2007). School-based interventions for aggressive and disruptive behavior: Update of a Meta-Analysis. *American Journal of Preventive Medicine, 33,* S130–S143.

Wilson, S. J, Lipsey, M. W., & Derzon, J. H. (2003). The effects of school-based intervention programs on aggressive behavior: A meta-analysis. *Journal of Consulting and Clinical Psychology, 71,* 136–149.

Woolf, S. H. (2008). The power of prevention and what it requires. *Journal of the American Medical Association, 299,* 2437–2439.

Yale Center for Clinical Investigation. (2011). *Principles and guidelines for community-university partnerships.* Retrieved on June 30, 2011 from http://ycci.yale.edu/community/index.aspx

Yuen, F., & Owens, J. (1996). Power in partnership. *International Journal of Nursing Practice, 2,* 138–141.

Zetlin, A., Ramos, C., & Valdez, A. (1996). Integrating services in a school-based center: An example of a school-community collaboration. *Journal of Community Psychology, 24,* 97–107.

INDEX

parent participants interview
protocol, 194–96
RPACI, 110–11, 201–7
scholarship students interview
protocol, 197–98
youth participants interview protocol,
192–93
Bridge Project evaluation plan, 111*t*
agency-university collaboration, 108–10
evaluation procedures, 110
IPEI model and, 108–12
measures, 110–12
procedures, 110
Bridge Project interventions, 70–94
after-school program, 66, 74–80,
128–30
literacy, math, and technology skill
training, xv, 74, 76, 121
participation in, 122*t*
risk and resilience framework, 66–70,
73
tutors and mentors for, xv, 74, 76,
121, 128–29, 132
Bridge Project Summer Program, 78

Calhoun, Molly, 87–88
Califano, Joseph, 40
Canada, Geoffrey, 22
caring and compassion, 25, 26, 27, 73,
111, 152
Castro, Richard, 65, 69
Catalano, R. F., 7, 30, 35
categorical funding, 41–42
Caucasian student achievement gap, 41–42
cause-and-effect relationships, 107–8
CCM. *See* community collaborative model
census data, 98
change assessment, 106
character, 25, 26, 27, 73, 111, 152
child. *See also* youth
as competent and prosocial, 24
development, xiii, 25
rights of, 4
saving movement, 4
child and youth behavior, public health
approach to, 8, 9*f*
child and youth problems
industrialization influence on, 4
poverty influence on, 4
prevention and treatment, 3–7

child and youth programs
interorganizational collaboration in,
37–56
PYD model for, 21–36
risk and resilience framework, 3–19
Child Insurance Health Program (CHIP),
44
client
flows, 50–52, 51*f*
as integral factors, 38
journals, 99
needs, 38–39
outcomes, 96
relationships, one-to-one, 86
Cloud, William, 64, 89
CMHC. *See* community mental health
center
collaboration. *See also* community collaborative model; interorganizational
collaboration
methods for increasing, 93*t*
between school personnel and staff
members, 115–16
for smart planning, 85
in work process, 48
collective client flows, 50, 52
collective conceptualization, 85
collective socialization, 124, 126
Colorado State Assessment Profile
(CSAP), 112, 154*t*, 155, 181
Communities that Care (CTC), 168
community activists, 68
nonprofit organizations creation by, 40
community and participant outcomes
from Bridge Project, 113–58
community-based after-school programs
advancing education policy in, 162–70
intervention and evaluation elements,
165–67
IPEI for, 163, 165
leadership element for, 166
limitations of, 165
policy elements, 167–69
PYD for, 165
recommendations for, 165
research elements, 169–70
risk and resilience for, 165
theory and program design, 165
university-community partnership
for, 163–64